Harmful Sexual Behaviour and Autism

of related interest

The Autism Spectrum, Sexuality and the Law
What Every Parent and Professional Needs to Know
Tony Attwood, Isabelle Hénault and Nick Dubin
ISBN 978 1 84905 919 0
eISBN 978 0 85700 679 0

How to Respond to Sexualized Acts
A Research-Based Guide for Families and Frontline Staff
Working with Neurodivergent Individuals
Kate E. Reynolds
ISBN 978 1 80501 010 4
eISBN 978 1 80501 011 1

**Children and Young People Whose Behaviour
Is Sexually Concerning or Harmful**
Assessing Risk and Developing Safety Plans
Jackie Bateman and Judith Milner
ISBN 978 1 84905 361 7
eISBN 978 0 85700 714 8

HARMFUL SEXUAL BEHAVIOUR and AUTISM

Working with Children and Young People

David Russell, Dr Sophie King-Hill, Stuart Allardyce and **Professor Clare Allely**

FOREWORD BY TONY ATTWOOD

Jessica Kingsley Publishers
London and Philadelphia

First published in Great Britain in 2026 by Jessica Kingsley Publishers
An imprint of John Murray Press

2

Content Warning: This book contains mentions of bullying,
sexual abuse, sexual assault and sexual violence.

A CIP catalogue record for this title is available from the
British Library and the Library of Congress

ISBN 978 1 80501 052 4
eISBN 978 1 80501 053 1

Printed and bound in the United States by Integrated Books International

Jessica Kingsley Publishers' policy is to use papers that are natural,
renewable and recyclable products and made from wood grown in
sustainable forests. The logging and manufacturing processes are expected
to conform to the environmental regulations of the country of origin.

Jessica Kingsley Publishers
Carmelite House
50 Victoria Embankment
London EC4Y 0DZ

www.jkp.com

John Murray Press
Part of Hodder & Stoughton Ltd
An Hachette Company

The authorised representative in the EEA is Hachette Ireland,
8 Castlecourt Centre, Dublin 15, D15 XTP3, Ireland (email: info@hbgi.ie)

This book is dedicated to all the children, young people and families we have had the privilege to support over our careers. We hope this book supports a better understanding of this subject matter, and gives autistic children and young people a voice across our sectors.

Contents

Foreword by Professor Tony Attwood 9

Acknowledgements from David Russell 11

Biography of Authors 13

Use of Language 15

Introduction 19

1. **The Context: Children, Young People and Sexual Behaviour** 25

2. **Socio-Ecological Model and Approaches to Assessment and Intervention** 65

3. **Individual Factors: Contribution to Assessment and Intervention** 93

4. **Wider Interpersonal and Familial Factors** 113

5. **Community Factors** 133

6. **Societal and Risk Management Factors** 143

7. **Prevention** 177

   Closing Remarks 187

   References 189

   Index 215

List of Figures and Case Studies

FIGURES

Figure 1. Autism socio-ecological model 66

Figure 2. Adaptation of the autism socio-ecological model for autistic children who have sexually harmed 68

Figure 3. Merging of the Traffic Light Tool and the Hackett Continuum. 68

Figure 4. Individual factors of the autism socio-ecological model 93

Figure 5. Interpersonal factors of the autism socio-ecological model 113

Figure 6. Community factors of the autism socio-ecological model 133

Figure 7. Societal factors of the autism socio-ecological model . . 143

CASE STUDIES

One: Technology-assisted harmful sexual behaviour 61

Two: Obsessional interests 111

Three: Harmful sexual behaviour 128

Four: Possession of child sexual abuse material 139

Five: Possession and distribution of child sexual abuse material . 174

Foreword

Professor Tony Attwood

There are many reasons why autism can be a contributory factor in harmful sexual behaviour, ranging from aspects of the diagnostic criteria for autism, such as a delay in interpersonal abilities, ritualised behaviour, unusual interests and sensory sensitivity, access to pornography, loneliness and peer rejection.

When an autistic child or adolescent engages in harmful sexual behaviour, we need detailed assessment procedures to determine the combination of factors that lead to such behaviour and to design an intervention programme for that individual. This requires that practitioners are knowledgeable in the many dimensions of autism, have a library of relevant assessment instruments, are up to date with the latest research on autism and theoretical models for harmful sexual behaviour and can determine which intervention programmes would be appropriate for the individual and the specific sexual behaviours.

In my extensive clinical experience, I have been referred autistic children, adolescents and adults who have engaged in harmful sexual behaviour. I have used that experience to determine the potential reasons for the behaviour and explain the reasons to the individual, those who support them and various government agencies. I am often asked for a professional opinion on the appropriate consequences for the behaviour, the risk of such behaviour occurring again and what can be done to minimise that risk. My professional opinion is based on combining clinical experience and knowledge of relevant research literature. However, I did not have a primary source of information on the appropriate theoretical models, assessments and interventions until I read the manuscript for *Harmful Sexual Behaviour and Autism*. At last, we have the seminal comprehensive guide for practitioners, academics and the legal system, who will greatly benefit from the authors' depth of knowledge, experience and compassion. I also know autistic individuals will benefit indirectly from their insights and wisdom.

Acknowledgements from David Russell

A sincere thanks to everyone who made this book possible. With the support and reassurance from Sophie, Stuart and Clare we have pulled together our knowledge and practice experience to create what I hope will support professional judgement and practice when supporting autistic children and young people. I would also like to acknowledge Professor Kieran McCartan for his ongoing support throughout this journey. I especially want to express my heartfelt gratitude to my fiancée Jason and my family for all their moral support.

Biography of Authors

David Russell is an expert in the field and has extensive experience specialising in work with children and young people with harmful sexual behaviour and / or who have experienced sexual abuse or exploitation. This includes providing assessments and interventions for vulnerable children, adolescents and adults within the field of sexual harm and violence. He has also worked in custodial and secure settings. David provides training on a range of themes on sexual violence, and has facilitated multidisciplinary training internationally. He currently sits on the NOTA (National Organisation for the Treatment of Abusers) Scotland Executive Committee, supporting professionals responding to sexual harm. He is the lead author of *Restorative Justice & Sexual Harm: The Voices of Those Who Have Harmed* and is currently involved in a research project in collaboration with the University of Birmingham, exploring prevention strategies within incel subcultures.

Sophie King-Hill is an Associate Professor in the Health Services Management Centre at the University of Birmingham. She specialises in sexual behaviours and assessment in children and young people, sexual health, sibling sexual behaviour / abuse, misogyny, relationships and sex education and the importance of youth voice. Much of her work is cross sector and cross disciplinary, and centred around participatory and stakeholder co-design approaches. Sophie also has an interest in policy implementation, transfer and success frameworks and evaluation strategies. Previously she worked extensively in the third sector in the field of education and sexual health with many diverse groups, such as teenage parents and young people with social, emotional and behavioural difficulties.

Stuart Allardyce is a director at the child protection charity The Lucy Faithfull Foundation. He has responsibility for Stop It Now services in Scotland. He has worked in the child sexual abuse field as a social worker for over 20 years, and is chair of NOTA (National Organisation for the Treatment of Abusers) UK and Ireland, the membership association for professionals working with adults and adolescents who perpetrate sexual harm. He is a visiting researcher at the University of Strathclyde and co-author (with Peter Yates) of *Working with Children and Young People Who Have Displayed Harmful Sexual Behaviour* and *Sibling Sexual Abuse: A Knowledge and Practice Overview*, as well as over 20 peer-reviewed articles and book chapters. He was a member of the Scottish Government's Expert Group on Preventing Sexual Offending Involving Children and Young People and their senior leadership group on tackling child sexual abuse.

Clare Allely is Professor of Forensic Psychology at the University of Salford and is an affiliate member of the Gillberg Neuropsychiatry Centre at the University of Gothenburg, Sweden. Clare is an Honorary Research Fellow at the College of Medical, Veterinary and Life Sciences affiliated to the Institute of Health and Wellbeing at the University of Glasgow. She is a Chartered Member and Associate Fellow of the British Psychological Society. Clare acts as an expert witness in criminal cases involving defendants with autism spectrum disorder and is a consultant for the Irish Prison Service. She has published over 150 academic peer-reviewed articles and book chapters. She is author of *The Psychology of Extreme Violence: A Case Study Approach to Serial Homicide, Mass Shooting, School Shooting and Lone-actor Terrorism* and *Autism Spectrum Disorder in the Criminal Justice System: A Guide to Understanding Suspects, Defendants and Offenders with Autism*.

Use of Language[1]

Language is an important aspect to consider when working in the field of autism and sexual behaviours. It is one of the principal ways in which values and ethical priorities are communicated. Throughout the book the term 'harmful sexual behaviour' is used. Although there is no consistent or universally agreed meaning of this term, we draw on the following definition:

> Sexual behaviours expressed by children and young people under the age of 18 years old that are developmentally inappropriate, may be harmful towards self or others and / or be abusive towards another child, young person or adult. (Hackett, Holmes and Branigan 2019, p.12)

The term is not therefore a synonym for sexually abusive behaviour, but instead covers a range of presentations, from inappropriate sexual behaviour that may sit outside social or developmental norms but not lead to victimisation through to behaviour that will constitute sexual offending in many jurisdictions and which is likely to lead to significant emotional and possibly physical harm to victims. The term 'harmful sexual behaviour' ensures a child-focused and strengths-based approach and reduces labelling. However, it still acknowledges the harm caused to self and others. This also applies to the term 'perpetrator', which is not used when referring

---

1   Please note that some of the quoted research in this book uses outdated language.

to children and young people due to the need to move away from their criminalisation.

Throughout the book we also use the term 'autism' to mean a life-long and unchanging neurodevelopmental disorder that impacts variably on a person's communication and social interactions (National Autistic Society 2023). Current diagnostic criteria in *The Diagnostic and Statistical Manual of Mental Disorders, Fifth Edition* (DSM-5) (see APA 2013) and *International Classification of Diseases*, 11th revision (ICD-11), focus on two core domains of impairment:

- Persistent difficulties with social communication and social interaction
- Restricted and repetitive patterns of behaviours, activities or interests.

For some young people there may be a co-occurrence with other conditions such as learning disabilities and other neurodevelopmental disorders such as attention deficit hyperactivity disorder (ADHD). Autism is a highly heterogeneous phenomenon and can include those who are high functioning as well as those who experience cognitive impairments (Wing 1997). Around 1 in 100 people in the UK are estimated to be autistic (Fletcher-Watson and Happé 2019; Gould and Smith 2011; NICE 2019; O'Nions *et al.* 2023), although this covers a wide diversity of different presentations.

There have been significant and positive shifts in how autism has been conceptualised over the last few years. The diagnostic criteria for autism was traditionally based on a medical model of disorders, with evidence of impairments through observed behaviours, such as lack of 'theory of mind' and 'mind blindness' (Fletcher-Watson and Happé 2019; Jack 2012). With the rise of access to the internet, autism networks and online forums have been able to develop their own autistic subculture and advocacy (Dekker 2019; Jackson-Perry 2020; Sinclair 1992), citing that autistic difficulties need to be considered as part of a social model rather than a medical model. Instead of focusing on impairments and what a child cannot do, this approach instead looks at environmental challenges for autistic people and society's failure to create a context where autistic people have the ability to engage and perform well socially. This approach also considers professional practice that does not adapt to work with autistic people. Throughout this book there is a focus on avoiding a deficit model in relation to autism and to embrace this socio-ecological model. Key to this is a focus on the many positive things about being autistic.

Throughout the book the terms 'autistic children' or 'autistic young people' are used rather than the person-first formulation 'children with autism'. However, it is acknowledged that different autistic individuals may have different preferences in relation to use of language. This is a sensitive issue in the autistic community, as many autistic people see autism as a part of who they are rather than as something separate. We have made efforts to respect this in this book.

We have also made the decision to use 'victim / survivor', to respect the fact that people who have suffered abuse relate to their experiences in different ways (see NSPCC 2024).

Finally, this book is about children and young people. The definition of childhood we have used is as set out in the United Nations Convention on the Rights of the Child (UNCRC; UN 1989) and the rights this document enshrines. So, throughout this book we use 'young people' when referring to post-adolescent individuals aged 12–18 and 'children' when referring to pre-adolescent individuals below the age of 12.

Children's rights are essential to this book. Sexually harmful behaviour that leads to harm to other children violates Article 34 of the UNCRC, which states that children and young people have the right to be protected from sexual abuse. However, all individuals under the age of 18 are children, and as such deserve particular protection from harm and abuse, and many of them will have experienced maltreatment or harm themselves. These children and young people who may harm others also have rights that need to be protected, and they – like their victims – should have their fundamental needs for respect, nurture, support, education, social inclusion and protection from harm met. Although working with autistic children and young people where sexual behaviour is concerning involves working in an area where rights may be in conflict, behaviour that may cause harm to others does not mean that the individual who has caused harm loses their rights.

Introduction

Beginning to understand and express sexual identity is a natural and healthy part of adolescent development. Sexual exploration and experimentation is incremental in children and young people. This is expected and commonplace, and follows on from the curiosity that younger children have about their own bodies and the bodies of the adults and children around them. Adolescent experiences then have a foundational role in shaping emerging adult sexual identity and understanding of healthy and appropriate boundaries and intimate relationships in adulthood. Because of this, children and young people have a fundamental right to learn about their growing bodies, relationships, sexuality and sexual health in ways that are appropriate to their age and stage of development.

Navigating the complexities of societal expectations in relation to gender, sex and sexuality can be challenging for any young person. This is especially true when learning about sex and sexuality, and early expressions of sexual feelings may take place in online spaces. While most children progress towards adult sexuality without any significant problems or difficulties, sexual development for some children may be more challenging.

An increasing body of research indicates that a significant proportion of the sexual abuse of children is carried out by children and young people themselves. UK data on recorded sexual crime confirms that more than half of those who carry out sexual harm against children are themselves under the age of 18 (NPCC 2024). The issue of young people who have displayed harmful sexual behaviour has been a significant focus of research and social policy over the last 20 years in the UK and beyond. Although there is no compelling evidence to suggest that autistic young people are more likely to display harmful sexual behaviour than neurotypical young people, most practitioners who work with this client group describe autistic children as being overrepresented in referrals.

The overrepresentation of autistic children and young people among services working with individuals who present a sexual risk of harm to others raises significant challenges. There are various screening, intervention and assessment models within the field of harmful sexual behaviour for supporting children and young people, but few provide explicit guidance on supporting autistic children and young people. Some are situated behind paywalls, making widespread use and accessibility problematic, and fostering a sporadic approach to intervention. With access to resources limited, professionals are often required to adapt them and make them autism-friendly. However, this is flawed due to the need for bespoke and evidence-based assessments and interventions that are specifically for autism.

The support provided for autistic children and young people in relation to healthy relations, boundaries, consent and sexual knowledge and expression have a critical role in helping those young people who may misjudge social context and who may struggle with the acceptability of expression of sexual feelings in adolescence, including online behaviours. These issues are exacerbated if autistic children and young people lack access to accessible and bespoke relationships and sex education (Davies *et al.* 2022; Ragaglia, Caputi and Bulgarelli 2023), or if adults are overprotective. This can then impact on how autistic young people learn the rules of relationships, acceptable boundaries around sexual expression and the subtleties of non-verbal signals in relation to consent (Chianese, Jackson and Souders 2021; Maggio *et al.* 2022). There is mixed evidence about whether autistic young people are more likely to seek out information about sex from the internet rather than from peers (Dewinter *et al.* 2016; Kellaher 2015). However, when this is the case, exposure to pornography and sexually explicit material can potentially contribute to confusion about norms about sexual behaviour among adolescent youth.

A range of studies has highlighted asexuality as a key component of autism rather than expected sexual development and expression of sexual thoughts and feelings among autistic youth (Ten Hoopen *et al.*

2020). There has been an increase in the number of academic studies published looking at autism and sexuality, providing an insight into sexual development among autistic people (Dewinter, Vermeiren and Vanwesenbeeck 2013; Hancock, Stokes and Mesibov 2017; Pecora, Mesibov and Stokes 2016). However, the research literature on social and sexual development in autistic children remains limited. Those working as practitioners in the field often lack a clear evidence base to help inform interventions to support autistic young people in relation to healthy sexual development.

Psychosexual development, the psychological development of aspects of sexuality, has become a focus of interest in policy and practice relating to autism. There is an overrepresentation of autistic children and young people who are gender questioning. Studies indicate that autistic young people can be up to four times more likely to experience gender dysphoria than those without autism (De Vries *et al.* 2010). The reasons for this overrepresentation are unclear, and it should be noted that not all studies have found a clear over-representation. Autistic people may be less aware of social pressures about societal gender stereotyping or are less likely to follow norms set by peers and adults. This could result in them potentially being less likely to conform to the social norms on gender (Davidson and Tamas 2015; George and Stokes 2016; Glidden *et al.* 2016; Lindsey 2008).

None of this resistance to gender norms and stereotyping need be negative. Ten Hoopen *et al.* (2020) highlight a new paradigm emerging where autistic people are developing their own sexual identities and definitions of relationships that are different to their neuro-typical peers. However, uncertainty about gender identity for some young people who find aspects of social interaction and understanding challenging, and who experience heteronormative sex education that does not meet their basic needs, could further find challenges in navigating their adolescent social and sexual development.

PURPOSE OF THE BOOK

This book has been written primarily for those who currently work with – or who plan to work with – autistic children who have displayed harmful sexual behaviour. It is aimed at practitioners as well as students, academics and researchers in social work, psychology, health, psychiatry, education, criminal justice, criminology, the legal professions, police and counselling and psychotherapy. It will be relevant to those who work with children up to the age of 18, but it may also be of interest to those who mainly work with adults involved with sexual offending and who wish to consider a developmental perspective in working with older adolescents and young adults up to the age of 25. It is written for a UK audience, but efforts have been made to ensure that the international nature of this issue is reflected.

A range of themes, theories and concepts are explored to support professionals, establishments, parents and carers in ensuring that they see the whole child or young person, and an unhelpful focus is not simply placed on behavioural traits that are only one part of who the child or young person is. We have combined our specialisms to produce a robust and holistic overview of the complexities of harmful sexual behaviour being displayed by autistic children and young people, exploring this via the socio-ecological model that encompasses the varying multilevel considerations that are required when planning approaches and interventions. This is underpinned by a child-centred and individualised response.

STRUCTURE OF THE BOOK

The book consists of seven chapters that are structured around the varied and complex elements that require consideration when working with autistic children and young people who display harmful sexual behaviour.

Chapter One considers the overarching contexts of children and young people and sexual behaviour, and how these relate to how sexual behaviour is framed in contemporary society. It explores the underpinning factors that result in the mutual exclusivity of sexual behaviours and childhood. Historical factors and perspectives on childhood are considered alongside the history of relationships and sex education and the impact this has on children and young people. The fluidity of sexual behaviours over time is outlined, as are inappropriate and problematic sexual behaviours. The chapter then goes on to provide an overview of harmful sexual behaviour and autism, index harm and victim attributes, and explores how defining sexual behaviour in autistic children and young people is approached. Technology-assisted harmful sexual behaviour and the impact of pornography is also considered in autistic children and young people.

Chapter Two outlines the socio-ecological model and how this has been adapted by Russell, McCartan and King-Hill (2025) for autistic children and young people into the ASEM (autism socio-ecological model) (subsequent chapters are then framed around the domains within this). Assessment approaches are considered and a discussion about staged interventions (including technology-assisted harmful sexual behaviour interventions), and the approaches required for autistic children and young people are critically discussed. This chapter outlines trauma-informed practice and the importance of this when considering harmful sexual behaviour in children and young people.

Chapter Three critically appraises the individual domain and range of considerations that are required when viewing and approaching harmful sexual behaviours in autistic children and young people, including vulnerability factors, wider behaviours, methods of engagement, working with denial and shame and anxiety. It also considers additional aspects of working with children under 12, and the importance of the voice of the child within assessment.

Chapter Four builds on this and considers the interpersonal and wider factors when harmful sexual behaviours present in children and young people. This includes discussions about parents, wider family environments, residential and secure care, the impact on restricted contact with peers, adult supervision, social maturity, impaired ability to guess age and facial expressions, paranoia, mistrust and issues with time to respond.

Chapter Five then considers the community domain and the impacts and needs of autistic young people displaying harmful sexual behaviour. This includes a discussion on moral and legal boundaries, literal thinking, impaired theory of mind and working with schools and local community groups.

Chapter Six goes on to outline the wider factors that impact on children and young people displaying harmful sexual behaviours that relate specifically to the societal domains that are pertinent to consider. It includes consideration of confidentiality for children, young people and parents or carers, safeguarding, risk management, autism and the justice system and offending behaviour. The chapter also includes a discussion on the need to recognise and understand some of the potential innate vulnerabilities in some autistic individuals charged with viewing indecent images of children, the important role that co-occurring mental health disorders play in offending behaviour in autistic individuals, the disproportionately higher risk of autistic individuals experiencing abuse and victimisation, autistic young people and police interactions, and important considerations for autistic young people in police investigative interviews and during courtroom proceedings.

Chapter Seven then draws all of the considerations together to offer a summary of the various aspects that relate to support a reduction and prevention of harmful sexual behaviours in autistic children and young people.

Throughout the book case studies are used to give examples of how the approaches suggested can be used in practice. All case studies are fictionalised or composites.

LIMITATIONS OF THE BOOK

Writing a book on a relatively new area of social concern is fraught with challenges. Although many autistic young people come to the attention of statutory services because of issues around sexual behaviour, it is unclear whether this is as a result of additional monitoring and surveillance in the lives of autistic young people or an indicator of a social issue that needs to be addressed.

This book will contribute to practice responses, solutions and policy, which mean that when sexual behaviour issues are identified among autistic children and young people, they are responded to within a context of understanding of neurodiversity as well as in a child-centred and effective way that helps promote child protection as well as positive social and sexual development. This ultimately means working with situations involving peer-led sexual abuse that foreground children's rights and what needs to be done to promote moral repair after harm has occurred.

CHAPTER ONE

The Context

CHILDREN, YOUNG PEOPLE AND SEXUAL BEHAVIOUR

This chapter explores three main contextual elements when considering the context of autism and sexual behaviours: the perspectives of children and sexuality, autism and sexual behaviours, and technology-assisted sexual behaviours in autistic children. It will critically examine the underpinning influences that result in the contemporary perception in Western society of children and young people and sexual behaviours. The fundamental elements of childhood and sexuality will be discussed and their temporal relevance examined in light of current perceptions.

Before considering autism and harmful sexual behaviours, it is first important to consider the position of children and young people as a whole in relation to developmentally appropriate sexual behaviours. This will allow for the contextualisation of the inappropriate, problematic and harmful behaviours displayed by autistic children and young people.

The chapter will then go on to explore harmful sexual behaviour through an autism lens. It will define harmful sexual behaviour among children and young people looking at the continuum of sexual behaviours ranging from normative through to abusive behaviours, both online and offline. Within the context of a discussion about the key characteristics of young people who display harmful sexual behaviour, we will look specifically at why autistic individuals are overrepresented in studies that have looked at harmful sexual behaviour in adolescence.

The chapter then outlines key psychological and contextual drivers that help us understand this overrepresentation, including limitations in sex education for autistic children, sensory sensitivity, misunderstanding of context, emotional recognition, emotional regulation issues, obsessional interests, disinhibited online behaviour, counterfeit deviance, sexual informants and environmental factors and influences.

The chapter concludes by critically exploring technology-assisted sexual behaviours and how these relate to current evidence, assessment and interventions.

THE MUTUAL EXCLUSIVITY OF SEXUALITY AND CHILDHOOD

It is important to consider wider perspectives on sexuality and children and young people before embarking on exploration that is specific to autism. This gives a foundation of knowledge that is useful when considering interventions with autistic children and young people in relation to sexual behaviours.

On examination of underpinning theories it is apparent that the views on sexuality and children and young people have many overarching influences. Many elements combine to impact on the negative perception of developmentally appropriate sexual behaviours in contemporary culture. These are wide-ranging and varied, yet all contribute to the negative connotations that are often attributed to the evolving sexual behaviours of children and young people, especially those who are autistic. The complexities surrounding sexual behaviours in children and young people appear multifaceted and not as straightforward as outside perceptions may suggest.

We refer to 'children and young people' as those aged 0–18, as defined by the UNCRC (UN 1989). There are two things to point out in relation to this. First, it is widely expected in contemporary culture that 18 is a milestone that results in children and young people becoming legal adults, yet it is important to consider that autistic children and young people may not demonstrate the capacity for these societal expectations. Second, the absolute age of 18 as the change from young person to adult for all children and young people is a simplistic view and is more complex than this simple premise, with the emergence of sexual behaviours incremental. We will discuss this complexity later in this chapter.

In contemporary culture sexual behaviours in children and young people are often seen as a binary opposition between 'good' and 'bad', with 'bad' being seen as sexual behaviours in children and young people overall and abstinence being seen as 'good', and with one position taking precedence over the other. Unpacking these positions is important, exploring why sexual behaviours in children and young people are seen as a 'bad' thing in contemporary culture, breaking down the contributory elements to smaller parts in an attempt to understand the social constructs that surround sexual behaviours in children and young people.

The elements that are important to explore are the perceptions and constructions of childhood, adolescence and sexuality. In this chapter we set out current societal views of sexual behaviours and discuss the converging influences, from sociology, evolution, philosophy and religion. Understanding this will provide the context and underpinning for discussions in the subsequent chapters on autism, children and young people and harmful sexual behaviours. It is equally important to examine the elements that assign meaning to children and young people and sexual behaviours within contemporary culture.

The historical underpinning of perceptions of sexual behaviour

When considering sexual behaviour and how it is conceptualised in contemporary culture it is important to understand the contributing and converging influences that result in how sexual behaviour is seen in the modern world. Many adults (including professionals as well as parents or carers) find it difficult to speak to children and young people about their sexual behaviours, and this is especially evident when considering autistic children. This stems from the mutual exclusivity between the perceptions of the child and conceptual notions that surround sexual behaviours, which will be explored later in this chapter. Understanding the converging factors that lead to this discord can support the planning of the healthy sexual development of all children and young people. This section provides a brief summary and overview of these aspects from a fundamental historical shift in perceptions of sexual behaviour in society, which is intended to give an underpinning for further discussions.

Prior to the 16th century sexual behaviour and sexuality were broadly perceived as a useful tool in contributing to the population growth and the labour force. While this changed with the rise of agriculture and paternal lineage becoming important due to inheritance of land and property, the commencement of menses was widely accepted as the start of childbearing. Post 16th century there were more organised gender roles within societal structures that needed to contribute to the labour market. However, concerns around population control and the need to maintain a labour force while preserving finite resources led to more explicit regulation of childbearing. This was closely tied to sexual regulation, with an emphasis on procreation being deemed acceptable only within the confines of marriage (Buss 2002).

With the Industrial Revolution children were needed in the workforce, so extended breastfeeding rates went down and birth rates went up. Economic productivity was the focus, and time wasted on sexual matters was frowned upon. This was reinforced by the normative sexual ethics that emerged with key standpoints on sexuality and concrete expectations of how sexual behaviour should play out (Stewart 1995). This standpoint was underpinned by a universal perspective of set 'rights and wrongs', with any variation to these being seen as a direct assault on morality (Soble 1998).

Key philosophical thinking at this time asserted that the internalisation of sex as only a means to procreate should be a societal norm (Soble 1998). This position was also reinforced by the dominant Christian religion in Western culture that advocated for sex within marriage for procreation only, and that lust was a mortal sin (Coogan 2010). Any sexual behaviour that varied from the expected norm was viewed as hedonistic, unethical behaviour (Foucault 1990, 1992a, 1992b; Gudorf 1994). It is important to note at this point that while the influence and popularity of the Christian church is currently declining in Western culture, these positions are still apparent, with sexual behaviour largely being seen as a set, fixed system of right and wrong, and any deviance being viewed as a direct offence to public morality (Soble 1998; Stewart 1995).

It is this normalisation of sexual behaviour via marriage and religion that has contributed to a modern, repressed attitude towards sex as shameful (Foucault 1990, 1992a, 1992b). This is then linked to power structures within society, social regulation and cultural control, and fosters feelings of shame around sexual behaviours, making even developmentally appropriate sexual behaviours difficult to discuss (McNay 1992).

Perceptions of childhood

When considering the sexual behaviours of children and young people it is pertinent to consider how children and young people are conceptualised in modern Western society. This perspective will support the further discussion in subsequent chapters of harmful sexual behaviours in autistic children and young people. To understand sexual behaviours in children and young people it is important to consider perceptions of the definition and expectation of children and young people, and what is expected of them in wider Western society and where this stems from.

As stated earlier, the UNCRC sets out that a child refers to every 'human being below the age of eighteen years unless, under the law applicable to the child, majority is attained earlier' (UN 1989). This statement, while giving an age for the end of childhood, still appears ambiguous and not representative of the fluidity in the perception of the child. While there are some issues with having a rigid age of adulthood, it is still vitally important to have this benchmark from the UNCRC to protect children and young people worldwide from all forms of exploitation. However, when considering how sexual development and behaviours are perceived in Western society, the age of 18 is not a simple line of transition from one state of being to another; rather, it is incremental. Quite often this age of adulthood is also associated with elements of transition such as the right to vote, control over property, legal responsibilities and, pertinently, sexual activity. However, these points of transition also vary – for example in the UK a person can legally have sexual intercourse at the age of 16 yet cannot vote.

Ariès (1962) argued that childhood itself is a social construct rather than a prescribed state of physical being. Postman (1994) reflects this view, asserting that before (circa.) 1850 perceptions of people between the ages of 7 and 17 were viewed as 'small adults' (under the age of 7 individuals were considered infants) as opposed to the contemporary view of children being 'unformed adults' (1994, p.36). Postman also points out that this age range is closely related with the acquisition and mastery of spoken language, which is a key point when considering autistic children. Cunningham (2006, p.15) builds on the premise of the social construction of childhood, stating that current perceptions are based on the 'many inventions of it that come to shape our ideas of it in the present' – therefore, with the perceived innocence of a child as being a cultural construction rather than an innate characteristic, in turn suggesting a fragility in this innocence and invoking a need to protect against corruption, including sexual behaviours.

The emerging perception of the innocent child and the need to protect them was enhanced by Locke in the 17th century (see Coogan 2010; Foucault 1992a) as well as the concept of the 'tabula rasa', that individuals are born as 'blank slates' that are open to environmental influences, and that it is the responsibility of adults to nurture development. Rousseau (Gudorf 1994) further reinforced the concept, likening childhood to a period of calm before the trails of adulthood, suggesting a split between the two states of being.

There was a shift in ideologies surrounding children in the late 19th century, changing from a useful commodity to the labour market, linking to the need for child labour, to innocent representations of future society (Ross and Rapp 1981). This is an important change to note when considering the perspective of sexual behaviours in children and young people. Compulsory schooling for children up to the age of 10 was introduced in 1880 in the Elementary Education Act (Ariès 1962), rising to 14 in 1918 with the Fisher Education Act (Ariès 1962), moving children from the workforce and into a social domain of their own, again reinforcing the perception of the specific nature of childhood. Ariès (1962) asserts that the emergence of 'childhood' as a recognised state was coupled with a perception of an innocence resulting in the concept of the current-day child, with the treatment of children, by society, dictating the elements of the domain of childhood rather than it being a natural occurrence. Taking all this into account, childhood appears to be an evolving concept, which is the result of convergent factors that have impacted on it. Childhood itself still appears to be difficult to define, a concept that can vary depending on many variable factors and perspectives as well as deeply embedded in the perceptions of those defining the 'child'.

A key aspect of sexual development and the perceptions of children and young people is the difficulty in defining childhood during adolescence, a transitory period between childhood and adulthood. The World Health Organization defines adolescence as 'the period in human growth and development that occurs after childhood and before adulthood, from ages 10 to 19'.[1] Yet, despite this assertion Western laws and the UNRC define an individual as a child until they are 18. Cousin (2006, p.139) refers to adolescence as a liminal space between the domain of the child and adult as being an 'unstable space in which the [individual] may oscillate between old and emergent understandings'. Adolescents are in a transitional phase of development, actively negotiating identity, autonomy and separation from childhood. This process often involves asserting independence and redefining their relationships with adults who may still perceive them through a childhood lens (see Grotevant and Cooper 1985). It is this apparent grey area of transition, where adulthood is beginning and the 'innocence' of childhood is disappearing, that causes conflicting perspectives, especially in the area of emerging sexuality.

THE MUTUAL EXCLUSIVITY BETWEEN CHILDHOOD, ADOLESCENCE AND SEXUAL BEHAVIOUR

The influential effects of the socially constructed perceptions of childhood, adolescence and sexuality appear to have impacted on the social disapproval that is linked to children and young people in Western culture, making any emerging and developmentally appropriate sexual behaviours in children and young people a contested issue. This link to immorality appears to stem from the conflicting moral-ethical viewpoints coupled with the changing perception of the realm of the child and the nature of sex (Soble 1998; Stewart 1995), with sexuality within this boundary being representative of the downfall of society (Coogan 2010; Foucault 1992a; Gudorf 1994).

Further compounding this point is the sociological perspective, which, as asserted by Meigham and Harber (2007), has a current focus on achievement and career, with the accepted age for childbearing increasing. With this perspective, sexual behaviour in adolescence, often associated and attributed to those from low socio-economic backgrounds, is seen as detrimental to current ideologies surrounding

---

1   www.who.int/health-topics/adolescent-health/#tab=tab_1

childhood, adolescence and employment expectations. The dominant values in Western culture appear to be those of family, work and nation, with familial ideologies tending to be based around conventional relationships of heterosexual marriage, viewing the male as the main earner and the female as the childbearer (see Lewis 1992; Miller 1990). This has been compounded in recent years by political perspectives, which can be seen in the UK with the rhetoric of the Conservative coalition and Conservative governments in the UK between 2010 and 2024. These ideologies appear to have impacted negatively on perceptions of emerging and developmentally appropriate sexuality, which will be explored later in this chapter.

All genders are viewed as potential contributors to the workforce and the economy. However, when individuals deviate from normative life trajectories due to, for example, teenage parenthood, they are seen as not able to enter the labour market, maintain stable education or contribute financially, and are often perceived as failing to fulfil societal expectations, despite the diversity of lived experiences and capacities (King-Hill 2013; Phoenix 1991). Lévi-Strauss (1966) refers to a functionalist perspective of society with clear definitions of wrong and right within contemporary social constructs based on majority norms. It is these unwritten rules that enable society to 'function', and with this in mind, sexual activity, even where developmentally appropriate, appears to be representative of the failings of this perceived functionality (see also Lewis 1992; Miller 1990; Williams 1989).

On further investigation, the reasons for sexual behaviours in childhood and adolescence are many and varied, with developmentally appropriate behaviours having many influencing factors such as hormonal changes, earlier onset of puberty, cultural expectations and media influences. Sexual behaviours in children and young people that are perceived as problematic, inappropriate and / or harmful can also stem from outside factors including sexual abuse, lack of knowledge and confidence in contraception, poor relationships and sex education (RSE), peer pressure and a skewed perspective of sex. It is these 'real problems' that form the intricate web of influences that impact on children and young people and sexual development rather than the lack of adolescents' abilities to control destructive and deviant impulses. This becomes even more complex for autistic children and young people due to the additional complexities that autism brings (Ashley, Jackson and Davies 2008; Boyer and Fine 1992; Cole and Putnam 1992; Gruber 2001; Polusny and Follette 1995; Schloredt and Heiman 2003).

As summarised earlier, current-day perspectives of sexual behaviours in the UK are as a result of factors that have converged from a range of perspectives and influencing factors. It is apparent that the views on sexuality in children and young people have many overarching factors. These elements are complex, yet all contribute to the negative connotations that are often attributed to sex and young people in the UK. To recap, over the years sex changed from something that was celebrated and regulated by extended breastfeeding to shifting to more regulation when paternity became important for inheritance, and sexuality and birth rates were controlled via gendered ideologies and age-related restrictions. Alongside this was a distinct shift in ideologies surrounding children, changing from a useful commodity to the labour market to innocent representations of future society.

Sex and morality have always been matters of public discourse. Influential perspectives of the universality of rights and wrongs in relation to sex are being consolidated into wider society, and any variation from the static ethical code is seen to be immoral behaviour. Historical religious ideologies have reinforced this thinking. These ideas embedded themselves into wider society, with the condemnation of any sexual variance outside marriage an assault on morality. This social regulation and cultural control then led to repressed and shameful attitudes towards developmentally appropriate sexual behaviour, making it a difficult discourse to address, especially in relation to children and young people.

Sexuality in children and young people is often held to be something dangerous that needs to be regulated. This is then coupled with the difficulty of defining a 'child'. Although the UNCRC states that a child is anyone under the age of 18, this becomes a particular issue in adolescence when sexuality begins to become more apparent, and is also especially pertinent when considering autistic populations. The concept of what constitutes a child is ever evolving in the UK, and this can be seen historically. Children and young people are often situated within the contradictory positions of innocent representations of future society or lacking agency and self-control. With this perspective, quite often developmentally appropriate sexual behaviour in children and young people is seen as detrimental to current ideologies surrounding childhood, adolescence and employment expectations. Coupled with this is the current position that all genders are now perceived as being part of the workforce, contributing to the economy, with sexual behaviour posing a risk to this ideology due to the 'risk' of childbearing and also the shame that is so often accompanied with sex.

Child health has also improved in recent years, and the age of first menarche has decreased. With this comes the associated sexual development. Adolescents are characters in flux, establishing self-assertion and separateness from childhood and the adults who perceive them within the childhood position. It is this apparent grey area of transition, where adulthood is beginning and the 'innocence' of childhood is disappearing, that causes conflicting perspectives, especially in the area of emerging sexuality. This, coupled with the widespread sexualisation of society, results in a mismatch between where children and young people are developmentally, and societal expectations and implications becoming more problematic for those who are autistic. Therefore, when childhood, youth and sexuality are combined, it makes conversations surrounding sexual behaviours difficult.

The context of relationships, sex and health education

It is important to recognise the educational and policy perspectives of relationships, sex, health and education (RSHE) when considering developmentally appropriate sexual behaviours in children and young people, and also inappropriate, problematic and harmful sexual behaviours that may be displayed by autistic children and young people. This should be considered alongside the underpinning knowledge of how sexual behaviours and children and young people are perceived within wider society. This section will consider the UK policy context as a backdrop to this discussion.

RSHE was not a formal feature in educational settings until after the Second World War. This appears to have been triggered by the move to reduce the rise in sexually transmitted infections (STIs) that were seen in postwar UK. However, education was embedded within science, with little reference to human sexual behaviour and relationships. A recognition of the importance of focusing on human relationships as an aspect of sexual behaviour emerged in the 1970s.

This was then furthered in the 1980s by the feminist movement with a renewed focus on gender roles within society. Within the context of the 1980s was also the fear mongering as a result of the AIDS crisis, which set back any progression in relationships and sex education that had been made, compounding the shame surrounding sexual relationships, especially those that did not fit within the heteronormative societal expectations. Education on sexual diversity was further inhibited with the introduction of Section 28, thus restricting realistic relationships and sex education (this was not repealed until 2000 in Scotland and 2003 in England and Wales).

In the 1990s there appeared to be a shift within this and a focus on the reduction of STIs and teenage pregnancy. It is useful to note at this point that the focus on sex-specific education was based around the prevention of negative outcomes rather than a focus on consent, pleasure, healthy relationships and developmentally appropriate sexual behaviours. This can be seen in the terminology used, moving from 'Sex Education' to 'Sex and Relationships Education' in 1999. This was linked to personal, social, health and economic (PSHE) education, although this was still not statutory. Many grassroots campaign groups recognised the importance of relationships and sex education, and the importance this held for their sexual development.

Despite the pressure on policy makers and commitments to redraft the RSE, policy work in this area slowed with the new Conservative coalition government in 2010. Movement was not seen in any great strides until a 2014 inquiry, which reignited the campaign for RSE to become statutory. This position was supported by the UNCRC, which, in 2016, recommended a statutory RSE policy for UK schools. This came to fruition in 2017 when relationships and sex education was legislated to be a statutory requirement. The guidance was updated in 2019 and relationships, sex and health education (RSHE) became statutory.

This was not the seminal moment it appeared to be, however, because in 2020, the Covid-19 pandemic resulted in subsequent school closures inhibiting work in this area. Since then the landscape surrounding RSHE has become especially fraught and politicised. An example can be seen via the production of a 'dossier' in Parliament by the then Conservative MP Miriam Cates in 2023, which purported that extreme sexual acts were being taught in RSHE sessions. On investigation (King-Hill and McCartan 2024a) it became clear that the assertions made in the document were not based on empirically based evidence, and that RSHE was being politicised. Despite this, a review of RSHE was brought forward.

Following a change of government in 2024, the revised statutory guidance for RSHE (Department for Education 2025) was published, which moved away from the politicisation and sensationalisation of the previous Conservative government's proposals. The 2025 statutory guidance represents a significant improvement in terms of clarity, structure and safeguarding emphasis; however, it remains notably limited in its attention to special educational needs and disabilities (SEND). Although the guidance acknowledges the need for differentiated teaching and references the importance of accessibility, it does not provide specific pedagogical strategies, suggestions for adapted resources or examples of best practice for autistic learners or learners with other neurodivergent profiles. This omission is particularly concerning given the unique challenges autistic learners may face in navigating relationships, consent and sexual health. Without tailored RSHE provision, these pupils risk being excluded from vital education that supports their safety, wellbeing and autonomy. Moreover, the lack of detailed SEND guidance places the burden on individual schools and educators to interpret and adapt content, often without sufficient training or support. As such, while the statutory status of RSHE is a step forward, the current framework does not yet fully meet the needs of all learners. There is an urgent need for evidence-based, autism-informed RSHE resources, alongside professional development for educators working with neurodivergent pupils.

The context of RSHE is especially important when considering autistic children and developmentally appropriate behaviours. The fraught nature of RSHE to date demonstrates that, even for those without additional support needs, the issues with teaching children and young people about relationships are evident. This links to the mutual exclusivity of children and young people and sexual behaviours, and also the perceptions of sexual behaviours within wider society and the associated shame and stigma stemming from the historical influences mentioned earlier. There is still an expectation that children and young people do not speak about or partake in sexual activity, and that sexual behaviour, especially in autistic children and young people, is seen as something that needs to be controlled and monitored. This is also strongly linked to the perceived risks associated with sexual behaviours and the conflict that these potentially have with the contribution to the labour market and career aspirations. However, this is in direct conflict with the highly sexualised society that children and young people find themselves in.

This is especially pertinent in adolescence, with the conflict of the adolescent seeing themselves transitioning to the adult domain yet often viewed as being firmly within the child domain, and lacking sexual agency and decision-making skills. It is this conflict and the sexualised society that makes RSHE particularly crucial for supporting developmentally appropriate sexual behaviours that keep children and young people safe, but that are also realistic. Evidence suggests that RSHE still often induces shame for children and young people, that good education and teaching in this area is sparse, and RSHE can be more damaging if it is carried out badly (King-Hill and McCartan 2024a; King-Hill, Gilsenan and McCartan 2023a; Pugh and King-Hill 2024). If shame is reinforced in RSHE it can put children and young people at risk as this negates safe spaces where they can ask for support and advice.

Evidence from a range of sources indicates that good RSHE results in the delay of sexual activity, rather than being an influencing factor for detrimental outcomes (evidence from Kirby 2007, UNESCO 2009 and the Sex Education Forum 2017). Despite this evidence, education on developmentally appropriate sexual behaviours in children and young people is still fraught with issues due to the perceptions of sexual behaviours and the position of children and young people and how they are perceived in wider society. Yet it is vital to keep in mind that children and young people are entitled to robust and evidence-based RSHE that can support them to negotiate the sexual world around them and help them make informed decisions about their own sexual behaviour. This should also be a priority for autistic children and young people, who are not asexual.

Given technological advances in recent years and widespread access to the internet and social media, this is even more pressing. Research indicates (Bragg et al. 2022; Ringrose, Regehr and Milne

2021; Setty 2022, 2023; Setty, Ringrose and Hunt 2024) that children and young people are increasingly using the internet to gain information about relationships and sex. For many children and young people the online and offline worlds have merged, and as a result of this, alongside other social interactions, many sexual behaviours have also moved online (discussed later in this chapter). This makes a case for the urgent need for a focus on online-based RSHE for children and young people, including those who are autistic.

Another urgent issue in relation to online access is the ease of access to pornography. Although technology-assisted harm will be discussed in depth later in this chapter, it is pertinent to highlight that children and young people are increasingly gaining education and information on sex and relationships from pornography. This needs to be addressed realistically via RSHE without the associated shame with the usage of pornography. Safe spaces for children and young people to explore and unpack what they have seen are still seriously lacking, and this is especially pertinent for the autistic child.

RSHE for all children and young people is vitally important to support them in the development of their sexual wellbeing. Well-designed and contextual RSHE is a key component in addressing the additional issues that autistic children may encounter when considering their own sexual development. Despite this, specific work in RSHE for autistic children is severely lacking and sporadic. Although this section highlights the historical issues with mainstream RSHE for all children and young people, specialist provision for those who are autistic is even more difficult to implement.

The discussion around RSHE demonstrates that there are a number of factors to consider when educating all children and young people on developmentally appropriate sexual behaviours. This also indicates the additional complexities that require consideration when working in this space with autistic children. RSHE should take into account the socio-ecological factors (discussed in Chapter Two) impacting on children and young people with these needs. Robust, evidence-based information on relationships and sex is needed for all children and young people, and this needs to be firmly supported by policy to enable the support of healthy sexual behaviours and prevent them developing into more inappropriate, problematic and harmful behaviours.

The changing context of sexual behaviour: The Natsal studies

There is a dearth of evidence and research that relates to developmentally appropriate sexual behaviour in children and young people. This is due to the converging factors discussed earlier that make discussions and work around sexual behaviours in children and young people difficult due to its contested nature, and the perceived mutual exclusivity of sexual behaviour and children and young people that makes research in this area ethically difficult. However, the British National Survey of Sexual Attitudes and Lifestyles (Natsal) studies do highlight that sexual behaviours, their context and what is considered 'normal' is fluid.

These three-phase studies are the largest sexual behaviour studies of their kind in the UK and have an explicit focus on human sexual behaviour. They consist of Natsal-1 (1990–91), which sampled 18,876 adults aged 16–59, Natsal-2 (1999–2001), which sampled 12,110 adults aged 16–44, and Natsal-3 (2010–12), which interviewed 15,162 adults aged 16–74; Natsal-4 is currently concluding, having interviewed 10,000 participants aged 16–59 (2022–23), with data being available from retrospective accounts from the 1930s. It is important to point out that these studies relate to those aged 16 and over; nevertheless they provide an important insight into the shifting perspectives of sexual behaviours.

The Natsal studies demonstrate that sexual behaviour is not static and is heavily steered by context, that sexual practice is complex and sporadic and has 'strong social determinants' (Mercer *et al.* 2013, p.1782). An example of the changing nature of sexual behaviours can be seen in the difference across the studies where vaginal sex had decreased and oral sex increased and then levelled out between Natsal-2 and Natsal-3 (Wellings *et al.* 2001). The studies also highlight that sexual experimentation increased over the duration of the three studies, and that changes in sexual behaviours are heavily dependent on social context and expectations such as legislation changes (e.g., legalities around homosexuality), national campaigns (e.g., Teenage Pregnancy Strategy) and STI epidemics (e.g., HIV / AIDS).

When focusing on children and young people in particular, the studies indicated that the range of sexual behaviours in children and young people was increasing, with vaginal sexual intercourse being the most common form of sex across the studies. The studies advocate for education and information to support healthy sexual development in children and young people (Mercer *et al.* 2013; Wellings *et al.* 2001). They assert that social influencing factors are a key aspect of sexual behaviour in the lives of children and young people, and that being informed is a vital aspect of keeping safe (Wellings *et al.* 2001). Vaginal and oral sexual experiences are the most common in the 16–24 age category, with a reduction in the median age of first sexual experience (Lewis *et al.* 2017), finding that the median age for sexual debut is 14 and first sexual intercourse at 16 (Wellings *et al.* 2001). Notably, prior to age 14 there is a lack of knowledge and data and no baseline exists.

When considering the educational needs of children and young people, the studies found that many young people lacked 'sexual competence' relating to mutual consent, contraception and decision making (Palmer *et al.* 2016, p.91). This shows the complexity and changing landscape of sexual behaviours in children and young people. When considering RSHE, the studies demonstrate that children and young people are gaining information about relationships and sex from social media rather than school-based education, advocating for more robust and varied RSHE in line with changing behaviours (Tanton *et al.* 2015). Since the publication of this paper social media and the internet has changed dramatically, with more and more children and young people accessing information via smartphones. The Natsal studies emphasise that staying abreast of the issues that surround children and young people is a crucial element in supporting them on their sexual journey, that this needs to be fluid and change with the shifting sexual landscape, and that as social influences change, so do sexual behaviours (Lewis *et al.* 2017; Mercer *et al.* 2023; Tanton *et al.* 2015; Wellings *et al.* 2001).

Defining inappropriate and problematic sexual behaviours

Inappropriate and problematic sexual behaviours (I/PSB), as set out in the Hackett Continuum,[2] are difficult to define due to a range of factors. Yet identifying these factors early for all children and young people can be a vital factor when preventing escalation to

---

2   https://centralsexualhealth.org/wp-content/uploads/sites/15/2022/11/The-Hackett-Continuum.pdf

more harmful behaviours. One of the difficulties relates to how sexual behaviours are perceived within different groups within society. I/PSB may be conceptualised differently between children and young people, parents or carers and specialist and non-specialist professionals. This results in disparities in how sexual behaviours are defined.

A robust understanding of what constitutes I/PSB is still lacking in Western society, and more research is needed to fully understand the 'tipping' point between healthy behaviours and I/PSB (King-Hill 2021, 2022). By understanding these complexities, the approaches to I/PSB can be planned for the contexts that children and young people are in. Relating these approaches to the socio-ecological model (discussed in the next chapter) will support both understanding and intervention in this area. This will give an insight into what is needed to de-escalate behaviours and to plan prevention measures. Nevertheless, research indicates that I/PSB sits within a grey area of definition and approaches between healthy and harmful sexual behaviours (King-Hill 2021, 2022).

Despite this disparity of understanding, I/PSB plays a crucial role in the escalation to more harmful sexual behaviours. Having an understanding of sexual behaviours of children and young people as a whole and how these are perceived, as outlined earlier, will support the recognition of I/PSB as an important point of intervention that should not be catastrophised or minimised, which is seen as a response to other sexual issues, such as sibling sexual behaviour (see King-Hill *et al.* 2023a, 2023b). Understanding that children and young people have an emerging sexuality and also a right to a healthy sex life should underpin considerations in this area, and a proactive approach to I/PSB should be taken to prevent it from developing. However, the perceptions of sexual behaviour and also how children and young people are seen may inhibit valuable work in this area.

The definitions of I/PSB are also dependent on many variables that include context and the difference in how behaviours are framed by children and young people, parents or carers and professionals (specialist and non-specialist). Across the board, I/PSB that is displayed in children and young people is hard to predict, and those demonstrating behaviours that are concerning are heterogeneous.

Understanding this 'tipping' point from healthy behaviours to l/PSB is not a simple linear process but requires an approach that accounts for many variable factors, and this is pertinent for autistic children and young people. As has been outlined, developmentally appropriate sexual behaviours are embedded within complex social viewpoints, therefore making considerations of l/PSB even more complex, yet pertinent. This complexity advocates, therefore, a multilevel approach.

Overview of harmful sexual behaviour and autism

A growing number of studies suggest that a significant proportion of harmful sexual behaviour is due to some of the features of autism providing the context of vulnerability rather than being due to any malicious intentions (Mogavero 2016). Allely and Creaby-Attwood (2016) reviewed studies that discussed some of these features of autism that can provide the context of vulnerability to engaging in harmful sexual behaviour. Some of these key features include:

- An obsession or preoccupation with certain things (e.g., women's underwear)
- Failure to conform to social conventions, impaired theory of mind (ToM) (ToM refers to the ability to explain and predict the behaviour of other people by discerning mental states including intentions, beliefs, desires or emotions; see Baron-Cohen, Leslie and Frith 1985; Gallagher and Frith 2003; Kana *et al.* 2015)
- 'Impaired ability to decode language and social gestures and a limited repertoire of appropriate behaviour' (Allely and Creaby-Attwood 2016, p.47)
- Impaired ability to appropriately interpret the victim's negative facial reactions (e.g., expressions of fear and distress) in response to their sexual advances (Freckelton and List 2009).

As discussed, terminology is critical when defining an element of behaviour present within a child or young person's life (Allardyce and Yates 2018). The misuse of the term 'harmful sexual behaviour' can have a significant impact on a young person's life and affect opportunities that at times include a safe and stable living environment. It is therefore important that the primary focus is on wider factors of the child or young person's life to ensure unnecessary labelling is not placed on them or their families. Sexual behaviour should be considered a continuum that is supported by an evidence base in determining factors of the level of behaviour the child or young person is displaying. It could be argued that a high proportion of concerning sexual behaviour displayed by children and young people is often problematic, which predominantly includes behaviours that impact on social isolation that can lead to a detriment in their own mental health and sexual development (Vosmer, Hackett and Callanan 2009).

Hackett (2014) suggests that children and young people displaying 'problematic, abusive or violent' sexual behaviours often show elements of 'compulsive' and 'intrusive' behaviours within the presence of the sexual behaviour. Compulsivity can be a prevalent factor in an autistic person's life (Hlavatá *et al.* 2018) that is often identifiable within bespoke interests or hobbies that can at times become all-consuming or a core part of everyday functioning (National Autistic Society 2020b). Taking this into consideration alongside an often hyper- or hyposensitive sensory (Marco *et al.* 2011) response to the world, we could suggest a link to problematic sexual development in relation to excessive use of pornography in which an autistic child or young person receives countless physical and psychological responses that support their specific needs.

The act of watching pornography often mirrors the elements that a person's autism may respond well to. These include predictability – the child or young person can ensure predictability is undertaken in deciding when the content starts and finishes. The act of masturbation offers a sense of predictability alongside the sensory return, such as the child or young person starts the process, controls the process and decides when they receive the sensory pleasure and when this finishes. A bespoke or intense interest that is sexualised, given the sensory return the act of masturbation and viewing pornography can give a young person, may influence an intense interest that is associated with autism becoming sexualised. Clinicians should consider the underlying function of the behaviour, whether it is sexually motivated or driven by features relating to autism (e.g., an autistic sensory need).

In defining harmful, abusive and violent sexual behaviour,

behaviours may include rape or sexual assault, creation, distribution or viewing of sexual abuse imagery of children and behaviours linked to emerging themes. Often these severe behaviours that would fall within the 'abusive' or 'violent' domain of Hackett's continuum of sexual behaviour would indicate that criminal justice systems would be present depending on the age of the child and legislation on age of criminal responsibility in the legal system in which they reside.

Although there is often an overrepresentation of this group among referrals to specialist services working with children who have displayed harmful sexual behaviour (Allardyce and Yates 2018), consideration should also be given to the minority that may be deemed sexually harmful and influence significant sexual violence either to satisfy psychological gratification or sexual arousal or that utilise physical violence to overpower another person to facilitate the abuse. The two motivations should be considered separately in identifying motivational factors that may show indicators of bespoke sexual interests or instances of paraphilias, such as sexual sadism in which a person requires another person's pain or discomfort to become sexually aroused (Allely 2020a). While not underestimating the impact any form of violence has on the victim, there are clear differences between the motivational factors each of these present with, and often require very different responses. It is critical that this domain is not misinterpreted by 'sexual fetishism' where consent is explicitly understood and an individual does not have a sole form of sexual expression.

In determining 'harmful sexual behaviour' being displayed by autistic children and young people, this chapter has begun to iden-tify the areas of complexity required in determining said behaviour in an already fraught landscape of sexual behaviours in children and young people, as outlined earlier. To understand core motivational factors in instances where victimisation of another has taken place, further exploration should be given to characteristics of the harm and the victim.

Sexual behaviours and the harm index
Children and young people who display harmful sexual behaviour are not a heterogeneous group, and the avoidance of generalising harmful sexual behaviour brings with it various issues. Allardyce and

Yates (2018) suggest a model of 'subgroups' that defines the following indexes of harm within harmful sexual behaviour: peer-on-peer; female; sibling or intrafamilial sexual abuse; learning disability; and pre-pubescent children. These groups form individualised factors that are present within each form of harmful sexual behaviour that highlights that generic responses are ineffective; this also advocates for a socio-ecological approach, as highlighted in Chapter Two. An example of this can be seen in identifying that the prevalence of sibling sexual behaviour and abuse has drastically improved in recent years, but children and young people are more likely to experience sexual abuse or harm within their own family (Yates and Allardyce 2021).

Approaches to this harm index vary, and although limited, some evidence suggests the use of 'restorative justice approaches' and 'family group decision making' can be of significant benefit in supporting a whole-family approach. In collating a psychosexual developmental assessment (Leonard and Donathy 2017) on the child's life from the point of being conceived, we can start to form an understanding of factors that include the information the child has utilised to be informed of sex; their experience and knowledge base within sex education; gender role modelling and attitudes around sex and gender; and initial sexual contact or experiences. In utilising evidence-based assessment and intervention models designed for supporting children and young people, the harm index can be explored to ensure an accurate representation is presented within professional or legal environments.

Victim attributes

The presence of a learning disability in a child or young person's life increases their vulnerability and likelihood of experiencing sexual abuse or harm (Franklin, Raws and Smeaton 2015). In determining a child or young person's ability to ensure victim compliance it is essential that an understanding of the victims themselves is gathered to assess elements of vulnerability that may have been exploited in instigating the harm. In understanding motivational factors of harmful sexual behaviour, identifying themes of victimisation in the following areas may support the assessment process: 'Was the victim or one of the victims a family member?' 'Excluding family, was the victim/s known to you?' 'Was the victim a current partner?' 'Was the victim an ex-partner?' 'Was the victim a stranger?' 'Did you first contact the victim online?' 'Was the victim a child under the age of 16?'

Approaches to defining sexual behaviour in autistic children

At the initial stages of the harmful sexual behaviour being displayed by autistic children and young people, prior to utilising specific assessment models on sexual behaviour it is useful to consider the contributory elements outlined in the socio-ecological model (set out in Chapter Two). These aspects are also demonstrated in King-Hill's Sibling Sexual Behaviour Mapping Tool (SSBMT) (King-Hill and Gilsenan 2023). While the SSBMT is aligned with sibling sexual behaviour, the domains set out in the tool provide a robust example of the range of socio-ecological factors that require consideration for harmful sexual behaviour in autistic children and young people. The model is arguably supportive within the context of autism as it requires a focus on environmental or social factors that have significant relevance for this condition. The model considers: the behaviour itself, those at risk, housing, schooling / education, home circumstances, health and development.

In this respect it is then useful to consider 'who' is at risk of the harmful sexual behaviour, and requires the team around the child or young person to explore factors of victim characteristics and potential mitigations of future risk. The 'who' is incredibly relevant for consideration of autistic children and young people, and may identify neurodiverse complexities such as an apparent power imbalance associated with age, but may highlight a theme of physical, social and sexual age of functioning that may be less present within a neurotypical population. Although the physical age difference between the child responsible for the harm and a victim is often referred to as a critical risk indicator (Hackett *et al.* 2013), an autistic child may be socially and emotionally functioning at a different age to their physical or sexual development, and therefore the intentional level of harm may become less clear (Hinnebusch, Miller and Fein 2017).

Explicitly outlining the incident(s) of harmful sexual behaviour within this domain initiates the next steps of required assessment and intervention, and the importance of this detail is often overlooked. The inclusion of families and professionals who have a sound understanding of the child's autism may support this step in determining the difference between sexual behaviours and potential sensory responses that are in tune with the child's autism. The exploration of the behaviour should be used to explore the individual incidents themselves and the potential crossover or co-morbid themes such as sensory requirement, in which the behaviour displayed could be misinterpreted as sexualised – such as the pressure or texture of clothing that may have required the child or young person to remove clothing in a public place to meet their sensory discomfort – therefore requiring an entirely different and less punitive intervention or response from adults. Similar to this is the area of intense interest – exploring the behaviour itself may provide further insight into the need for adults or support networks to support distraction techniques to encourage the child or young person to a safer or more age-appropriate interest.

As indicated in both the socio-ecological model (see Chapter Two) and the SSBMT, the environmental factors in which the behaviour has taken place are vitally important to consider, as well as their contribution to opportunistic or pre-meditated behaviours that were supported or influenced by the environment in which the harmful sexual behaviour took place. Various studies highlight the importance of the presence of routine and predictability to support the needs of an autistic child or young person (Boyd, McCarty and Sethi 2014; McAuliffe *et al.* 2017). Although the core purpose of environmental factors awareness is to consider the environment in which the harmful sexual behaviour took place, this also echoes the need for a child-centred and holistic approach, which, in terms of autism, would benefit from further exploration into environmental traits that are potentially causing the child or young person distress and influencing harmful behaviour. This approach also needs to consider the provision of boundary setting, structured and informed time and triggers caused by the environment in relation to sensory requirement.

Included in the contextual considerations should be identifying potential triggers of the harmful behaviours being displayed and themes that may be linked to a disruption in routine, structure or environment. It is also key to consider elements of opportunistic techniques that may be used by a child or young person, such as instances of limited adult supervision or in semi-private areas such as bathrooms. These themes require further assessment in identifying any elements of deviancy or the intent to harm, and at times may indicate the need for additional supervision. This multisystemic understanding should also consider historical elements to inform a robust understanding of the child or young person's psychosexual development. Punitive measures at this stage are potentially unhelpful in the reduction of the behaviour, yet it is important that this is not misinterpreted as justification for the behaviour but rather as a method to gather chronological information on the child or young person's life to understand the wider factors that may have influenced the harmful sexual behaviour. Autistic children and young people often have a less informed or non-existent input on sex education (Gougeon 2010) due to societal perceptions that can at times fail to see them as sexual beings with sexual needs and requirements. This understanding can support the identification of misinformation or understanding within the context of sex education and social boundaries that may identify alternative approaches to a harmful sexual behaviour intervention that require a bespoke and child-centred psychosexual education input.

In utilising a multilevel approach, practitioners can gather in-depth information in regards to a number of aspects of the child or young person's life that can support effective interventions and a factual and accurate assessment. Although utilising such models can be of significant support in the creation and delivery of an intervention, many tools currently in circulation do not provide bespoke guidance in supporting additional support needs, and often require professional skill and experience in transferring models into a more palatable approach for autistic children and young people. However, careful consideration should be given to this approach not to characterise autism as one definitive additional need, as it can and will present differently for each person (APA 2013), and caution should be taken not to simply consider a 'neurotypical' and 'neurodiversity' approach that loses the benefits to child-centred processes.

Many myths and misconceptions are associated with autism, some of which include suggested static factors that generalise social or communicational abilities. Empathy is a component frequently described in various assessment models for both children and adults responsible for sexual harm (Briggs, Hill and Kennington 2020), often lacking the presence of an evidence base for its relevance. Alexithymia (Young 2019), a concept in which an individual is impaired in their ability to recognise their own or other people's emotions, linked closely to social clues and cues, raises questions as to an autistic person's ability and capability to display what society deems as empathy. The ability to recognise and display emotion evidently can be an area of difficulty for an autistic child or young person (Stagg, Tan and Kodakkadan 2022). A cold or unresponsive display does not mean that a child or young person is simply deviant, cold or uncaring, but may highlight the need to differentiate between empathy and physical display.

It is also essential that empathy, which describes a person's ability to feel on behalf of another, is not confused with sympathy, which describes feelings of pity or sorrow for another. Arguably in relation to harmful sexual behaviour the presence of empathy and / or sympathy may give an indication to the child or young person's ability to hold some form of responsibility to the behaviour in which they have harmed another, although the sole focus should not be placed on the term 'empathetic', which may take considerable time to determine (Li et al. 2023).

TECHNOLOGY-ASSISTED HARMFUL SEXUAL BEHAVIOUR

Digital technologies are now an essential part of the lives of all children and young people. For younger children, going online includes a range of aspects such as playing games, entertainment and learning. Online spaces also create opportunities for communication and connection, and for many young people, social media additionally becomes a space for creativity and self-expression through content creation.

Going online is an unavoidable part of growing up. A report by Ofcom (2024) found that 96 per cent of 5- to 7-year-olds in the UK went online and 100 per cent of 12- to 17-year-olds. Different age groups may have different ways of accessing online spaces. Children aged 12–17 are more likely to use a mobile phone to go online than any other device, while those aged 3–11 are more likely to use a tablet for this purpose (Ofcom 2024). However, irrespective of the method of accessing the internet, online technologies have revolutionised many aspects of adolescent development.

Online media and digital communication are now embedded in children's daily experiences and routines, and it is complex to separate online activities from other aspects of their physical social lives. Children's internet use has become continuous, filling up the gaps between daily activities, with the internet being used to help synchronously contextualise activities and experiences. The Covid-19 pandemic has also led to increased use of the online environment for a variety of daily activities, and has widened access and engagement for many children and young people, further blurring the lines between online and offline experiences.

There are regular concerns in the media about negative impacts on children of overusing technology, and smartphones 'rewiring' childhood so that they are more vulnerable to anxiety and mental illness (Haidt 2024). However, Ofcom (2024) found that young people also describe digital technologies contributing to a sense of wellbeing, stating that social media or messaging apps / sites contributed to the happiness for two-thirds (67 per cent) of 8- to 17-year-olds all or most of the time. It is difficult to integrate a comprehensive picture of both opportunities and risks online as researchers generally focus on risk or resilience, and rarely both together (Smahel *et al.* 2020).

These findings also hold true for autistic children. For many autistic individuals, social isolation is a significant challenge. Online platforms and digital communication tools often provide an accessible alternative to face-to-face interactions, offering a space where social anxiety may be reduced and / or more easily managed, and communication can be more controlled. Emerging research in particular suggests that autistic people have a greater preference for using social media than non-autistic people (McGhee Hassrick *et al.* 2021). Autism-related content online spaces can also help build community through connection, understanding and inclusion for young people starting to explore their identity online, including their identity as autistic individuals (Gilmore *et al.* 2024).

Autistic young people often use the internet in slightly different ways to other children. Some caution is necessary here as research notes that gender, race / ethnicity and social-economic status significantly impact online behaviour, and may be more important factors than neurodiversity in explaining how young people access and use the internet. However, research has found that autistic adults and young people may prefer to communicate over the internet instead of in-person, although some find online platforms a source of anxiety (Brownlow and O'Dell 2006). In particular, research also indicates that video calling can cause stress for some autistic adults (Zolyomi *et al.* 2019). Research also suggests that autistic individuals are more likely to prefer certain interfaces such as personal computers over smartphones (Iglesias, Gómez Sánchez and Alcedo Rodríguez 2019). Nonetheless, exploring and using digital technologies is an essential aspect of the lives of autistic young people, as it is with young people who are neurotypical.

It is pertinent to consider how technology can be used for negative purposes and has led to new opportunities for criminality and anti-social behaviour. Typical cybercrimes involve fraud and scams, extortion and use of ransomware, use of malware, identity theft and online harassment. However, sexual offences can also occur using digital technologies. Online harmful sexual behaviour can take many forms, such as:

- Accessing child sexual abuse material (CSAM) online
- Sexual conversations with children
- Online solicitation of children
- Sexual harassment of peers and adults online
- Sharing of self-produced sexual images without consent
- Exposure of a child to harmful online content with sexual intent
- Livestreaming of sexual abuse and exploitation
- Sharing sexual material with children or young people
- Online stalking.

Those who commit online sexual offences are typically assumed to be adults, and in the main it is adults who carry out these behaviours online. However, data about online harm is complex. A study carried out in the US of a nationally representative sample of 2638 18- to 28-year-olds asked them about their experiences of technology-assisted harm in childhood. The study used the concept of 'online child sexual abuse' (OCSA), incorporating non-consensual image taking or sharing, forced image recruitment, threatened sharing of sexual pictures, unwanted sexual talk, questions or sexual act requests by adults, and commercial sexual exploitation, involving sex talk, images or other sexual activity. The study found that 16 per cent of those in the study reported experiencing one or more of these forms of abuse or exploitation online before they turned 18. However, one of the key findings from the study was that those carrying out the behaviours in most categories were predominantly dating partners, friends and acquaintances, not online strangers. Additionally, young people in the study were more likely to experience sexual harm from peers than from adults (Finkelhor, Turner and Colburn 2022).

The finding that children are harmed by the sexual behaviour of peers at least as often as they are by the sexual behaviour of adults is replicated in a study that focused on young people's online experiences. The tech non-governmental organisation (NGO) Thorn (2023) looked at whether young people used online tools to block those intending sexual harm after experiences of sexual and non-sexual harm. They had a sample of 1142 children aged between 9 and 17 and asked whether they had experienced specific forms of harm online. Minors reported experiencing online sexual interactions with peers and individuals they perceived to be adults at similar rates.

These findings suggest that technology-enabled sexual behaviour carried out by young people that causes harm to others is widespread, and that children may be as likely to be abused or exploited by peers online as they are by adults. This is congruent with studies that explore young people's experiences of online dating. Technology can also be used within intimate or dating relationships to initiate, maintain or escalate abuse (Stonard 2020). Typical technology-assisted behaviours reported by adolescents within their relationships include the sending of insults, threats, humiliation, non-consensual sharing of images, sexual pressure, monitoring messages or whereabouts, demanding passwords to social media accounts, deleting contacts or preventing an individual using technology (Stonard 2018). These harmful and controlling behaviours typically fall into three categories – digital monitoring and control, digital direct aggression and digital sexual abuse (Reed *et al.* 2021) – but are often multifarious and can be enacted across a range of devices and platforms, meaning that they can be extensive and highly intrusive.

Aside from studies looking at children's experiences of sexual exploitation and abuse online, young people who carry out online harm is also borne out by criminal justice data. In the UK, the *National Analysis of Police-Recorded Child Sexual Abuse and Exploitation Crimes Report 2022* found that online child sexual abuse and exploitation made up at least 32 per cent of all the sexual offences involving children as victims in England and Wales. Overall, perpetrators up to the age of 17 account for 64 per cent of the online offending age demographic. That works out as 16,401 of 25,561 offences being perpetrated by under-18-year-olds (NPCC 2024).

It is sometimes assumed that abuse experienced online has less impact on a victim than abuse experienced offline. As with contact forms of sexual abuse, the impact of sexual harm in online contexts varies widely and can be severe and lifelong. If images of a child have been shared, for example, the child is revictimised each time they are viewed. This can extend into adulthood, with adult survivors of online harm experiencing distress knowing that images of themselves in childhood continue to be shared in perpetuity. More generally, experiences of online sexual harm can lead to feelings of guilt, shame and self-blame, and can make children vulnerable to further sexual harm (Hamilton-Giachritsis *et al.* 2020). Additionally, there is no evidence to date to suggest that online harm carried out by young people themselves is any less impactful on victims than abuse perpetrated by adults (Allardyce and Yates 2018).

Recognition among professionals and practitioners that young people can be the cause of sexual harm as well as the subject of such harm has led to the development of the term 'technology-assisted harmful sexual behaviour'. This has been defined as involving under-18s using the internet, or other forms of technology, to engage in sexual activity that may be harmful to themselves or others:

> One or more children engaging in sexual discussions or acts – using the internet and/or any image-creating/sharing or communication device – which is considered inappropriate and/or harmful given their age or stage of development. This behaviour falls on a continuum of severity from the use of pornography to online child sexual abuse. (Hollis, Belton and Team 2017, p.11)

These behaviours could include taking, making, possessing or distributing indecent images of children (including self-produced images or 'sexts'); making, viewing or distributing extreme pornography; grooming; and soliciting or sexual harassment online (Hollis *et al.* 2017; Lewis 2018).

Technology-assisted harmful sexual behaviour (TA-HSB) can be solely evident or can be displayed alongside 'offline' contact sexual behaviours. In one study of referrals to a UK forensic child and adolescent mental health team, 289 referrals over a 4-year period were of children who had displayed harmful sexual behaviour. Of those, 60 per cent (N = 173) had engaged in some form of TA-HSB. This consisted of 15 per cent (N = 43) who had engaged in TA-HSB and 45 per cent (N = 130) who had engaged in both offline and TA-HSB (Galvin *et al.* 2024).

Research into young people who have displayed TA-HSB is surprisingly underdeveloped for such a significant social issue (Lewis 2018). Studies suggest that children who engage in harmful sexual behaviour in online contexts are predominantly white males (Hollis *et al.* 2017; Vaswani *et al.* 2022). Those who display harmful sexual behaviour solely in online contexts have been found to be typically older at the time of referral to services in comparison to young people involved with contact-only harmful sexual behaviour. They are also likely to have fewer mental health or behavioural difficulties, come from more stable family backgrounds and perform better at school (Belton and Hollis 2016; Hollis *et al.* 2017). There is contradictory evidence in relation to trauma and victimisation across studies (Hollis *et al.* 2017; Vaswani *et al.* 2022).

Autism and technology-assisted harmful sexual behaviour

Professionals working with children who have displayed harmful sexual behaviour often describe an overrepresentation of autistic individuals among the children and young people they work with. This is echoed by safeguarding colleagues in educational settings who often describe it as commonplace for autistic young people to get into trouble because of their online sexual behaviour.

One study by Vaswani *et al.* (2022) highlights this as an issue. The study looked at 61 young people in Glasgow who had come to the attention of services because of online harmful sexual behaviour. In 36 per cent of cases the young people had a mental health condition, learning disability or autism, either diagnosed or suspected (Vaswani *et al.* 2022). Establishing that autistic young people are significantly more likely to be involved with such behaviour remains minimal, and it has not been identified as a factor in the literature to date (Lewis 2018).

Clinical consensus appears to align with the premise that autistic young people are overrepresented among youth who are involved with TA-HSB. However, the dearth of research in this area may be for a number of reasons. Studies that have looked at young people who have displayed TA-HSB have typically used small sample sizes. Moultrie (2006) had sample sizes of 7 and 6 respectively, while samples of young people with TA-HSB in Hollis *et al.* (2017) were 21, Aebi *et al.* (2014) 54 and Galvin *et al.* (2024) 43. It may be that small sample sizes are insufficient to identify a minority where there are issues around autism. Studies that have looked at young people who come to the attention of statutory services as a result of such behaviour may identify children with autistic traits, but many will not have been formally assessed or received a diagnosis. In a minority of situations a young person having contact with the criminal or youth justice system may be the first time that a formal assessment for autism has occurred.

Reporting of autism among young people who have displayed TA-HSB may be an example of confirmation bias or even labelling all young people who may have a presentation that is unusual, but may have an explanation beyond neurodivergence. Even if that were the case, the general prevalence of online harm carried out by young people would mean that services still need to be adequate for young people who display these behaviours, whether they are autistic or not.

It is worth noting that this issue is paralleled in the relevant adult forensic literature. Although there seems to be a clinical consensus among practitioners working with adults who have sexually offended online that autism is overrepresented, and there appear to be good theoretical reasons for why autistic adults may be vulnerable to online sexual offending (Creaby-Attwood and Allely 2017), this does not seem to be borne out by the findings of studies that have looked at demographic data in relation to accessing CSAM or other forms of online sexual crime (see, for example, Babchishin *et al.* 2018).

A note of caution is urged here. Even if there was robust evidence that young people who have autism are overrepresented among young people who have displayed TA-harmful sexual behaviour, it may be that this is not because more autistic young people are displaying this behaviour than would be expected (bearing in mind around 1 per cent of the population is estimated to have autism). It may be just that autistic young people are more likely to be caught for online transgressions. For instance, they may be less aware that their behaviour is causing harm to others, and may therefore make no effort to hide the behaviour, or they may be less likely to deny it when questioned.

Autism and online sexual development

Despite the lack of data linking autism to adolescent TA-HSB, there may be aspects of adolescent sexual and social development of young people that mean that autistic young people are more vulnerable to display TA-HSB.

Children are often involved with developmentally expected exploration about sex from a young age, which involves a natural curiosity about their own bodies and those around them. This is often a way of making sense of gender and their own physicality. In early adolescence key changes occur that are typically linked to biological changes. Although there is considerable diversity, and a small proportion of adolescents report no sexual feelings or behaviour in their adolescence, typical behaviours in adolescence sequentially include:

- Increased sexual thoughts and interests
- New experiences of physical sexual arousal
- Self touch and masturbation
- Sexual interests and preoccupations with peers and adults (including those who are famous)
- Discussion with close friends about sexual attraction
- Flirting
- Dating behaviour
- Kissing.

By age 16, around half of young people in the UK will have experienced some sexual intimacy (mutual touch, oral sex, etc.), with some having experienced sexual intercourse (Allardyce and Yates 2018).

The lack of separation between online and offline experiences means that many of these experiences are now mediated in online ways. For instance, flirting may take place in online spaces with peers known to them or who may even be strangers, with dating apps targeting adolescents now being available. In the highly visual cultures of online youth that are characterised by value instilled by the number of 'likes' received by others, sharing a sexual image with a peer may be one of the first sexual encounters that a young person has.

Navigating this terrain of sexual development online and rules of contemporary courtship for young people can be difficult for a range of reasons for autistic young people. This is compounded by the fact that autistic young people may feel that they are more able to control online engagement and relationships than real-life relationships, and are therefore more likely to be attracted to sexual expression that is mediated online.

Key vulnerabilities for autistic young people include:

- Delayed social maturity. Peterson, Slaughter and Paynter (2007) compared social maturity levels among 16 neurotypical young people and 27 autistic children aged 4–12, and found that those who were autistic presented lower social maturity levels than their neurotypical peers. This may, in turn, impact the capacity of autistic young people to interact with peers, potentially leading to increased social isolation and withdrawal. This may then reduce opportunities to naturally gather sexual knowledge from peers and explore emerging sexual thoughts with peers (Brown-Lavoie, Viecili and Weiss 2014), as well as increasing the likelihood of being dependent on online interactions, sometimes with individuals who are outside their natural school and community-based peer group.

- Lesser sexual knowledge. Most studies that have explored this factor have found that autistic young people generally have less sexual knowledge than their neurotypical peers, and receive less sexual education from social sources (e.g., parents or carers, teachers). Because of this they may be more reliant on social sources for knowledge about sex and sexuality from the internet (Brown-Lavoie *et al.* 2014; Mehzabin and Stokes 2011; Ousley and Mesibov 1991).

- Cognitive differences that impact on sexual decision making. Some autistic individuals may have a limited understanding of what is socially acceptable behaviour and struggle with concepts of privacy, consent and boundaries. These challenges can be compounded by difficulties in interpreting non-verbal signals, which play a crucial role in navigating intimate and sexual relationships. These signals may be more difficult to navigate online than in real-life situations.

- Restricted and repetitive behaviours and interests (RRBIs). RRBIs are important to consider with autistic young people and their potential vulnerabilities online. For instance, some individuals may develop an intense focus on specific topics, including sexual content, which can lead to problematic online behaviour if not guided appropriately. This can include rigidity in interests and sexual-related fixated interests (Murrie *et al.* 2002). Sensory processing difficulties and sexual-related sensory stimuli may also be a factor (Haskins and Silva 2006).

- Impaired theory of mind (ToM), making it difficult to know right from wrong. Some autistic young people may struggle to understand that children have been harmed in child sexual abuse material (CSAM), particularly if any evidence of exploitation is absent in the static images or videos themselves.

- Modelling / imitation. Young people may imitate a behaviour without appreciating or understanding the meaning, complexity or context behind it – for example, behaviours they have seen on the television / internet. Coercion, often through immature expressions of gendered behaviour and influence of peers (sometimes relating to negative hypermasculine social media messaging), can be a factor for young people. Exposure to pornography at an early age before they are developmentally able to process and appraise what they are seeing may also be a factor.

- Lack of opportunities / restrictive environment. Lack of outlets for typical sexual expression and normative sexual exploration with peers is a factor, as can be the overprotectiveness of parents or carers who may feel uncomfortable in relation to the social and sexual development of their child in adolescence.

- Difficulties with imagination / empathy, that is, not understanding what other people are thinking, and difficulties understanding consequences of actions. What an autistic youth may experience as confidently expressing their sexual interest to a peer may be experienced by the peer as persistent and continuing, despite exhibiting clear social cues that the sexual interest is not mutual.

Autism and negative experiences online

Vaswani *et al.* (2022) found that autistic young people were overrepresented in their sample of young people who displayed TA-HSB. Another finding was that the majority of young men who displayed TA-HSB had themselves experienced sexual exploitation online. Many would not have described their experiences this way, often minimising their experiences to avoid appearing vulnerable. Nonetheless, some of the young people in the study had experienced significant, distressing and often repeated sexual interactions with adults and other peers online.

Discussions in relation to online harm tend to be binary, separating groups into those who harm and those who have been harmed. Research on cohorts of young people who display harmful sexual behaviour complicates this picture. Hollis *et al.*'s (2017) UK study looked at 21 young people involved with online-only offending and 35 young people engaged with both online and offline harmful sexual behaviour. A quarter of the online-only group reported that they themselves had been sexually groomed or abused online, echoing the findings of Vaswani *et al.* (2022). Moultrie (2006), in their small-scale study of young people who displayed TA-HSB, found that at least one person who had been arrested for possession of CSAM had themselves been sent this material by an adult.

Although experiences of sexual harm and exploitation online are insufficient explanations for the sexually harmful behaviours themselves, it may be the case that for some autistic young people, negative sexual and relational experiences model unhealthy boundaries, and this is a risk factor for further behaviour that may harm others. When these happen in a social context with other participants or bystanders who do not actively stop the harm happening, it may be difficult for the autistic child to understand that what has happened to them was wrong.

Autistic people who are socially isolated in adolescence may spend more time online, which, in turn, makes them vulnerable online. There also may be risks that flow from misjudging contexts and relationships, which make autistic young people more open to exploitation. Cyberbullying is a significant problem experienced by up to two-thirds of autistic young people, which can lead to experiences of anxiety and distress.

There is some research to suggest that autistic girls and young women are three times more likely to be sexually assaulted than neurotypical girls and young women (Cazalis *et al.* 2022). In one study of 95 autistic adults and 117 neurotypical adults, 78 per cent of the autistic respondents reported at least one occurrence of sexual victimisation compared to 47.4 per cent of the comparison group. Male adults with autism are also more likely to experience victimisation compared to males without autism, in relation to contact sexual abuse, coercion and rape (Browne-Lavoie *et al.* 2014).

A recent review of studies looking at the experience of online sexual exploitation of children with disabilities and autism found studies that were theoretically rather than empirically grounded on this subject (Álvarez-Guerrero, Fry, Ly and Gaitis 2024). However, it is likely that this gap in research will be filled in the future, and may help us understand the links between vulnerability and the onset of harmful sexual behaviour online.

Pornography and autism
There has been an emergence of data on exposure of children and young people to pornography and the impact of that exposure on

young people. In a study of 1000 young adults asked about their childhood experiences in the UK, the average age at which children first saw pornography was 13. By age 9, 10 per cent had seen pornography, 27 per cent had seen it by age 11, and half of the children who had seen pornography had seen it by age 13 (Children's Commissioner 2023). Seventy-nine per cent had encountered violent pornography before the age of 18, and frequent users of pornography were more likely to engage in physically aggressive sex acts.

This study does not discuss whether there are particular issues in relation to exposure of autistic children to pornography. This has, however, been picked up in the clinical literature, which often describes ritualistic collection of pornography among autistic young people and adults who are referred to clinical and forensic settings. For instance, Aral, Say and Usta (2018) reported the case of an autistic girl who had searched the internet for photos of famous naked children. The authors note that the scale of collection in this case was not an indicator of scale of deviance, but rather an example of the repetitive behaviour of this young person.

It would be a reasonable hypothesis that lack of access to sexual information and experience in adolescence, social isolation, high levels of dependence on online experiences and ritualistic, repetitive behaviours and lack of understanding of social context were factors meaning that autistic young people were more likely to seek out online pornography than other young people and also more likely to be negatively impacted. To date there is no empirical data to back this assumption, but it is theoretically possible. We also know from studies such as that undertaken by the Children's Commissioner's Office (2023) that early and / or regular exposure to pornography may affect sexual development and be a factor in the development of harmful sexual behaviour. This is common in clinical presentations, but to date, empirically based research on this subject is lacking.

CASE STUDY ONE: Technology-assisted harmful sexual behaviour

Dan, a 17-year-old autistic male, was referred to a specialist harmful sexual behaviour service due to concerns around his apparent reliance on what was described as an 'addiction to mainstream pornographic material'. The content Dan was reported to watch would often be videos of men and women engaging in sexual acts within public spaces. Dan was reported to spend up to eight hours at a time repeatedly watching videos while masturbating. A number of concerns were raised:

- Sleep deprivation. Dan was often accessing pornography late into the evening, and at times he would report himself that he 'lost sense of time'.
- Physical health. The repetitive act of masturbating was causing physical abrasions to Dan's penis, leading to bleeding and pain.
- Social understanding. It became evident that Dan struggled to differentiate between pornography and intimate sexual relationships.

Dan had received little access to relationships and sex education (RSE) during his time at school due to a key focus of his education being around partial attainment and in facilitating a part-time timetable. The specialist service highlighted that the behaviour Dan was displaying was not necessarily defined as harmful sexual behaviour but rather, problematic, affecting his own social, emotional and physical health. On the team's initial meeting with Dan it was clear that any discussion around sex or Dan's pornography use was going to be embarrassing, even shameful, for him.

Early in the intervention Dan had made the practitioner aware that he was an avid *Star Wars* fan, which allowed the practitioner to utilise Dan's interest to create a child-centred intervention plan. Two key areas were identified to prioritise in the intervention, one being to support Dan's understanding of time, and the other to help him identify the differences between pornography, intimacy and consent. *Star Wars* was a core part of this, with the practitioner supporting Dan to explore characters within the film, creating a timeline and visual artwork around the characters' lives, romantic partners and family. Once this was completed the same exercise was repeated, this time looking at the actors' lives playing the characters, which allowed the practitioner to open up a discussion around the differences between acting and everyday experiences. This approach supported Dan's understanding of the key messages professionals wanted him to grasp in relation to pornography, being mindful of the impact of shame that a direct discussion may have created in the initial stages of the intervention.

As the support continued, practitioners were acutely aware of the unhealthy role pornography had played in Dan's life, both as an unhelpful source of sexual information but also as an apparent coping strategy for Dan to respond to stress in periods when he became dysregulated. Dan expressed a view that he himself was at times surprised to learn how long he had watched pornography, stating he had 'lost the sense of time'. To support Dan the practitioners chose a harm reduction approach during the initial stages, acknowledging that removing all access to pornography in the interim may cause significant distress to Dan.

To help Dan understand time better, he was given a stopwatch. The stopwatch would support Dan to understand the time he had spent viewing pornography, and a scheduled timetable, noting times Dan was to set on his stopwatch, supported him to reduce the time being spent on this activity. Over the course of a few months, it was noted that Dan's pornography use appeared to decrease, and that he started utilising the stopwatch strategy in other non-sexual aspects of his life, such as painting cartoon figures.

This case highlights the need for practitioners to think dynamically and to acknowledge alternative approaches that may be considered as soft interventions but that can have a significant impact. Alongside this work Dan gradually began to become more comfortable in engaging in a bespoke RSE programme, with practitioners noting he had many unanswered questions, just like many other young people. This space ensured Dan had the equal opportunity to be curious about sexuality as his peers.

CONCLUSION

This chapter has explored a range of factors that require consideration when exploring autism and sexual behaviours. The mutual exclusivity of childhood and sexuality and the historical underpinnings of sexual behaviour provide a backdrop to perceptions of sexual behaviour in children and young people, and are particularly pertinent to autistic children and young people. This is coupled with the importance of the context of relationships, sex, health and education in the UK. It is also important to note that sexual behaviour is not static, and longitudinal studies on sexual behaviours indicate that societal norms and behaviours shift over time and are fluid. Definitions of inappropriate and problematic sexual behaviours, and how harmful sexual behaviour and autism are, are also important factors when considering sexual behaviours in autistic children and young people. The index of harm and victim attributes demonstrate the complex nature of sexual behaviours in autistic children and young people. The importance of recognising the pertinence and proliferation of technology-assisted harmful sexual behaviour in autistic children and young people is also an important part for the considerations that need to be given.

Overall, the context of sexual behaviours in autistic children and young people is complex and multifaceted, with many aspects that require consideration when harmful sexual behaviours are displayed in this cohort.

CHAPTER TWO

Socio-Ecological Model and Approaches to Assessment and Intervention

In assessing harmful sexual behaviour in children and young people it is crucial that professionals only utilise assessment tools and approaches designed for children, and do not rely on or transfer adult offence management frameworks that are unsuitable and inappropriate within this population (Allardyce and Yates 2018). Prior to undertaking a specialist harmful sexual behaviour assessment, practitioners should first consider the value the proposed assessment will provide. This should consider carefully the purpose of an assessment such as risk management to determine recidivism or to support an intervention approach. It is critical that care is taken in initial assessments to avoid unnecessary overestimation of risk (Chaffin, Letourneau and Silovsky 2002; Hackett 2014) and wider factors are taken into account to support a reduction in harm. This chapter will explore the socio-ecological model and its relevance to autism and harmful sexual behaviour assessment and intervention. Assessment and intervention will then be discussed in depth, underpinned by the socio-ecological model.

THE SOCIO-ECOLOGICAL MODEL AND ASSESSING BEHAVIOURS

Collectively, many approaches focus on similar domain criteria when determining risk and factors that may have contributed to the emergence and / or perpetuation of harmful sexual behaviours (Prentky and Righthand 2003; Worling and Curwen 2001). However, a socio-ecological approach to assessment is underpinned by considering the wider socio-ecological domains within a child or young person's life (HM Inspectorate of Probation 2023). This framework can be a helpful method to prepare intervention needs based on a child or young person's wider needs, taking into account a contextual safeguarding approach that addresses vulnerability and risk factors that may have collectively influenced harmful or criminogenic behaviour.

The socio-ecological model explores this via four foundational domains: individual, interpersonal, community and societal. These fundamental domains give guidance in taking into account the factors that may contribute to an effective and whole-systems approach to the child or young person's whole identity as opposed to an over-behavioural focus that only addresses the harmful sexual behaviour. It is important that an assessment framework takes into account the child or young person's strengths and prosocial factors on a multisystemic level that may be supportive in tackling behaviour or dynamic risk factors.

This approach can be aligned to the socio-ecological framework (HM Inspectorate of Probation 2023) (see Figure 1).

INDIVIDUAL	INTERPERSONAL	COMMUNITY	SOCIETAL
Factors in an autistic child or young person's biology and personal history that increase the possibility of committing harmful sexual behaviour	Factors within an autistic child or young person's closest relationships history that increase the possibility of committing harmful sexual behaviour	Factors in the community such as relationships with schools, workplaces and neighbourhoods that increase the possibility of an autistic child or young person committing harmful sexual behaviour	Societal or cultural norms that increase the possibility of an autistic child or young person committing harmful sexual behaviour
Focus: Individual development	**Focus:** Interpersonal relationships	**Focus:** Community bonding, social inclusion	**Focus:** Creating and maintaining broad social norms

Figure 1. Autism socio-ecological model
Source: HM Inspectorate of Probation (2023)

This model highlights a number of key factors that should be considered when identifying and approaching inappropriate and problematic sexual behaviours (I/PSB) that relate to individual, interpersonal, community and societal factors.

The socio-ecological model is a multilevel population-based approach that considers how to engage with different people at different stages of social engagement: individual (the person themselves), interpersonal (one-on-one or close personal relationships with family, friends and peers), community (relationships within the different communities people are members of) and societal (interactions with the society people live within). The socio-ecological model allows a population-based approach to social and behavioural problems that takes account of the different institutions, agencies and social dynamics that people are party to.

The model is rooted in a public health approach and theory. Epidemiological Criminology (EpiCrim) sees sexual abuse as a health, wellbeing and justice issue (McCartan *et al.* 2025). For autistic children and young people, the socio-ecological model allows us to understand, respond to and prevent their engagement in harmful sexual behaviour with regard to their biology and personal history (individual), their engagement in close relationships (interpersonal), the various communities, online and offline, they are involved with (as well as the varying dynamics of these communities) (community), and how society engages with and understands them (societal), as set out by Russell *et al.* (2025) in their ASEM (see Figure 2). The socio-ecological model enables professionals, policy makers and society more broadly to understand how social dynamics drive behaviours, and allows us to understand how to build effective interventions.

Definitions of I/PSB are important to consider. As defined by the National Society for the Prevention of Cruelty to Children (NSPCC 2021), both inappropriate and problematic behaviours align with the amber categories of the Brook Traffic Light Tool and the Lucy Faithfull Foundation Parents Protect Tool (PP) (2023[1]) (see Figure 3).

---

1   https://shorespace.org.uk/about-us or www.lucyfaithfull.org.uk/shore

INDIVIDUAL	INTERPERSONAL	COMMUNITY	SOCIETAL
Factors in an autistic child or young person's biology and personal history that increase the possibility of committing harmful sexual behaviour	Factors within an autistic child or young person's closest relationships history that increase the possibility of committing harmful sexual behaviour	Factors in the community, such as relationships with schools, workplaces and neighbourhoods, that increase the possibility of an autistic child or young person committing harmful sexual behaviour	Societal or cultural norms that increase the possibility of an autistic child or young person committing harmful sexual behaviour
Examples: Autism, neurodiversity, offence supportive beliefs, history of abuse, addictions	**Examples:** Association with peers, family members or partners who condone anti-social or criminological behaviours, being in abusive environments	**Examples:** General tolerance of crime and anti-social behaviour, lack of support from the police, weak community sanctions against perpetrators	**Examples:** Inequality due to an individual's gender, neurodiversity, race or class or due to economic and social policies
Interventions: Medication, psycho-educational programmes	**Interventions:** Restorative justice, mentoring programmes	**Interventions:** Mentoring programmes, community participation programmes (Circles of Support and Accountability, CoSA)	**Interventions:** Cure Violence, a new generation of policing
Focus: Individual development	**Focus:** Interpersonal relationships	**Focus:** Community bonding, social inclusion	**Focus:** Creating and maintaining broad social norms
Across primary, secondary, tertiary and quaternary (medical harm) prevention levels	**Across primary, secondary, tertiary and quaternary prevention levels**	**Across primary, secondary, tertiary and quaternary prevention levels**	**Across primary, secondary, tertiary and quaternary prevention levels**

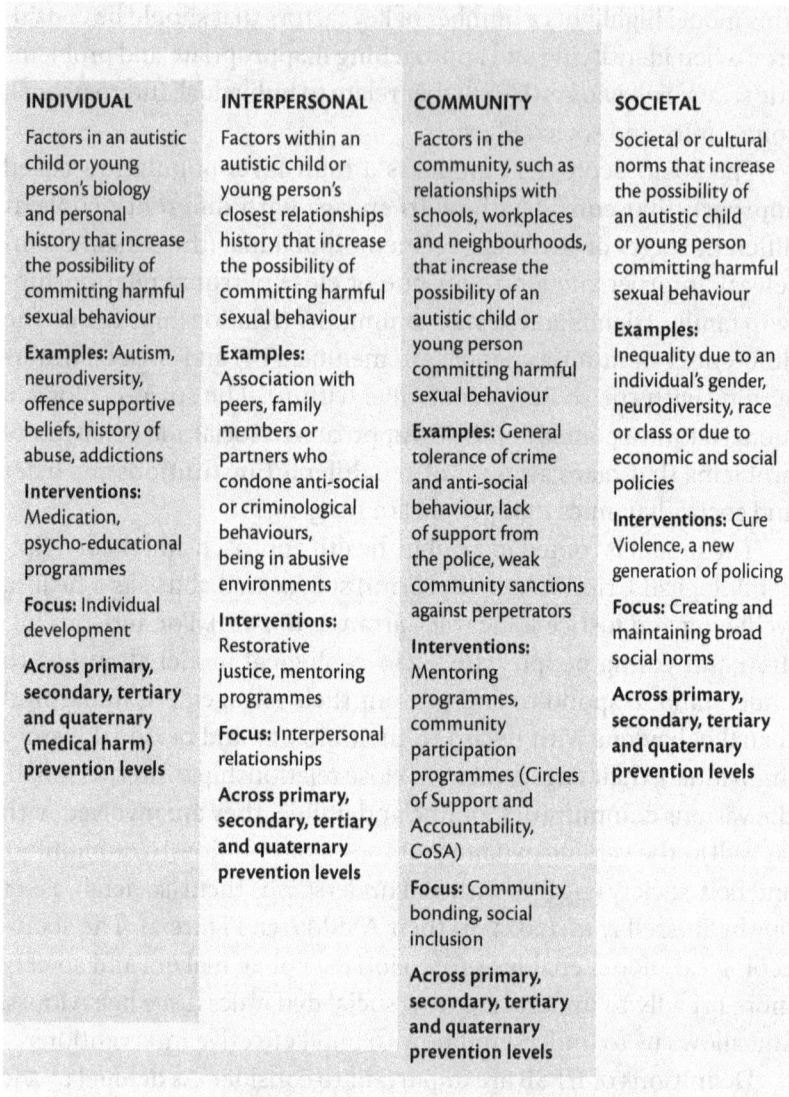

Figure 2. Adaptation of the autism socio-ecological model
for autistic children who have sexually harmed
Source: Russell et al. (2025)

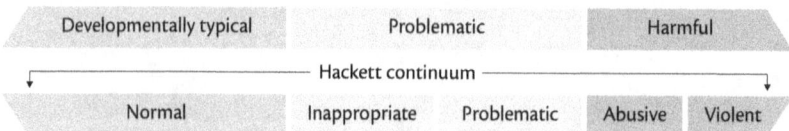

Figure 3. Merging of the Traffic Light Tool and the Hackett Continuum
Source: NSPCC (2021)

One of the key difficulties in defining I/PSB is the contested and fraught nature of how sexual behaviours are conceptualised in Western society, as outlined in Chapter One. This makes ascertaining what is normal and I/PSB difficult due to differing and conflicting ideas as to what pertains to be developmentally appropriate, and this becomes even more difficult in autistic children and young people. It is useful to note that sexual behaviours that are deemed harmful (abusive / violent) are more straightforward to identify in children and young people and to plan interventions for. The difficulty in defining I/PSB was outlined in a study by King-Hill (2021, 2022) that highlighted professional disparity in understanding of what constitutes I/PSB, which then led to sporadic and inconsistent interventions. Due to these issues around the definition of I/PSB there is no freely available specific guidance and support available for children and young people, parents or carers and professionals. This is also the case for national, autism-specific, freely available support, guidance and intervention models.

As outlined in Chapter One, it is normal for sexual behaviours to develop incrementally in children and young people (NSPCC 2021). However, there is an inherent expectation that professionals and parents or carers will be able to identify when this behaviour is I/PSB. This becomes even more difficult when children and young people are autistic. There is a complexity of issues surrounding this, and it is compounded by the confidence of parents or carers and professionals when addressing sexual behaviours in children and young people. The NSPCC (2021) do offer a steer when identifying I/PSB, but still require mapping onto the socio-ecological model when considering differing contextual influences:

- Single instances of developmentally inappropriate sexual behaviour
- Behaviour that is socially acceptable within a peer group but would be considered inappropriate outside that group
- Generally consensual and reciprocal
- May involve an inappropriate context for behaviour that would otherwise be considered normal
- Developmentally unusual and socially unexpected behaviour
- May be compulsive

- Consent may be unclear and the behaviour may not be reciprocal
- May involve an imbalance of power
- Doesn't have an overt element of victimisation.

These contextual elements are a key indicator of I/PSB, and a focus should be on these factors rather than just the behaviour itself that is presenting. These aspects may explore age, ability, other children, education, home life, perceptions of consent, understanding of sexual behaviours, socialisation and, most importantly for the autistic child, developmental ability and understanding (HM Inspectorate of Probation 2023).

Shame, in relation to sexual behaviours in children and young people, can be particularly damaging. When sex is coupled with shame, in wider society and also in RSHE sessions, it inhibits a young person's ability to report and highlight I/PSB (King-Hill 2024a) (see Chapter One). Implying that children and young people should be ashamed or embarrassed about sexual behaviours leads to an awkwardness when discussing sexual matters, and inhibits the vital communication that is needed. This becomes even more complex with autistic children and young people where social cues may be missing. Pleasure is also not an aspect of sexual behaviour that is discussed with children and young people. This is often around the skewed perspective that it will encourage rather than inhibit sexual behaviours, despite research indicating otherwise (see King-Hill 2023, 2024b; McGeeney and Kehily 2016; Wood et al. 2019).

Another key aspect linked to disclosure, choice and understanding is the high number of sexual harassment behaviours being seen in the education system. An example of this can be seen in a recent Ofsted report (2021) finding that sexual harassment and violence was a normal part of school life in England, with the majority of these behaviours being displayed by boys against girls. However, this finding is not remarkable, and a large amount of data from many fields demonstrates that sexual violence against women and children (VAWC) is commonplace. For instance, a website called Everyone's Invited has captured over 50,000 testimonials of sexual harassment in schools since 2020 (Hickman & Rose 2023). In 2020 a quarter of recorded child sexual abuse reports were carried out by under-18s, and 90 per cent of rapes of 13- to 15-year-olds were committed against girls (Radford *et al.* 2020). The 2020 NSPCC report (Bentley *et al.* 2020) found the highest rates of sexual abuse in under-25s being 15- to 17-year-old girls. These examples clearly highlight that enough is not being done to address and understand I/PSB in children and young people, and the problem is endemic. Specifically, this aspect of I/PSB in autistic children and young people should be considered when designing interventions and education with additional needs being accounted for.

ASSESSING SEXUAL BEHAVIOURS IN AUTISTIC CHILDREN

This section sets out considerations when assessing autistic children and young people who have displayed harmful sexual behaviour. It provides an overview of multidimensional approaches that consider developmental, cognitive and social factors that support and inform assessment and plans to reduce harm and achieve positive outcomes for children, young people and families. This will be framed around the socio-ecological model.

Prior to undertaking any form of harmful sexual behaviour assessment, caution should be given to define the purpose of the assessment itself, and consideration given to the potential stigmatisation this may have on a child or young person (Allardyce and Yates 2018). Initial screening of the level of behaviour and harm, if present, should be carried out and provide a case for an intervention. The assessment should not only focus on the child but should also provide professionals with additional knowledge to ensure intrapersonal and community safety and effective decision making. Only if initial screening suggests the behaviour lies outwith normative or expected developmental pathways should a more comprehensive assessment – including risk assessment – be undertaken.

There has been significant growth in the use of risk assessment tools within the harmful sexual behaviour field since the early 2000s, with a growing range of assessment tools to choose from. However, research remains inconsistent in the predictive accuracy of these tools with this population to predict recidivism (Allardyce and Yates 2018). Many tools have been developed in accordance with what is considered good professional practice to support practitioners in determining risk factors that can be targeted as part of intervention plans and approaches. However, robust evaluation of approaches is still lacking in the field.

It is important that the focus of assessment remains on the child as opposed to merely reducing anxiety within professional networks (Myers 2007). Many assessment frameworks and tools for children and young people who have displayed harmful sexual behaviour have shifted from scoring or categorising risk as low, medium and high, acknowledging that risk is often dynamic and contextual in nature, and strongly linked to the domains of the socio-ecological model (Allardyce and Yates 2018; King-Hill 2021, 2022, 2024b).

In the context of autism, this leads to a more inclusive approach, acknowledging that risk factors can be relative to wider domains including health and social abilities. As previously noted, social isolation is often referenced within this group, and many suggest that it is an increased factor within autistic populations. However, it is critical that social isolation is given wider consideration in its presence within a child's life, which may vary depending on other factors, including access to education and social situations, which may be removed from a child by a parent or carer or institution – which is arguably different from a child choosing to self-isolate or withdraw.

Currently there is no imperative evidence to suggest that an autistic child or young person is less or more likely to display harmful or problematic sexual behaviours. The behaviours often expressed in referral documentation to specialist services highlight themes, including:

- Perceived misunderstanding of social or environmental situations. Themes can include:
  - Social or communication issues, including social clues and cues
  - Misinterpretation of emotional recognition and ability to emotionally regulate
  - Misunderstanding socially expected and appropriate behaviours relating to differing environments
  - Social naïvety in communication with others the child or young person has a sexual or emotional connection with.

- Inappropriately seeking physical touch and contact. Themes can include:
  - An increased desire for sensory responses, such as touch of others
  - A heightened response to pressure and weight, which can, at times, be overwhelming for recipients
  - A lack of awareness of others and self's personal space and appropriate levels of physical contact.

- Repetitive behaviour. Themes can include:
  - Behaviours with sensory reward, including sexual behaviours, can be present in what may seem excessive with the child or young person's daily routine.

- Fetishist preoccupations and collection of sexual material. Themes can include:
  - A typical or bespoke sexual interests that at times consume aspects of the child or young person's sexual identity due to excessive reliance
  - Sexual behaviours that include the presence of physical sensory objects (transvestism, diaper fetishism, bondage, discipline, sadism and masochism, BDSM)
  - The collection of pornographic, sexual or indecent and illegal sexual imagery.

The impact of assessment should never be underestimated, and care should be given alongside practice experience and supervision to ensure a robust and holistic approach is upheld in determining assessment conclusions and decisions for all children and young people. Professional practice should be supported by the use of assessment tools and frameworks, influencing and shaping interventions and positive goal settings for children, young people and families.

INTERVENTIONS

Assessment often responds to immediate need based on a reactive response; however, in achieving better outcomes for children and young people, effective and child-centred interventions often have greater impact on achieving the desired behavioural change (Reitzel and Carbonell 2006). Research appears to be inconsistent in determining the effectiveness of interventions in responding to harmful sexual behaviour (Allardyce and Yates 2018; Caldwell 2016), specifically in considering autistic children and young people. An effective assessment framework should indicate the level of intervention for a child or young person, and consider wider aspects of the child or young person's life, including developmental factors that may require substantial but differing approaches to a harmful sexual behaviour intervention. These aspects align with the domains of the socio-ecological model. A harmful sexual behaviour intervention may require less focus on the instances of harmful sexual behaviour but rather a model of psychosexual education to promote positive sexuality to support desistance in further instances of harmful sexual behaviour forming due to inaccurate or unhealthy perspectives and views of sex and sexuality. Other approaches may highlight additional support for unresolved trauma that may have been a contributing factor to the harmful sexual behaviour due to early exposure to adult sexual behaviour, material or abuse.

Research on harmful sexual behaviour at the time of writing (2024) has often specifically focused on sexual recidivism of young people, with an absence of longevity or life outcomes for children and young people who have displayed harmful sexual behaviour. In 2024, Hackett and colleagues published 'Life course outcomes and developmental pathways for children and young people with harmful sexual behaviour' exploring the life outcomes of young adults who, in their childhood, received a professional intervention in relation to harmful sexual behaviour. The study provided empirical evidence for the need to move away from formal risk management approaches and to encourage practice around wider socio-environmental factors to support greater life outcomes and resilience. The study goes further, highlighting the benefits of supporting children and young people to build on social and emotional awareness that the authors, among others (McNeil, Reeder and Rich 2012), suggest are dynamic factors that young people, with support, can develop further to achieve better life discourses. The study highlighted unsuccessful or variable outcomes that were often related to wider factors such as unstable housing, poverty, anti-social behaviour and / or substance use, showing the need for multidisciplinary approaches with harmful sexual behaviour interventions for families and young people.

In defining an intervention, we must first consider the rationale in forming an intervention plan, considering key aspects of assessment that have been identified as areas of concern for the child or young person. Although the intervention itself may have been instigated to respond to harmful sexual behaviour, an assessment may have highlighted specific areas of need that may have influenced the harmful sexual behaviour occurring.

The 'Good Lives Model (GLM)' (Print 2013), albeit mainly used with adults in responding to sexual and violent crime, has many transferable attributes in relation to children and young people. The model focuses on the strengths and goals of the client, promoting a holistic framework that can guide an intervention. Schnitzer, Terry and Joscelyne (2020), however, suggest that the GLM approach may be more effective within neurotypical populations, with aspects of the model being less effective in supporting autistic individuals. They go on to suggest that interventions involving a focus on social skills, supporting children and young people, may increase outcomes within this population, highlighting the need for interventions to be dynamic and individualised, based on need. However, the GLM highlights the benefit of a strengths-based approach to support positive destinations in people's lives, which ties in firmly with the socio-ecological model approach.

Any intervention addressing harmful sexual behaviour will arguably tackle the sexual behaviour that has instigated the need for intervention; however, in considering outcomes for children and young people we must consider areas of strength that may support the desistance of further harmful sexual behaviour. This may include embedding education or employment opportunities within the intervention and safety plan to address social isolation or disengagement from social activities, education and / or employment as advocated by the socio-ecological model. Autistic people are up to four times more likely to experience social isolation (Williams 2023), with some studies highlighting the prevalence of social isolation as a contributing factor to harmful sexual behaviour and sexual offending (Seto and Lalumière 2010). These themes highlight the need to transfer the assessment domains into practice by addressing and considering aspects of the child or young person's life that may be in need of additional support, alongside responding to the harmful sexual behaviour.

Allardyce and colleagues (2021) conducted a literature review exploring the direction of harmful sexual behaviour interventions, and highlighted the following key findings:

- There is growing evidence of the relationship between disruptions in children's psychosexual development and harmful sexual behaviour.

- Different forms of intervention need to be available in responding to differing demonstrations of harmful sexual behaviour often within subgroups such as siblings, learning disability, children under 12 and females.

- Intervention effectiveness may be achieved in ensuring relationships established between practitioners, the child and their families, the level of involvement of families and education stability.

- Intervention targets that are focused on wellbeing and welfare needs can achieve better outcomes for children across their life.

- Effectiveness of a harmful sexual behaviour intervention is dependent on the skills and experience of a practitioner undertaking the work, highlighting the need for practitioners to be well versed, trained and provided with adequate levels of supervision.

- Education stability is suggested to be a protective factor, highlighting the benefit of contextual safeguarding approaches in responding to instances of harmful sexual behaviour.

The review provides a helpful note for practitioners and service providers, to consider 'Does your intervention or programme do the following' (Allardyce, Yates and Gurpreet 2021, pp.71–72):

- Use assessment tools or a standardised measure to measure change with each treatment goal

- Not only deliver psychoeducation but teach skills and provide ample opportunity to practise newly learned skills

- Rely on evidence-based approaches with respect to each component of your intervention

- Provide reflective supervision on a regular basis, including space to explore impact of the work

- Provide adequate training of staff to promote skills and knowledge

- Pay attention to diversity

- Be culturally sensitive and safe (working in a culturally safe way means recognising the importance of working with broader kinship and community systems, and helping young people to maintain connection to community)

- Consider subtypes and appropriate intervention approach in line with current evidence

- Show evidence of being
    - Holistic
    - Multimodal
    - Developmentally orientated
    - Strengths-based
    - Proportionate
    - Delivered via a multi-agency approach

- Tailor interventions so they are responsive to the young person's particular needs and lived contexts

- Show flexibility is used in determining who the protective / supportive adults are, what broader systems of care need to be involved in the treatment plan and strategies to ensure their engagement over the treatment period

- Work at and with young people's developmental capacities, which means taking into account age, gender, pubertal development and particular intellectual, cognitive and other factors that shaped the young person's understanding of themselves and their relations with others

- Assess atypical sexual interests and provide evidence-based interventions to help young people develop understanding and target sexual regulation skills where appropriate

- Have processes in place to identify young people with low motivation at assessment stage and whether your approach addresses factors underpinning poor motivation

- Provide aftercare support

- Have child-friendly consent forms and reports

- Use language that puts the child first, such as a child who has displayed problematic behaviour

- Considered the influence of operating environments on enacting good practice.

In considering an intervention, the method can initially be a key point to consider. There are various models to facilitate interventions with equal limitations and strengths in their approach, such as one-to-one support, groupwork, restorative approaches and cognitive-behavioural therapy.

One-to-one support

One-to-one (in-person) interventions can cover a range of themes but often involve a practitioner and a child or young person in an environmentally trauma-informed space, which can vary depending on the child or young person's preference. This links to the individual domain of the socio-ecological model. One-to-one approaches often support a trusting relationship that, alongside the development of a professional client relationship, can support discussion-based and interactive approaches to address the harmful sexual behaviour and wider factors impacting the child or young person's life.

Although one-to-one approaches are often the most preferred method of interaction, they are not without their limitations. Often a great deal of pressure and responsibility is placed on the practitioner to build and maintain constructive relationships, which can, at times, be disrupted due to factors such as child protection process or reporting disclosures that the intervention may encourage, often conflicting with the professional relationship with the child or young person. This highlights the requirement for an open dialogue between the practitioner and the child or young person to ensure they are aware from the initial stages of which professionals will respond to concerning information, and how the child or young person will be supported throughout the lifespan of the intervention as well as post intervention.

Another point to consider is the maintenance of the relationship that a one-to-one environment promotes. Practitioners and children and young people will spend significant periods of time working with each other, with relationships often growing in strength. It is critical that practitioners promote resilience factors for the young person, and do not form an unsustainable or unrealistic relationship that may cease due to factors including funding, staff moving on or young people transitioning to adult services. This last point highlights the importance of exit planning and practitioners consistently exploring options of safe and supportive exiting or transitioning to achieve the best possible outcomes for the children and young people they support.

Group support

Groupwork often consists of professionals providing psycho-education or therapeutic interventions within a group setting that focuses on reducing future harmful sexual behaviour and links to the intrapersonal domain of the socio-ecological model. Although this is considered a standard and effective way in which adults who have sexually harmed are supported, it is deemed less effective in children and young people as it does not offer a child-centred approach dependent on individual need (Allardyce and Yates 2018). This is particularly notable when considering autism, with limited evidence highlighting groupwork's effectiveness in supporting children and young people in this population.

To engage within a group context certain expectations are often placed on children and young people, including an ability to exchange with others via a range of communication strategies; an understanding of socially acceptable behaviours; an understanding of social clues and cues; a shared tolerance of others' interests; and emotional regulation and recognition of others. These factors show the foundational issues that may create difficulties for an autistic child or young person engaging in group dynamics with others due to a range of communication and social impairments often associated with autism. It is not that all group dynamics are unsuitable, and at times the group setting itself may provide a positive prosocial impact on the child or young person by providing them with the opportunity to learn and develop with peers and potentially exchange effective coping strategies.

Restorative approaches

A restorative approach, or restorative justice (RJ), is often used in the case of intrafamilial or sibling sexual abuse, and considers the possibility of reunifying the victim and person responsible for the harm if and when appropriate. This relates to the interpersonal domain of the socio-ecological model. The Restorative Justice Council advocates the following six principles (RJC 2016):

- Restoration – to address and repair harm
- Voluntarism – RJ is based on a voluntary approach for both parties
- Neutrality – non-judgement and non-biased approaches for both parties
- Safety – key to the process, and RJ considers both parties' emotional and physical safety throughout
- Accessibility – non-discriminatory and available to all affected by the conflict or harm
- Respect – respectful of the dignity of all affected by the conflict or harm.

A key component to an RJ process is that the process and outcome is victim-focused, so RJ would not be a sole intervention but rather an approach to support the young person in displaying empathy and responsibility to either restore the relationship or support the victim's recovery. As RJ often involves the exchange of emotional awareness and a demonstration of empathy, this can, at times, be problematic, for an autistic child or young person may appear visually different to their internal emotions, giving an inaccurate presentation to the victim and facilitators.

Cognitive behavioural therapy (CBT)

The model of CBT is a common factor within services providing harmful sexual behaviour interventions (Allardyce and Yates 2018; McGrath *et al.* 2010), with a core focus often being on behavioural change to support individuals to desist from future harmful behaviour. This relates to the individual domain of the socio-ecological model. Many of the interventions that utilise the CBT model often explore behavioural change approaches, supporting young people to desist from further harmful behaviour, thoughts or feelings (Allardyce and Yates 2018). It is important to consider, however, the role in which CBT is being placed in relation to responding to harmful sexual behaviour displayed by an autistic child or young person. Although the CBT intervention may explore issues associated with autism that may have contributed to harmful sexual behaviour, CBT should never be used or considered for the intention of shifting autism to neurotypical processing, which is both unethical and unrealistic (Grossman 2021).

TRAUMA-INFORMED PRACTICE AND AWARENESS

Although harmful sexual behaviour is in some instances related to previous adversity or trauma experienced by the child or young person displaying harmful sexual behaviour, it is pertinent to acknowledge that not all children and young people who display harmful sexual behaviour will have experienced adversity. However, trauma can be nuanced and its impact depending on a number of factors often post adversity, such as family support and early interventions targeting the harm that has been caused. Experiences of trauma and adversity are suggested to be more prevalent within an autistic population.

When supporting autistic children and young people who have displayed harmful sexual behaviour, we must consider the relationship between symptoms of autism and their similarities at times with trauma, as they may be contributing factors that are co-occurring with trauma and autism (Allely 2022). For children and young people within this population who are initially identified as having no apparent experiences of trauma or adversity, caution should be taken in exploring themes in their own experiences and life that professionally we may not consider as a traditional traumatic or adverse experience, such as bullying, which can lead to forms of post-traumatic stress in later life. Whether a child or young person has experienced trauma adversity or not, practitioners should always uphold best practice and support a trauma-informed and adversity-aware approach to ensure trauma is identifiable, and the child or young person feels safe to explore and potentially disclose themes of adversity.

It is important that trauma or adverse experiences are identified early within assessment and intervention stages as this will often shape the approach the practitioner takes and areas they will have to prioritise in the initial stages of an intervention – an example being if a child or young person has a significant background of adversity, including themes such as sexual abuse and neglect, these will arguably take priority within a harmful sexual behaviour intervention to ensure the child or young person has received support prior to focusing on behavioural-focused work.

A recent Swiss study provides more nuance to the discussion, examining the adverse childhood experiences of 687 young people known to social services because of harmful sexual behaviour. Barra and colleagues (2017) found particular clusters of certain kinds of negative experiences were characteristic of different kinds of offence and victim characteristics. Those with neglect-only backgrounds were more likely to abuse pre-adolescent children rather than peers, as were those who had experienced bullying and social rejection among their peers. This latter group were also more likely to have been involved with a penetrative sexual act with their victim. Those who had adverse experiences in the family environment were more likely to sexually abuse others within the context of a wider range of other delinquent and non-sexual offending behaviour. Multiple experiences of adversity were linked to having multiple victims, although not statistically associated with penetrative abuse. Our understanding of the exact timing and combinations of adverse experiences that may predict later sexually abusive behaviour is still at a primitive stage, however, as is how these kinds of findings map onto the growing literature about subtypes among young people who have displayed harmful sexual behaviour (Dillard and Beaujolais 2019).

PRACTITIONER AND PROFESSIONAL IDENTITIES

Practice across the sector of harmful sexual behaviours varies depending on the organisation or agency responsible. Currently across the UK, harmful sexual behaviour services are delivered by a range of statutory (youth justice and children and families) and third sector agencies. Despite the organisational source, many suggest similar requirements and advisories to practitioners in the field of harmful sexual behaviour. Practitioners working in the field of harmful sexual behaviour will require skills such as an ability to demonstrate empathy and maintain relationships and positive communication strategies, although other professional qualities are also essential (Allardyce and Yates 2018).

Practitioners will often be faced with a range of complexities when responding to harmful sexual behaviour, and it is critical they have a sound knowledge of child protection processes and legislation and adequate training (Scottish Government 2014). Professional identities across the field may fluctuate from social work, youth work and offender management and education, depending on the level of behaviour being reported and displayed. In some instances, behaviours such as 'problematic' (Hackett 2014) may not reach the statutory threshold but nonetheless require an intervention of some degree. Despite the professional qualifications, any practitioner undertaking an intervention within harmful sexual behaviour should have access to robust and supportive supervision (Allardyce and Yates 2018) to ensure cases are reviewed and practitioners have support for their own wellbeing and decision making, which can, at times, be complex to navigate.

A STAGED APPROACH TO INTERVENTION

Information gathering is a productive initial stage to gain a strong understanding of the young person's cognitive and learning abilities, knowledge of the their interests that can be used in achieving engagement, setting expectations and boundaries using visual and literal methods and a sound and explicit safety plan in place, which is created with the input of the young person, parents or carers and other professionals. This information gathering should be underpinned by the socio-ecological model.

Where possible, an agreed time and environment should be ensured with the young person, which should be upheld on a predictable and frequent basis. To encourage engagement, preparation findings and interests should be used that are important to the young person; these could be used to form an exercise such as understanding the young person's view on their own harmful sexual behaviours. The young person should be allowed to initially feel safe in the environment, such as where and how they position themselves. How they choose to stand or walk, whether they use fidget spinners, Play-Doh, paper and pens etc., may be helpful in helping them settle and feel safe. For example, emojis for five visual expressions can be a helpful way in supporting the young person to give a non-verbal or less shameful way to express how they are feeling.

In supporting autistic children and young people we must consider ways to capture their understanding of why they are receiving an intervention. Language can be a key element to this, ensuring we are being literal and explicit, and being aware of the language the young person uses can help us understand their motivation – for example, a young person who uses language familiar to that of a police interview may be replicating language and explanations they believe are the right thing to say, similar to that of echolalia. Breaking down words like 'bad' can help to ensure that the young person is aware of what they are describing and feeling.

Autistic young people are more likely to experience adversity, stigma and low self-esteem, factors that can impact on self-efficacy and resilience. Practitioners must be conscious of this and adapt a realistic approach to promoting resilience. Consider factors in the young person's life that could be amended in promoting resilience, such as home environment or education settings.

A variety of studies have indicated that autistic people have similar desires for sexual and intimate relationships with others (Byers, Nichols and Voyer 2013). We must appreciate that sexual urge and need can be an area of great frustration for autistic young people, with studies indicating a high number of them having had little or no education relating to sex or sexual behaviour (Stokes, Newton and Kaur 2007). With a recurring theme for this subgroup of social and peer isolation, these could be considered factors in influencing sexual dysfunction and harmful or problematic sexual behaviours. This may be worth consideration during the early stages of interventions. Consider the following points:

- What sex education has been available to the young person?
- What knowledge have they gained from sexual informants?
- What is their understanding of sex?
- Has anyone explained masturbation to them?
- How do they sexually identify?
- Do they have sexually specific interests or motivators?
- What do they think a relationship is, and have they been in one, either offline or online?

It is essential not to shame the young person or make them feel uncomfortable, hence this stage comes at a point where a therapeutic and trusting relationship has been established. It is important to gain insight into how the young person views their harmful sexual behaviour and what understanding they have on this. In identifying the young person's perspective on sexual arousal and introducing this approach into allowing them to consider how sexually aroused they were at the time of the behaviour, we can start to map sexual interests and motivators for the young person. Depending on the form of the harmful sexual behaviour that took place, such as contact abuse or technology-assisted abuse, this will determine the direction of work. A useful method for exploring harmful sexual behaviour can be utilising a young person's learning type and creating a timeline (visual or artistic) to explore what sparked the behaviour, how it started and how it escalated, and at the end of this, exploring how the young person felt post incident. This requires professional judgement and an awareness of the young person's motivation.

Although most harmful sexual behaviour interventions are time-limited, in some instances autistic young people will require long-term support mechanisms in their life, so an ending may be different. The harmful sexual behaviour is only one part of the young person, and throughout the intervention the practitioner should be supporting parents or carers in gaining an understanding of their young person's sexuality and behaviour, which will require them to continue a level of supervision within the home environment. This can be disarming to parents or carers, and make them feel they are on their own. Ensuring we have revised an amendable safety plan can support this exit and remove views of rejection or isolation.

Professionals undertaking this work vary in profession and qualifications, so it is important to consider the wider factors of the young person and their family, and consider referrals to additional services that may support unmet themes throughout the harmful sexual behaviour work, such as the need for occupational therapy, additional assessments, education support and mental health support.

Within the autistic group, it may be apparent that the concerns are focused on the sexual behaviour; however, to improve this one domain in a young person's life the focus may have to be on wider behavioural factors. There is research to suggest that behavioural interventions can increase an autistic young person's ability to emotionally regulate and recognise emotion and increase their ability to socially interact with others. These are areas that may be strong factors in discouraging recidivism. Focusing solely on the sexual behaviour with this group may bring little positive change or engagement due to other factors driving the behaviour, which may include lack of routine, underlying anxiety leading to behaviours that generate predictability, and sensory issues. There is an argument that by reacting to negative behaviour, we increase the likelihood of seeing this more frequently.

For the autistic person, the world can be a frighteningly unpredictable place. Any behaviour that leads to predictable reactions will be reinforced (even by negative consequences). If we consider distraction strategies, we can see the use of 'distraction techniques' that encourage us to initially ignore negative behaviour and react in a positive manner when seeing behaviour we want to encourage. This distraction is not a short-term measure. It is fundamentally about setting a more positive agenda and reinforcing behaviours that we want to see. As it involves adults setting the agenda, it reduces the distress that the child experiences, and thus we should see a reduction in harmful or problematic behaviours. If we do not, then that is an indication that something else is going on. In working with autistic children and young people our initial thoughts should be around what autistic-specific approaches are in place. Without these strategies being used it will be difficult to tell what behaviours are due to autistic needs not being met and what are due to other causes.

NHS Lothian created an assessment tool named 'The Big Question' (2006). This is a questionnaire assessment that uses images and verbal narrative to assess a child or young person with learning disabilities' knowledge on sex and sexual behaviour. It is primarily led by using images of scenarios to allow the young person to provide a narrative to each, which gives the assessor an insight into the young person's views and knowledge of sex. This can be an effective tool in assessing poor knowledge, abusive views and distorted or confused views. The assessment is scored in three categories with a summary overview that can support an intervention and assessment on the child or young person's sexual knowledge and need for relationships and sex education (RSE) that may influence their desistance of future harmful sexual behaviour. A benefit to this visual assessment model is that it can contribute to initiating an intervention model due to its verbal provoking nature and the opportunity it gives the young person to ask further questions to encourage learning.

The range of the child or young person's autism will determine what tools are used in the intervention process. For children and young people who are non-verbal in communication style, or for those with a learning disability, the intervention will likely be focused on responding to the child or young person's sensory needs, which may include aspects of sexual behaviour such as masturbatory activities and practitioners supporting children and young people to communicate their needs.

The Picture Exchange Communication System (PECS) (Bondy and Frost 1984) allows the child or young person to use single images to communicate what they want to do or need, such as to use the bathroom or to ask for food or a drink. This method of exchange would require significant skill for a practitioner to undertake alongside an intervention and would likely take place with a child or young person who has significant adult supervision in their life, with the intervention predominately in place to respond to aspects of environmental behaviour and need.

ASSESSMENTS AND INTERVENTIONS

This section considers particular adaptations necessary when an autistic child has displayed harmful sexual behaviour online.

In the first instance, careful screening for whether the behaviour is genuinely problematic or abusive may be necessary. It is common for the 'technology' aspect of the behaviour to raise anxieties among parents or carers and professionals as it underlines the element of 'unknown' and 'secret' aspects of the young person's life. Caution is needed in particular with issues relating to sharing of self-generated sexual images or 'nudes'. These can range from behaviour that is consensual in the context of a relationship to behaviours that are attention-seeking in nature or that involve a misjudging of context, through to behaviour that is coercive and very clearly abusive. Some behaviours of this sort may technically be criminal but may not warrant anything further than advice about harm reduction in the context of risk-taking, but relatively normative, behaviour. For instance, a 16-year-old who shares a sexual image of themselves with a romantic partner in the context of a consensual relationship is technically committing a crime, and the behaviour will be investigated if, for instance, their partner's parents find the image and report it to the police. However, it is unlikely they would be prosecuted (at least in the UK) unless there was a context of coercion or lack of consent. The behaviour is risk-taking nonetheless, as ultimately they have little control of what happens to this image, especially if the relationship ends.

In the instance of online and technology obsessional behaviour, where the young person struggles to identify a need in their use of technology, we can start to influence positive and reward-led use. For example, if a young person continues to access online sexually explicit content in an inappropriate environment, such as an education setting, we can try to divert this use into something productive. This could be completing a set task by a teacher that requires technology to complete, such as a poster to raise awareness about harms related to technology. At times professionals and parents or carers will remove all access to technology, but this, in general terms, is an unsustainable approach and may, at times, increase anxiety and stress and drive the behaviour into more harmful directions to meet the young person's needs. It is also likely to impair building of resilience in using technology in positive and constructive ways.

For those young people involved with more concerning behaviours, risk assessment within the context of a comprehensive assessment of need will be necessary. It was highlighted earlier that some behaviours in relation to youth-produced sexual images and online harassment behaviours may have more in common with intimate partner violence than downloading and viewing CSAM. Careful assessment of the behaviour will help to determine the most appropriate intervention, which may have to draw on models outside the harmful sexual behaviour field. It is also becoming apparent that a significant proportion of harmful sexual behaviours displayed by young people now have both online and offline dimensions.

Although there is some evidence of increasing numbers of young people involved with online harmful sexual behaviour being referred to specialist agencies (Hackett, Branigan and Holmes 2019), the practice literature around assessment and intervention is still limited. Henshaw, Ogloff and Clough (2015), in a literature review in relation to adult online offending, suggest that risk assessment tools for sexual reoffending are likely to overestimate the risk of reoffending for downloading images of child sexual abuse. It is unclear whether this is the case with adolescents at this stage, and risk assessments should focus on identifying intervention goals and proportionate risk management measures rather than predicting risk.

Interventions need to be holistic and systemically orientated, integrating relevant support from parents or carers and schools. Providing accessible and autism-specific education on sexuality, privacy, consent and online safety is crucial. Messaging about taking responsibility for the content created is also an important psycho educational theme. Young people also need to know that because something is on the 'surface net' and shared by peers, this does not mean that it is legal. Generalisation of skills across devices, apps and platforms etc. is vital, that is, the same 'rules' apply whether you are viewing material on varied platforms and websites. This may involve 'reteaching' the same lessons for different areas on the internet to ensure that they generalise this learning.

This education should be tailored to the individual's cognitive level and should include practical examples and role-playing exercises to reinforce understanding; this relates to the individual domain of the socio-ecological model. Pre- and post-learning opportunities, that is, breaking down what you learn about, learning it and checking the learning, is important. Lessons that build on each other in sequential ways can help support this. Parents or carers also play a crucial role in monitoring online activities and guiding appropriate behaviour. This relates to the interpersonal domain of the socio-ecological model. Encouraging open communication about online experiences, setting clear rules and using parental control tools can help mitigate risks. The heterogeneity of behaviours that may constitute problematic or abusive online sexual behaviour makes it difficult to establish any one single intervention approach. No specific treatment programmes have been evaluated as yet, although some resources, particularly in relation to early intervention, are emerging, such as the Inform Young People's programme, which is currently being independently evaluated at the time of writing.[2]

Nonetheless, a number of intervention principles emerge from the research. The overlap and potential blurring of boundaries between online and offline realities and behaviours for children and young people may mean that an assessment of online risk needs to be integrated into standard risk assessments assessing offline risk. Understanding a young person's online world will need to be an aspect of any assessment undertaken with young people involved with offline-only harmful sexual behaviour. Completing a timeline examining the experiences the young person has had online (first experience of the internet, key positive and negative experiences, first exposure to sexual material online), in parallel with their offline experiences, can be an important foundation in this work.

Young people can be victims online as well as perpetrators. This needs to be explored in the course of an assessment and responded to in the context of interventions. There is some research suggesting

2   See www.stopitnow.org.uk/inform-young-people

that safe and confidential spaces for young people can support them to explore worries about their own sexual thoughts and behaviour, particularly with respect to sexual attraction to younger children (Beier *et al.* 2016). It is likely that online self-help resources may be particularly valuable as young people may find this is a less stigmatising way of obtaining advice and support with these issues (McKibbin, Humphreys and Hamilton 2017). Free resources, such as the Shore resource in the UK (Lucy Faithfull Foundation 2023[3]) and What's OK in the US,[4] are promising resources that are currently being evaluated.

Assessment of sexual preoccupation and compulsivity will be particularly relevant for those involved with downloading CSAM. When relatively large collections of images and videos are found, screening for autism spectrum disorder / condition may be indicated. It is particularly important for autistic people to know applicable rules and social norms about internet-based sexual communication (e.g., age of consent, legal versus illegal pornography).

CONCLUSION

Although research remains limited in demonstrating the effectiveness of interventions in response to harmful sexual behaviour (Allardyce and Yates 2018), this may be due to the intervention holding too much focus on the incidents of harmful sexual behaviour. New frameworks and approaches are supporting a wider approach to both static and dynamic factors that may be impacting on the child or young person's wider social, emotional and cognitive functioning (Russell *et al.* 2025). This is particularly important when interventions are supporting autistic children and young people who are displaying harmful sexual behaviour who will most likely require additional consideration within the intervention by ensuring social, cognitive and developmental wellbeing is held in the utmost importance. Alongside these factors, practitioners must carefully utilise a multidimensional assessment to look at the wider child or

---

3   https://shorespace.org.uk/about-us or www.lucyfaithfull.org.uk/shore
4   www.whatsok.org

young person's behaviours, as well as aspects of vulnerability that may require additional support, perhaps even lifelong.

Using the socio-ecological model that has been adapted for autistic children displaying harmful sexual behaviour by Russell *et al.* (2025) (see Figure 2) is a robust approach to assessment and intervention as it encompasses all elements of the young person's personal life in a strengths-based approach, recognising the importance of the individual, interpersonal, community and societal domains in approaches to assessment and intervention.

Individual Factors

CONTRIBUTION TO ASSESSMENT AND INTERVENTION

OVERVIEW OF THE INDIVIDUAL DOMAIN

This chapter explores the aspects of harmful sexual behaviour in autistic children and young people that relate to the individual domain (see Figure 4) set out by the autism socio-ecological model (ASEM) (Russell *et al.* 2025). A range of biological and social factors within the child or young person's life are considered, including early years experiences of trauma, adversity or abuse that relate to the individual factors of the ASEM (see Figure 2).

Individual: Factors in an autistic child or young person's biology and personal history that increase the possibility of committing sexual harm

Examples: Autism, neurodiversity, offence supportive beliefs, history of abuse, addictions

Figure 4. Individual factors of the autism socio-ecological model
Source: Russell et al. (2025)

SEXUAL BEHAVIOURS ASSESSMENT

Considering the sexual behavioural aspect of any assessment model in responding to harmful sexual behaviour requires a wide and holistic view of the child, and an appreciation that the behaviour displayed is not the entire child but rather an element presented within their life. Critical care is required in this particularly sensitive section of any harmful sexual behaviours assessment, as a core risk in misidentifying behaviours can ultimately lead to extensive stigmatisation or unnecessary labelling of the child or young person (Allardyce and Yates 2018; Hackett 2014). An initial screening of the sexual behaviour can be helpful in trying to understand the context and severity of the behaviour, which may include themes such as the presence of penetration or attempts to penetrate a victim. Documentation of the sexual behaviour itself needs to be detailed and specific and not include jargon and / or slang (King-Hill and McCartan 2024b).

The context and actions that have been displayed can help in understanding the seriousness of the behaviour, which can give an indication as to the intensity of the intervention and response required. However, the nature and frequency of the behaviour – and harm caused – needs to be considered alongside a number of other factors that relate to the child as an individual. Hackett's continuum of sexual behaviour proposes that all sexual behaviour displayed by children and young people at any age sits on a spectrum, ranging from developmentally expected to abusive and violent. Although a young person may be responsible for a single instance of 'abusive' or 'violent' sexual behaviour, this does not mean that they should be labelled 'sexually violent' or 'harmful'. The concerning behaviour may be the culmination of an escalation of problematic behaviours over time and / or may exist alongside healthy or expected traits.

Careful consideration needs to be given to the child or young person's psychosexual development, including considering non-sexual drivers in relation to the presentation of harmful sexual behaviour. The ASEM can provide some context to the child or young person's sexual life journey, which includes factors that have potentially misinformed them of what is healthy or socially acceptable. Approaches to assessment need to be strengths-based, looking for positive indicators that can support adequate interventions, including signs and indicators of healthy sexual development or expression.

The individual perspective in the ASEM can account for many aspects of a young person's life and perspective, and one example of this can be in regards to consent. The Rape Crisis England & Wales website defines consent as 'Someone consents to sex when they agree by choice and have the freedom and capacity to make that choice'. They go further, stating, 'If someone seems unsure, stays quiet, moves away or doesn't respond, they are not agreeing to sexual activity. In fact, it's really common for people who have experienced sexual violence to find they are unable to move or speak'.[1] Although these are general statements, they may highlight nuances in relation to autism.

The NeuroLaunch (2024) website suggests that consent requires significant communication and a mutual understanding in adhering to consent. A key theme highlighted is the at times lack of communication and social skills for autistic children and young people, acknowledging that consent often requires an emotional and physical understanding of others, including recognising non-verbal communication such as facial expressions and body language, areas that are well evidenced to cause difficulty within autistic populations. When considering consent within the context of harmful sexual behaviour, care should therefore be taken in exploring how consent is relative to other areas of the child or young person's life, and consideration given to areas of deficit that may have contributed to the harmful sexual behaviour being displayed towards another.

DEVELOPMENTAL ASSESSMENT

A formulation of developmental adversity and trauma and the possible links to sexual aggression and harm are essential aspects of the individual domain of the ASEM (Foy, Furrow and McManus 2011). Autism can mediate a child's experience of developmental adversity, so it is important to consider an individual's trauma responses, and that the autistic characteristics are not diminished or exaggerated, and the symptoms of trauma are identified in line with standard trauma-informed practice (Scottish Government 2021).

At times the developmental assessment takes a less holistic approach and focuses on a professional's view of adversity, often concluding with limited consideration given to the child or young person and their own perspective of the adversity they have experienced and how their narrative is defining its impact. This is an area

---

1   See https://rapecrisis.org.uk/get-informed/about-sexual-violence/sexual-consent

that holds significant nuances. A transferable example of this can be seen in instances of sibling sexual behaviour and abuse (SSB/A). SSB/A is often described as a family trauma (King-Hill *et al.* 2023a; Yates and Allardyce 2021), but in supporting children and young people, it is important that consideration is given as to how the SSB/A was experienced by the child or young person who carried out the behaviour, and not assume that this was perceived as purely negative, abusive or violent for the victim / survivor. Some victims / survivors of SSB/A share feelings of confusion and worry, and at times, shame. These feelings may come from a range of places, but one example may be siblings instigating age-appropriate games in which they receive physical arousal responses (and the male child achieves an erection during play). In the absence of appropriate adult supervision or education, the siblings may graduate to less age-appropriate play, which can lead to sexualised behaviours between them. This experience may not include an individual victim, but can leave a child or young person with feelings of confusion, fear and shame.

Many academics have highlighted the importance of attachment within child development (Bowlby 1969; Hughes 2004). Positive attachment is also considered to have a positive impact on a child's sexual development (Tracy *et al.* 2003), supporting the child or young person's basic understanding of intimacy as opposed to control within a sexual or intimate relationship. It is critical that attachment is not mistaken as existing positive relationships that may not have been present throughout early years in which the child and carer are exchanging emotional messaging. This emphasises the importance of considering the child's chronological life as opposed to simply their current emotional and physical situation, which may differ significantly from their early years.

REGULATION ASSESSMENT

Emotional regulation is often used to describe a person's management of emotional experiences and the way they respond. It can manifest in different ways for an autistic child or young person, including a continuum in how behaviours are displayed, such as 'meltdowns' or 'shutdowns' (National Autistic Society 2020a). These methods, often generated in response to an emotional situation, can, at times, be misinterpreted as negative behaviour. With a 'shut-down', the risk is that adults in the child or young person's life may misinterpret their behaviour as resilience, but in fact the emotional experience may be too much for them, and so methods of 'shutdown' are used to cope or block the experience (Embrace Autism 2018). Empathy again becomes present, and it is critical that consideration is given in assessing empathy within an appropriate and neurodiver-gent approach.

For autistic children and young people, consideration should be given to their general ability to regulate with everyday tasks, and their own needs, for themes such as predictability in a daily routine, managing stressful or distressing situations, coping mechanisms, support from others, methods and abilities to problem solve, and social and emotional competence. This takes into account a young person's perspective on responsibility in relation to the harmful sex-ual behaviour.

Although autism should be central in considering this domain, attention should also be given to the young person's 'brain matu-ration' (O'Rourke *et al.* 2020), which, arguably, will support consid-eration of their ability to express remorse or responsibility for the harm caused. It is essential that the impact of childhood adversity within this domain is considered, specifically the potential damage that exposure to themes such as sexual abuse, domestic violence and neglect may have had on the young person's understanding and ability to regulate appropriately (Allardyce and Yates 2018). Educa-tion within a harmful sexual behaviour intervention should again be noted here, as the assessment of self-regulation may identify areas of support to enhance a young person's mechanisms in coping and managing everyday challenges, including relationships and sexual functioning.

A factor within this domain considers the person who has caused the harm and the perspectives they have on the harm that may have been caused, either directly or indirectly, to others. This may be dis-played differently for an autistic child or young person as they may present as cold or stern; hence it is critical to further explore this within a neurodivergent context, utilising a practice style that meets the needs of the young person. Within the context of self-regulation, a child or young person's ability to problem solve should also be considered, including their methods and strategies in navigating and managing difficult or complex incidents or environmental situations. For autistic children and young people, this may highlight additional themes to consider, such as the way they process sensory or social situations, which may, at times, demonstrate as an impairment or a challenge within social settings. This may also include identifying social communication deficits such as the literal processing of language, which may, at times, impair logical thinking.

VULNERABILITY ASSESSMENT

The impact of vulnerability factors experienced historically or currently within the child or young person's life should be acknowledged, including childhood adversity and trauma, as well as factors that are static in nature. The impact of these, combined with the presence of autism, may have significant influence in the negative, or in some instances harmful, sexual behaviour being displayed. Alongside the risk factors in children or young people displaying harmful sexual behaviour, the risk from others that autism brings should also be considered. Children and young people with a learning disability are at significantly higher risk of being the victim of sexual abuse and / or exploitation (Helton, Gochez-Kerr and Gruber 2018). Various studies have highlighted that harmful sexual behaviour is statistically associated with childhood adversity (Hackett 2014). Because of this it is critical that a full chronology of vulnerability factors is viewed alongside existing risk factors, and their impact is not minimised due to the harmful behaviour being displayed.

For autistic children and young people, a number of factors may have placed them at an increased risk of abuse or trauma. These can include an increase in time spent with adults, including personal care support, social exclusion and communication impairments. In terms of autistic children and young people displaying instances of harmful sexual behaviour, additional consideration should be given to the prevalence of vulnerability factors that may have led to or instigated elements of the harmful sexual behaviour. This may include online communication, which has become their main source of social interaction and has become their single outlet for sexual experiences, ranging from direct communication with others to the viewing of pornographic, indecent or illegal material. In this context the child or young person's psychosexual development may have been founded by visual and non-contact experiences that often lack the communication and social interactions required within a physical, sexual or intimate experience. Determining the basic psychosexual developmental traits should be a key component to the assessment process, providing a holistic understanding of the child and young person's developmental and social abilities that can support the approach to intervention.

WIDER BEHAVIOUR ASSESSMENT

Young people who have displayed harmful sexual behaviour are more likely to come to the attention of the criminal justice system later in young adulthood because of non-sexual offending (including non-sexual violent offending) than because of later sexual offending (Caldwell 2010). To support an extensive and holistic assessment, other behaviours outside a sexual context should be considered, including the child or young person's social abilities and any demonstration of anti-social behaviour.

For an autistic child or young person this is a critical area to consider due to some within this group presenting behavioural traits that sit outside societal norms. An area to consider that may vary from neurotypical populations is the presence of intense interests or hobbies, which may often pose no reason for concern. However, it is worth identifying factors within these interests that may graduate to unhealthy coping strategies or addictive tendencies, such as substance use, which some suggest may be more prevalent within autistic populations (Weir, Allison and Baron-Cohen 2021).

Various studies highlight that autistic people are more likely to be the victims of offending behaviour as opposed to perpetrating such behaviours (Allely 2022). However, some research suggests that individuals with co-occurring mental health disorders, such as psychosis or schizophrenia, may at times drive violent behaviours (Allely and Faccini 2019). It is therefore essential that consideration is given to the wider social, emotional and mental impairments that may coincide with autism, which may lead to harmful, criminal or unhealthy non-sexual behaviours. We should also carefully consider the pertinent theme of vulnerability within this group, and the increased likelihood of autistic people experiencing exploitation and bullying, which may, at times, include them being taken advantage of (Arora 2014), leading to forms of criminal or harmful behaviours influenced by others.

METHODS OF ENGAGEMENT

No matter the intervention approach, whether it be one-to-one or a group setting, intervention methods should be considered based on the child or young person's own learning style and capabilities. To support autistic children and young people displaying harmful sexual behaviour we should remain focused on the child or young person's everyday communication and engagement styles, to maximise the intervention's effectiveness. This may include aspects of visual, sensory, verbal and written-based techniques.

Visual techniques may include the use of existing tools used to support the child or young person's daily functioning, such as a visual timetable that demonstrates the child or young person's daily routine, which can be used either throughout the day or at times when additional support or direction is required. Visual communication guides can be most effective when created alongside the young person and their own interests, ensuring they are logical and clear, and suit the child or young person's learning and communication styles. They can be used in a variety of scenarios and may include aspects of supporting the child or young person's healthy sexual development, such as supporting their understanding of safe and appropriate spaces to masturbate or simply to be naked. Studies have shown that routine and structure are a key element in supporting autistic children and young people (Rodger and Umaibalan 2011), and that disruption to everyday routine can influence negative or aggressive behaviours (Sevin, Rieske and Matson 2015). Harmful or problematic sexual behaviour may present via this route, and by utilising visual aids we may encourage the young person's own self-efficacy and enhance their interpersonal skills, reducing future negative behaviour in some instances.

Sensory techniques may provide comfort throughout an intervention when supporting hyper- or hyposensitive children or young people, such as fidget spinners, sensory art techniques (e.g., finger painting) and using physical items to help describe narratives. Sensory techniques may also ensure the child or young person is comfortable and feels safe in the environment the intervention is taking place in – from the texture of the seat in a room to the feeling of the carpet between the soles of their shoes and feet.

Most interventions will promote a model of verbal communication in some capacity, which will vary depending on the child or young person's communication style. Verbal communication may be utilised intermittently throughout the intervention and combined with other approaches to reduce shame or embarrassment. In exploring the harmful sexual behaviour within the intervention, the concept of shame should be noted, and the impact it may have on the child or young person and the professional relationship. At times the instance of the harmful sexual behaviour can be difficult for the child or young person to express, and aspects of denial or minimisation may become present. The intervention can support a safe and trauma-informed approach to support the child or young person's responsibility taking, and a range of approaches can be utilised to do so.

Often children and young people have a strong indication of why they are receiving the intervention, and the harmful sexual behaviour may generate anxiety within the therapeutic space due to them being unsure of when they will be asked or prompted about the harmful sexual behaviour. An approach that can sometimes be of use is a written method, where the child or young person writes either a journal or a letter and gives it to the practitioner to read. This experience can demonstrate to the child or young person the practitioner's non-judgemental style, and allow for further psychosexual conversations to be explored prior to the harmful sexual behaviour itself being discussed, therefore reducing stress and anxiety for the child or young person at an early stage of the intervention. In instances where children or young people have difficulty writing, alternative non-verbal approaches can be taken, such as visual and artistic methods.

A variety of intervention models are available to support individuals who have or who are displaying harmful sexual behaviour, but there is a real gap in specific evidence-based and well-evaluated intervention models in supporting both harmful sexual behaviour and autism.

WORKING WITH DENIAL AND SHAME

Aspects of denial can often be a factor in supporting children, young people and families within harmful sexual behaviour (Harkins, Beech and Goodwill 2010). A component of assessment, the presence of denial can influence the approach to the intervention based on the child or young person's rationale of the harmful sexual behaviour. Denial is a multilayered issue and should not be assessed without a full understanding of factors that may be influencing the denial itself. The child or young person's account of the harmful sexual behaviour may vary, from full denial that the instance of harmful sexual behaviour occurred to minimisation, such as acknowledging elements of the harmful sexual behaviour with either a minimised or reduced understanding of the severity and the impact this had on others.

It is also essential that the messaging parents and carers are giving to the child or young person is considered, as well as their own account and understanding of their child or young person's harmful sexual behaviour, which may range from minimisation and denial to an overreaction to the behaviour. As opposed to simply considering that the denial is coming from a place of deviancy, when supporting autistic children and young people consideration should also be given to their understanding of the harmful sexual behaviour, and whether or not their own social or emotional impairments or difficulties have impacted on their understanding of the impact that their behaviour has had on themselves and others. This highlights the importance of a multimodal approach to an intervention that considers the child or young person's social, emotional and developmental functioning.

Taylor's 'continuum of denial' (Taylor and Armor 1996) highlights the benefit of considering denial as a spectrum and a staged approach. The model considers the relationship between hope and hopelessness, demonstrating the use of minimisation or denial in reducing shame, embarrassment and fear for a child or young person. Rather than providing an immediate or reactive assessment to the denial, the level of denial should be considered, such as the child or young person highly minimising the impact of their behaviour but still indicating aspects of a specific incident that they acknowledge happened in some capacity. This use of denial may be an indication that the child or young person is frightened or ashamed to disclose further the harm they have caused, but allows practitioners to initiate an intervention, which, alongside positive relationship building, may see the denial progress positively through the continuum. This resource can also be useful in defining parent or carer responses and attitudes to their child or young person's behaviour by gaining an insight into aspects of minimisation or victim-blaming narratives that may be detrimental to the child or young person receiving an intervention due to reinforcement of unhelpful messaging from parents or carers, which can stem from gender inequality, shame, stigmatisation and a family's overall psychosexuality.

In considering the initial stages of an intervention to address a child or young person's harmful sexual behaviour, shame, and the role it can have within client disengagement, should be given careful consideration. The 'compass of shame' developed by Nathanson (1992) explores symptoms of shame and suggests a list of ways shame can impact individuals, such as withdrawal, attacking others, avoidance and attacking self. These themes can often indicate how an individual may currently be managing shame, which can, at times, be misinterpreted as behavioural deficits, such as physical aggression or outbursts of verbal anger.

ANXIETY

Another area that is important to consider is anxiety in autistic individuals. This can significantly affect their ability to understand what is said to them and to make themselves understood during court proceedings, for example. Anxiety in autistic individuals may be heightened during court proceedings due to being in rooms and buildings that are not familiar to them, having to engage in communication with people who are not familiar to them, and changes to usual routines and also to what is expected – for instance, there may be delays in the trial scheduling or changes of location. Indications or signs that a person is anxious might not be immediately obvious. It may just be things like coughing, picking at skin or yawning.

Autistic individuals may exhibit stress-adaptive (although atypical) behaviours during a suspect interview if they are experiencing feelings of increased anxiety. Either consciously or unconsciously, many autistic individuals will avert their gaze from the questioner or engage in repetitive movement to self-regulate hyperarousal (Collis *et al.* 2022). Stereotypically these non-verbal behaviours are associated with deception (see, for example, Hartwig and Bond 2011).

Additionally, the individual themself may not recognise that they are feeling anxious. Many autistic individuals lack emotional awareness or have an impaired ability or difficulty in identifying and describing feelings and being able to distinguish feelings from the bodily sensations of emotional arousal. This is known as alexithymia, where the individual is not able to recognise or describe their own thoughts and emotions (Berthoz and Hill 2005; Bird and Cook 2013). In their systematic review and meta-analysis, Kinnaird, Stewart and Tchanturia (2019) noted studies that have found that alexithymia is heightened in autistic individuals (Berthoz and Hill 2005; Fitzgerald and Bellgrove 2006; Hill, Berthoz and Frith 2004). Specifically, research indicates that between 40 and 65 per cent of the autism population are alexithymic (see, for example, Berthoz and Hill 2005; Hill *et al.* 2004). Alexithymia is a multidimensional construct that consists of three components:

- Difficulty identifying one's own feelings (DIF)
- Difficulty describing feelings (DDF)
- An externally orientated thinking style (EOT), whereby individuals tend not to focus their attention on their emotions.

Individuals who have high levels of alexithymia find it difficult to focus their attention on their emotional states (EOT) as well as having difficulty in accurately appraising what those states are (DIF, DDF) (Preece *et al.* 2017). There are a variety of measures for alexithymia, such as the Toronto Alexithymia Scale (TAS; Bagby, Parker and Taylor 1994), which is the most commonly used measure.

The TAS-20 is a self-report scale with a total of 20 items, and has three subscales:

- DDF subscale used to measure difficulty describing emotions; five items: 2, 4, 11, 12, 17.

- DIF subscale used to measure difficulty identifying emotions; seven items: 1, 3, 6, 7, 9, 13, 14.
- EOT subscale used to measure the tendency of individuals to focus their attention externally; eight items: 5, 8, 10, 15, 16, 18, 19, 20.

Some examples of the questions in this self-report scale include: 'It is difficult for me to find the right words for my feelings'; 'I prefer to analyse problems rather than just describe them'; 'I am often puzzled by sensations in my body'; 'People tell me to describe my feelings more'; and 'I often don't know why I am angry'. Items are rated using a 5-point Likert scale whereby 1 = strongly disagree and 5 = strongly agree. Five items are negatively keyed (4, 5, 10, 18 and 19). The total alexithymia score is calculated by summing the responses to all 20 items, while the score for each subscale factor is the sum of the responses to that subscale. The TAS-20 uses cut-off scoring: equal to or less than 51 = non-alexithymia, equal to or greater than 61 = alexithymia. Scores of 52–60 = possible alexithymia.

Regarding the reliability of the TAS-20, studies have found it to demonstrate good internal consistency (Cronbach's alpha = 0.81) and test-retest reliability (0.77, $p<0.01$). Research using the TAS-20 demonstrates that it has adequate levels of convergent and concurrent validity. It has been found that the three-factor structure is theoretically congruent with the alexithymia construct. The TAS has been found to be stable and replicable across clinical and non-clinical populations (Bagby *et al.* 1994).

ASSESSING CHILDREN UNDER 12

Practitioners and services have noted an increase in children under the age of 12 displaying problematic or harmful sexual behaviour, with the severity of behaviour increasing for older children. A number of factors may be accountable within this prevalence, such as the growth of social media, accessibility and exposure to pornographic content. However, careful consideration should be given to determining the nature and rationale of harmful sexual behaviour within this younger population and the impact of wider factors within the child's life, such as the role of family and the child's social, cognitive, emotional and physical development in relation to their age.

In considering autism within this population, Lordan, Storni and De Benedictis (2021) highlight the controversy around 'treatment', which is often echoed by those who consider themselves autistic or with lived experience, highlighting heterogeneity within this population. It is, however, well evidenced that autistic children and their families can benefit from support specifically within domains such as social communication, to enhance social functioning and ultimately increase the quality of their lives. In responding to harmful sexual behaviour within this group, a child's social and cognitive functioning should be considered, although caution should be taken when comparing cognitive and social development with sexual behaviour that may have been displayed.

It is essential that consideration is given to the nature of the sexual behaviour in context to the child's social, emotional and cognitive functioning, but also being mindful that although a child may be considered younger than their physical age, the sexual behaviour may be symptomatic of this factor but still requires immediate intervention due to harm they may pose to themself or others. Care should be taken by practitioners in using assessment models that are designed for harmful sexual behaviour within neurotypical populations, and consider the socio-ecological impact autism has had within this behaviour that has been identified as concerning.

Harmful sexual behaviour being displayed by a child under the age of 12, whether autistic or neurotypical, raises significant concern that they are displaying behaviours that are an advancement on expected developmental behaviours unexpected within such a young population. Children under 12 displaying harmful sexual behaviour are suggested to have been more likely to experience child sexual abuse or to have been exposed to adult sexual behaviour or material (including exposure to online sexually explicit material) and other forms of adversity. This, coupled with the previously noted prevalence of child sexual abuse experienced by children and young people with learning disabilities, highlights the importance of considering trauma, adversity and abuse within initial stages of any assessment.

THE VOICE OF THE CHILD WITHIN ASSESSMENT

Autistic children and young people and their families will often have been exposed to robust assessment processes, either within health institutions or statutory services, that may, at times, have induced anxiety. When considering the initial stages of completing a harmful sexual behaviour assessment of any kind, we should think about how we ensure children's rights are upheld throughout this process, and that they have the opportunity to share their own views on factors we are professionally judging on their behalf. It is critical that an assessment is based on factual information as opposed to assumptions we may have prior to meeting a child or young person. A practitioner can gain a great deal of direct information if positive engagement is achieved with the child or young person, building on a trusting professional relationship (Allardyce and Yates 2018). This includes working alongside families, specifically parents or carers, who themselves may be anxious due to negative experiences of assessment processes or with professionals more broadly.

THE RITUALISTIC AND COMPULSIVE NATURE OF COLLECTING CSAM

The desire for CSAM can end up being markedly excessive and compulsive in the same way as other preoccupations and interests for autistic children and young people (Mesibov and Sreckovic 2017). It is common in cases of autistic individuals who have been charged with CSAM-related offending to have substantially large collections due to the ritualistic / compulsive nature of autism, with hundreds and hundreds of files on their computer / devices, many of which are unopened (Mesibov and Sreckovic 2017). For a small subset of autistic individuals, the internet, coupled with sexuality, can lead to what Mahoney has referred to as a 'lethal combination' (2009).

There are cases of autistic individuals charged with possession of CSAM who have engaged in extensive categorisation of the material.

Take the following example of an adolescent autistic male we will call Jeffrey, who is 15 years old. Jeffrey said that he did not set out with any aim but would just go on to various websites (Twitter, Instagram, etc.) to see what he could find to collect; on some occasions this would also include going on to foreign sites. He would categorise the material according to a variety of different features, such as eye colour, hair colour, skin colour and age (roughly). There were numerous times when he would have the same image in more than one folder because it fell into two categories. If there were a number of individuals in the image / video, they would be categorised into a group folder.

When Jeffrey was visiting the various websites where he would collect his material, he would initially put all the material into the same folder, which he would later categorise, or he would categorise as many as he could in a certain time. He said that he would spend hours organising the material. He said he found some of the images he collected morbidly disgusting. When asked to give an example, he said that there were images / videos of corpses (not always people having sex with a corpse, when I asked about this specifically). It was just another type of material that he could categorise and organise into certain folders. He also collected images of animals and would categorise these into different folders according to the type of animal. He would collect images from films and would have subcategories (with electronic folders for each character). The characters were both male and female. He would name the folders according to the character he was collecting images of. He would do this for both 'real-life' films as well as cartoons or anime.

Jeffrey reported that he found it frustrating that he could not get the exact ages of the individuals in the material in order to categorise them accurately. He would have to try and infer their age and put them into folders, such as individuals aged between 20 and 30 or mid-40s / early 50s. Jeffrey's frustration at not being able to get the exact ages for the purposes of detailed, specific and accurate age categorisation is consistent with the features of autism.

A commonly held assumption is that there is an association between the level of risk that the individual poses and the quantity or nature of the content of the CSAM they possess. This is due to the widely held assumption (by criminal justice professionals, the police, etc.) that the larger amount of CSAM an individual possesses, the greater the obsession, and, therefore, the greater the risk of acting on these urges (Sugrue 2017). However, no studies provide any support for this assumption in neurotypical populations (Mahoney 2009; Stabenow 2011). For autistic individuals, this association may be even more inappropriate as it fails to factor in the relationship between the volume of collected indecent images of children and the compulsive and obsessive features associated with autism.

PARAPHILIC, FETISH-BASED BEHAVIOURS AND AUTISM

According to *The Diagnostic and Statistical Manual of Mental Disorders, Fifth Edition* (DSM-5) (APA 2013, p.685), paraphilias are defined as 'any intense and persistent sexual interest other than sexual interest in genital stimulation or preparatory fondling with phenotypically normal, physically mature, consenting human partners'. Only a modest number of studies have looked at paraphilias in autistic individuals (see, for example, Fernandes *et al.* 2016; Hellemans *et al.* 2007), and most are case studies (such as Bowler and Collacott 1993; Chesterman and Rutter 1993; Cooper, Mohamed and Collacott 1993; Coskun and Mukaddes 2008; Dozier, Iwata and Worsdell 2011; Kobayashi 1991; Kolta and Rossi 2018; Milton *et al.* 2002; Silva, Leong and Ferrari 2003). One study found one autistic individual in a sample of 20 institutionalised autistic male adolescents and young adults with borderline / mild mental retardation who exhibited a variety of paraphilias such as olfactophilia (sexual arousal by smells and odours emitted from the body, particularly the sexual areas), podophilia (where the individual has a sexual attraction to feet, a foot fetishism) and zoophilia (where the individual experiences a sexual fixation on a non-human animal) (Hellemans *et al.* 2010).

The behaviours demonstrated within this population can often manifest as problematic, and at times involve self or unintentional victimisation, such as exposing others to sexual behaviour (Beddows and Brooks 2015). Although these behaviours highlight sexually preoccupied behaviours, it may be that they are symptomatic of other aspects of the child or young person's life, and actually mirror the way they operate in all behavioural attributes and are not exclusively sexual. This highlights the importance of considering the wider context of the child or young person's developmental functioning, which will give clarity and context to the harmful or problematic sexual behaviour that may be displayed in accordance with their ability to self-regulate and cope.

Some colleagues suggest fetish-based interests and developmentally unexpected sexual interests may be more common within the autistic population (Schöttle *et al.* 2017). This does not necessarily indicate deviancy, and most interests themselves will arguably be safe and legal; however, when considering a young person for assessment who has displayed harmful sexual behaviour, it is important to focus on apparent sexual interest that may be an influencer or trigger to hypersexual behaviours that may have led to the harmful sexual behaviour. It is also critical that we do not simply assume that these behaviours, albeit sexual in nature, hold solely sexual purposes, as they may also be related to an intense or sensory interest in which an object gives the young person sensory reward or satisfaction.

In their study 'Sexuality in autism', Schöttle and colleagues (2017) suggested an increased likelihood that autistic individuals may be more likely to develop non-normative sexual behaviours as opposed to neurotypical populations due to deficits in social functioning and hypo- / hypersensitivities. The study went further in identifying higher rates of prevalence within this group displaying signs of hypersexuality and paraphilic fantasies or behaviours; this was, however, considered as increased prevalence within male populations.

Fetish-based interests can at times raise concern for both the young person and also their parents or carers, with behaviours often being considered as developmentally unusual and socially unacceptable. However, it is important that a balanced perspective is upheld, and that the young person is given the same opportunity to safely and age-appropriately sexually explore sensory and sexual experiences without societal prejudice and, at times, the overprotective view of autistic people. Arguably many young people may seek a range of sensory sexual experiences that may include the use of atypical items and / or fantasies, and it may be that an overrepresentation within research could be indicative of autistic young people again being subjected to increased adult supervision and on some occasions their lack of social awareness that places them as more identifiable within this area.

CASE STUDIES INVOLVING AUTISTIC INDIVIDUALS ENGAGING IN ZOOPHILIA OR BESTIALITY

Zoophilia is a paraphilic disorder involving intense recurrent sexual fantasies, urges and behaviours involving animals. In the DSM-5 zoophilia is categorised under 'other specified paraphilic disorder', with paraphilia classified as 'any intense and persistent sexual interest other than sexual interest in genital stimulation or preparatory fondling with phenotypically normal, physically mature, consenting human partners' (APA 2013, p.685).

Autism can be associated with zoophilia in a number of ways. For example, it may be associated with sexual interest in animals as a highly restricted fixated interest that is abnormal in intensity, relating to criteria three in the second domain of the diagnostic criteria for autism: 'B Restricted repetitive patterns of behaviour, interests, or activities' (namely, 'B3 Highly restricted, fixated interests that are abnormal in intensity or focus; such as strong attachment to or preoccupation with unusual objects, excessively circumscribed or perseverative interests') (APA 2013, p.50). It is also possible that it is related to the third criteria of the first domain of the diagnostic criteria for autism, where there is an impaired ability to develop and maintain social relationships (specifically, 'A3 deficits in developing and maintaining relationships, appropriate to developmental level (beyond those with caregivers); ranging from difficulties in adjusting behaviour to suit different social contexts through difficulties in sharing imaginative play and in making friends to an apparent absence of interest in people') (APA 2013, p.50). Such difficulty can make it challenging for some individuals with autism to develop and maintain normal intimate and sexual relationships with other humans, which may lead to other forms of sexual expression (Dr Miyuru Chandradasa, 2019, personal communication).

CASE STUDY TWO: Obsessional interests

The 'obsessional' interests commonly displayed by autistic individuals typically only contribute to harmful sexual behaviour if they have a sexual element or are perceived by the individual to have a sexual element (Haskins and Silva 2006; Murrie *et al.* 2002). RM was a 17-year-old male with a diagnosis of autism, and he was found guilty of several counts of theft and criminal damage. He would steal cotton lingerie from washing lines and he stole similar items from the linen baskets in people's homes. Sometimes he would watch clothes spinning around in a front-loading washing machine while using the stolen items as a masturbatory aid.

RM was charged with assaulting the interviewing police officer during an assessment, when the police officer suggested to RM that his intention had been to commit burglary. RM's only intention, from his perspective, had been to use the homeowner's washing machine. RM was referred to a specialist harmful sexual behaviour service to receive an intervention to address the behaviour that was bringing him into conflict with the law.

This case illustrates how autistic individuals' sexual preoccupations make them vulnerable to engaging in offending behaviour (Chesterman and Rutter 1993; Creaby-Attwood and Allely 2017). In RM's case, the practitioners were required to consider a multimodal approach to address a range of factors that were impacting the RM's wider social and emotional wellbeing. A main focus for the intervention also had to consider how RM's sexual behaviour, which arguably was problematic as opposed to harmful or abusive, was influencing his non-sexual criminal behaviour, such as theft and breaking and entry to people's properties.

CONCLUSION

To conclude, the ASEM's individual domain provides an overview of the contributing factors to harmful sexual behaviour and the areas practitioners must consider while supporting autistic children and young people who have displayed harmful sexual behaviour. It is important that prior to undertaking an intervention or assessment for a child or young person, professionals identify the nuances of autism and differing approaches required to ensure engagement to best achieve outcomes across a child or young person's life.

The next chapter will explore how wider factors support an autistic child or young person who has displayed harmful sexual behaviour, and tackle themes such as societal impact and best approaches to prevention.

CHAPTER FOUR

Wider Interpersonal and Familial Factors

OVERVIEW OF THE INTERPERSONAL DOMAIN

This chapter explores the aspects of harmful sexual behaviour in autistic children and young people that relate to the interpersonal domain set out by the ASEM (Russell *et al.* 2025) (see Figure 5).

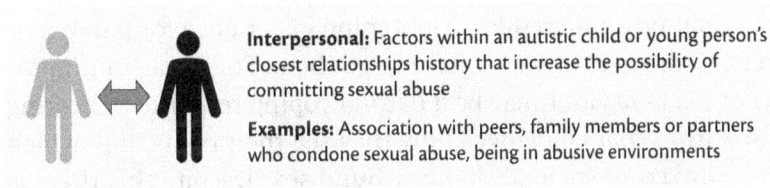

Interpersonal: Factors within an autistic child or young person's closest relationships history that increase the possibility of committing sexual abuse

Examples: Association with peers, family members or partners who condone sexual abuse, being in abusive environments

Figure 5. Interpersonal factors of the autism socio-ecological model
Source: Russell et al. (2025)

Aspects in this chapter explore developmental and interpersonal factors that have been formed within the home environment or wider family eco-systems. These include parenting models, attachment styles and how early years and family dynamics influence the attitudes and social behaviours in a child or young person's later life (explored in greater depth in Chapter Five).

Within the context of sexual behaviour, parents often play a significant role in their child's emotional and physical sexual development.

PARENTS

The importance of parent or carer engagement is frequently highlighted within the field of harmful sexual behaviour (Allardyce and

Yates 2018; King-Hill and McCartan 2024), with many stating that the nature and quality of professional engagement with parents and carers during assessment and interventions is closely linked to outcomes for the child or young person. Parenting is a critical factor in supporting all children and young people to achieve social, emotional and physical development (Rees 2007). This is particularly true for autistic children and young people.

Autism is often described as an unchanging developmental impairment, which, in some instances, may require lifelong or permanent support packages, either from parents or carers, family members or professionals (Dudley and Herbert 2014). Although a great deal of harmful sexual behaviour interventions are structured on change for the future, aspects of autism, such as repetitive behaviour or obsessional interests, may require additional and longer term support to help desistance from future harmful sexual behaviour.

Parental responses to a child or young person displaying harmful sexual behaviour can vary. Finding out that your child's sexual behaviour sits outside developmental norms and / or has caused harm to others can be an incredibly frightening experience for parents or carers, with some unsure where to get help. For some, minimisation of the behaviour may be a natural coping response to hearing information that challenges how they see their own child, which can be linked to societal shame around sex. Despite this there is little specific support for parents or carers in relation to the sexual behaviours of children and young people.

It is incredibly important that parents or carers are included in developing the plan to respond to their child or young person's harmful sexual behaviour, and are key partners in delivering this plan. Children and young people will typically spend more time within the family home or living environment than at school or any other setting (including time with services focusing on harmful sexual behaviour), highlighting the benefit of engaging parents or carers in the early stages to gather correct information and to ensure safety planning is adhered to, to the best of their ability.

A number of factors must be given to this domain and the impact it has on children and young people's ability to productively engage in a harmful sexual behaviour intervention. Both parental attitudes and parents' own behaviour have a substantial impact on the child's life outcomes, and detrimental behaviour displayed by parents or carers can influence a child or young person's likelihood of engaging in anti-social or harmful behaviour (Blechman and Vryan 2000; Bremer 2001; Heller *et al.* 1999). When this is considered within an autistic context, research suggests that parent or carer or adult contact and supervision is often higher, highlighting the importance of their role within a harmful sexual behaviour assessment and intervention process.

Gaining an insight into parents' or carers' beliefs and views of the harmful sexual behaviour and the impact on a victim helps the practitioner determine how the messaging the child or young person is receiving is an important factor in the socio-ecological interpersonal domain. For example:

- Does the parent or carer display empathy themselves to the victim, indicating that they fully understand the impact of the harm? This scenario can support the child or young person's engagement. However, this would be if the parent or carer can hold a balanced view and response and not escalate the harmful sexual behaviour, such as referring to the child or young person as an 'adult sex offender'.

- Does the parent or carer minimise or deny the harmful sexual behaviour their child or young person has displayed? The role of responsibility or admission is assessed to determine the child or young person's perspective, and consideration should be given to the impact of the parent or carer themselves holding victim-blaming views or denial.

- Does the parent or carer excuse the harmful sexual behaviour through rationalisation of autism? This narrative can also become victim-blaming in failing to identify the impact of the harmful sexual behaviour despite the child or young person's autism.

- Does the parent or carer fail to see that certain features of the autism may be contributing to (or providing the context of vulnerability to) the harmful sexual behaviour?

FOSTER CARERS

Foster carers often support children and young people who have experienced significant trauma or adversity prior to coming into their care. Environments vary within the care context, and individual carers vary in their approach to supporting children and young people within their care. This variation can influence a range of areas including the response, if and when required, to support a child or young person in care who has or is currently displaying harmful sexual behaviour. In a study that considered the individual, family and abuse characteristics of 700 British children and young people who had displayed harmful sexual behaviour, Hackett and colleagues (2013) found that two-thirds of the sample had experienced some form of abuse or experience of adversity. This is not an uncommon finding, with a range of studies highlighting similar themes (Creeden 2013; Vizard *et al.* 2007).

Given that many children and young people find themselves in foster care due to experiences of abuse or adversity, it is apparent that this group may demonstrate prevalence in relation to harmful sexual behaviour. However, it must be argued that children and young people in care, including foster environments, often experience an unjustly heightened experience of adult supervision. Children and young people in care are often highly supervised, and this can, at times, appear unfair in comparison to children living within family settings. Many children and young people will at some stage demonstrate behaviours that are inappropriate across a wide spectrum, which, we could argue, is developmentally normative. However, for children and young people in care, residing under strict supervision or increased professional input, many of these developmentally normative behaviours are identified and at times escalated as they are considered to be inappropriate. When we consider that autistic children and young people often already receive increased adult supervision, a child or young person in this context may experience further heightened levels of professional or carer supervision that may, at times, become restrictive and punitive.

RESIDENTIAL AND SECURE CARE

Residential living environments, whether close support or secure care, albeit offering children and young people a place of safety, are not the ideal living environment for children and young people in which to grow and develop. Staff are often managing a range of complexities in terms of the developmental and emotional needs of the children, and although positive relationships are encouraged and often evident between staff and the young people in their care, these are often inconsistent due to staff moving on or annual leave and sickness. For autistic children and young people, however, these environments, due to rigid and predictable routines, often offer stability and structure, which can be well received. A key area to consider, however, is what defines a 'home'.

Although residential environments are often set out as the young people's homes, which is well meaning, the routine and living structure do not match that of a typical family home environment. When considering the basics around social scripts in which they explain to children and young people about person space and appropriate public and private behaviours, we may often cause confusion, particularly within neurodiverse populations. When considering an intervention to support a child or young person residing in care who has displayed harmful sexual behaviour, it is important to assess the environment's response to sexual behaviour. Within a family environment we have discussed the need to consider parental tolerance, boundaries and openness to support conversations and behaviours around sexual development. The residential environment is no different, with the exception of the thresholds for tolerance throughout the staff team.

It is critical to determine if the staff collectively give children and young people in their care a consistent message and if boundaries are well defined. In the initial stages of assessment it may be helpful to determine what collective messages the organisation and staff team are giving children and young people in their care (Russell *et al.* 2025). These factors may include access to sexual information, such as imagery, material, language and access to sexual content, either online or offline, what language is considered acceptable and unacceptable, exposure to other young people's sexual behaviour, boundaries and safe / private spaces, and rules and regulations on pornography. For autistic children and young people, it is particularly important to have clear social rules.

WIDER FAMILY ENVIRONMENTS

Families play a significant part within both the facilitation of harmful sexual behaviour and preventing further instances occurring. A range of studies highlights prevalent themes, such as parental separation, domestic violence, parents in conflict with the law, intrafamilial sexual abuse, lack of environmental sexual boundaries, substance use and parental mental health (Manocha and Mezey 1998) – these can be statistically associated with the emergence of harmful sexual behaviour.

However, not all instances of harmful sexual behaviour displayed by children and young people necessarily relate to an experience of adversity. Many autistic children and young people have romantic experiences or experiences involving sexual expression, often within the context of an overprotective parenting style and high levels of monitoring, which can, at times, limit a child or young person's access to sexual knowledge or information (Torralbas-Ortega et al. 2023). It can be challenging managing an autistic child's social, sexual, emotional and physical development and needs, which may limit their access to developmentally appropriate information and education on matters around sex, relationships and intimacy.

The role parents or carers and the wider family play within this is critical. Without the presence of a supportive living environment that has clear sexual boundaries in place, which support the dialogue of sexually developmental themes, harmful sexual behaviour can create a level of anxiety and fear that families often feel ill equipped to manage (King-Hill and McCartan 2024). Autistic children and young people often have increased parental or carer supervision or guidance in their life, which can, at times, be an area of great strength, but when an instance of harmful sexual behaviour occurs, this can often fracture existing relationships or lead to parents or carers struggling to manage this one aspect of their child or young person's life.

It is important that we resist a blame culture on parents or carers and instead consider their own support needs to achieve the best possible outcomes for their child or young person, such as sharing knowledge or resources around sexual health and education that they can utilise with them. In responding to the harmful sexual behaviour it is important that appreciation is given to the behaviour's occurrence, which may be a single or multiple incidents. However, in progressing with a whole-family support approach, Duane and Morrison (2004) suggest that practitioners should work alongside parents or carers to increase their capacity to manage the home environment and to enhance their capabilities. They also highlight an interesting theme that is significant within autism, which is to support parents or carers in managing the child or young person's structured time and socialisation, an effective approach that is well evidenced within approaches to autism in managing difficult or unwanted behaviours (Autism Speciality Group 2021).

INTERGENERATIONAL EXPERIENCES AND PSYCHOSEXUALITY

Many parents or carers will struggle with finding out that their child has acted in a way that caused sexual harm to others. However, for some, their responses may, in turn, be influenced by their own psychosexual experiences. In particular, for some adult survivors of sexual abuse, their own childhood experiences may influence their ability or willingness to provide effective and emotionally aware education, and at times generate fear of physical or intimate connection with their child (Jay *et al.* 2018). For some, the impact of childhood sexual abuse may lead to overprotective parenting and the effective provision of sex education within the family environment, amplifying challenges that often exist in parenting autistic children generally.

Other themes that should be assessed include parental gender role modelling and expectations on the child or young person's gender based on their own experience of gender expectations and tolerance of gender fluidity. Some of these issues are intergenerational, and sensitive discussions with parents or carers about their own experience of being parented are appropriate. For those who are adult survivors of child sexual abuse, some may have preconceived beliefs around gender based on the gender and relationship of the person responsible for harm, often supporting narrow views on gender, usually males.

The role fathers have in relation to gender socialisation may also be a critical one that should be explored at the assessment stage. Often fathers or father figures in a child or young person's life can give early information on gender expectations and how masculinity is articulated within the family environment and wider community. Hackett *et al.* (2013) carried out a study where they consulted with 676 children and young people who had been referred to specialist services for harmful sexual behaviour. Overwhelmingly 97 per cent were male, with a mean age of 14, demonstrating a prevalence of male children and young people displaying harmful sexual behaviour. Recognising that most children and young people who have displayed harmful sexual behaviour are boys or young men – as well as the fact that most victims are girls – the influence of fathers in the formation of attitudes and values in relation to girls and women is worthy of assessment. The role of fathers may therefore be significant in how gender and sexual messaging is exchanged and taught. This role arguably collates themes including consent, equality and positive male role modelling that will often be intergenerational through the fathers' own experiences in early years.

The concept of masculinity is one that varies across cultural, societal and religious contexts (Philaretou and Allen 2001). The cultural, societal and religious demographics of communities will often impact a male's fluidity of how masculinity is perceived and taught (Hopkins 2006). Ensuring a child has access to a fluid and tolerant environment of masculine fluidity may influence their own interpretation of their gender and ways in which they express themselves, emotionally and sexually. Gender expectations of male children may also be prevalent within their early attachment between themselves and their mothers. For example, if a mother has been affected by male-perpetrated sexual violence or early years child sexual abuse, she may have strong expectations of her child prior to birth, such as a hope she gives birth to a female child, or that her male child grows up to be a 'safe' male (Leonard and Donathy 2017).

As detailed in Chapter One, relationships and sex education (RSE) remains inconsistent in its delivery across the UK (Sex Education Forum 2022), especially for autistic children, which can often influence a model of peer learning on such matters as opposed to meaningful and emotionally connected conversations with parents or carers that often don't take place due to shame, own experiences, lack of information and fear (Jackson, Rhodes and Kotera 2022). Although peer learning has its strengths, young people often require additional information based on sexual curiosity and a desire to understand more about their sexual and emotional feelings, which can, at times, place them in situations or environments that increase their risk of harm, such as online indecent communication or receiving unhelpful or harmful sexual information from other sources, including pornography.

IMPACT ON RESTRICTED CONTACT WITH PEERS

Predecessing factors that may have contributed to social isolation or social development skills, careful consideration should be given to further restricting peer interactions. Decision making on this factor should primarily focus on preventing further harm, but also the impact further peer isolation may have on the child or young person. The assessment of victim attributes should be explored to identify prevalent risk groups in which the child or young person poses risk of sexual harm. This may support the safety plan to establish a rationale on potential restricted contacts, but offer a continued prosocial environment as and when appropriate, which may require additional supervision as opposed to removal of all contact.

ADULT SUPERVISION

Autistic children and young people often experience increased and prolonged adult supervision throughout their lives, a factor to consider in how the harmful sexual behaviour was identified. The behaviour of autistic children and young people may often be identified at an earlier stage due to the level of professional or parent or carer supervision and monitoring. When considering the supervision to respond to harmful sexual behaviour, an assumption of existing strengths within supervision should be avoided, and supervision for preventing further harmful sexual behaviour should be considered independently. It may be that current levels of supervision are adequate and require redirecting to areas of the child or young person's life that have received less attention and potentially encouraged opportunities for the harmful sexual behaviour to occur. To ensure the child or young person has the opportunity to develop resilience and coping strategies it is important that an overprotective practice approach is avoided, and based on a child-centred approach on need.

SOCIAL MATURITY

It has been well covered in the literature that the social and behavioural impairments that characterise autism could have a negative impact on the sexual development in some adolescents who have this diagnosis (see, for example, Sevlever, Roth and Gillis 2013). There are a number of possible explanations for this, including, for example, that the autistic adolescent may not have positive peer support and relationships. They may also have limited sexual education from adults – both at home and in school (Brown-Lavoie *et al.* 2014). This impacts them individually.

Some autistic young people may use the internet in order to seek information about sex / sexual relationships or to satisfy sexual needs due to a lack of sexual outlets with peers / friends (Attwood, Hénault and Dubin 2014). Autistic children and adolescents tend to prefer the online world as it is easier to predict, it is logical and it does not involve emotional communication – it is a place where they feel safer (Mahoney 2009). It is important to emphasise here that it is a misconception that when autistic children or adolescents spend a lot of time online that they are anti-social and do not like being with other people in the real world. This is typically not the case. Rather, the anxiety or fear of the unpredictability of meeting up with friends in a café (for example) may make them stay at home. The online world is also devoid of many of the challenges of face-to-face interactions. For instance, online communication with others or friends means that they can take their time to respond, and it is clear when the person has finished speaking as the message is sent. There is also not the same distracting or overwhelming amount of stimuli such as facial expressions, different tones of voice, non-verbal body language, background noise, etc. to manage when interacting with others.

It is well established that autistic young people have sexual interests, as does any other young person. Despite this, numerous studies have found that autistic individuals, when compared to typically developing peers, may get less formal and informal sexual education (see, for example, Ballan 2012; Holmes and Himle 2014). When compared to their typically developing peers, autistic young people have been found in numerous studies to be less likely to receive knowledge about sex from parents or carers, teachers or peers. Additionally, they are also more likely to use media and pornography as a means of obtaining knowledge about sex (Barnett and Maticka-Tyndale 2015; Brown-Lavoie *et al.* 2014; Stokes *et al.* 2007). Autistic individuals report that they rely mostly on television as opposed to their parents or carers, teachers or peers for education or information on sexual issues (Brown-Lavoie *et al.* 2014; Mehzabin and Stokes 2011; Pecora *et al.* 2016).

When some autistic young people use the internet in order to seek information about sex / sexual relationships or to satisfy sexual needs (Attwood *et al.* 2014), they may focus on circumscribed fields of interest and can quickly become intensely attached, leading them to download and look at or watch more pornographic material (Mahoney 2017). When the autistic young person has a circumscribed interest, their searches online will not remain limited to a superficial internet search as it typically would with non-autistic young people. They will search obsessively and extensively, which may increase the chances of them being exposed to CSAM (Aral *et al.* 2018; Tantam 2000).

An autistic individual can have a level of intelligence that is average or above average while their social maturity can be significantly well below average and closer to that of a much younger person. This spiky profile can often lead them to prefer and feel safer in the company of younger people, who are emotionally or socially at a similar level to them (Cutler 2013). Therefore, they may share the same interests and the level of communication may be preferable – for instance, young children tend to say what they think. Adult interactions, however, can often be very complex and contain a lot of subtle nuances – it is quite common for adults to say one thing but mean something else, for example.

IMPAIRED ABILITY TO CORRECTLY GUESS
AGE AND FACIAL EXPRESSIONS

An impaired ability to accurately or correctly estimate the age of the individuals in the images or videos they are looking at online is another contributory factor as to why some autistic individuals may inadvertently view CSAM. It is crucial that this impaired ability to correctly guess age and the presence of blurred boundaries between adult and child is considered given that the age of the victims in the material determines the legality and severity of the offence (Mahoney 2009). This impaired ability can be further exacerbated by the media, which is full of images, where the boundary between an adult and a child is intentionally blurred. Young teenage models are made to look much older and older models are made to look 'barely legal'. For some autistic individuals, such images can be particularly confusing and challenging to discern as being illegal (Mesibov and Sreckovic 2017).

An impaired ability to recognise facial expressions, in particular negative facial expressions, in many autistic individuals is another potentially contributory factor that might lead an autistic individual to inadvertently engage with CSAM and not obviously recognise that it is illegal, that there is a victim in the material. They may have an impaired ability to recognise the negative facial expressions (e.g., fear, distress) of the minors in the material. It is widely established in the empirical literature that autistic individuals are, overall, impaired in their ability to recognise facial expressions (see, for example, Uljarevic and Hamilton 2013; Woodbury-Smith *et al.* 2005), in particular negative emotional expressions (de la Cuesta 2010; Dziobek *et al.* 2008; Woodbury-Smith *et al.* 2005), which has obvious implications when such individuals are viewing CSAM. The fear, distress or sadness in the faces of the minors they are looking at may not be recognised, which would be a clear indicator that they are victims as opposed to willing, happy participants.

AUTISM AND STALKING BEHAVIOUR

There is a real need to explore how certain features of autism may provide the context of vulnerability to engaging in stalking behaviour (Stokes and Newton 2004). To date, no empirical studies have explored this. However, there is a growing amount of anecdotal evidence of autistic individuals who engage in stalking behaviour when seeking friendships or an intimate relationship (see, for example, Church, Alisanski and Amanullah 2000; Clements and Zarkowska 2000; Green *et al.* 2000; Myles and Simpson 2002; Stokes and

Newton 2004). An autistic individual may misinterpret a person's social niceties as evidence or an indication that the person is romantically interested in them. The autistic individual may then engage in the pursuit of a romantic relationship with that person.

Freckelton and List (2009) described such a case where an autistic man was charged with assault after he rubbed a female stranger's body (her lower back and upper buttocks) after she had briefly smiled at him. When he was questioned as to whether he experienced any feelings of excitement when he did this, he responded: 'It wasn't, it wasn't sexual. It wasn't for excitement or sexual. It was more a way of me trying to get to know her, to see if something would come out of it; a relationship or something' (Freckelton and List 2009, p.26).

In both autistic adolescents and adults, Stokes *et al.* (2007) investigated the influence of learning sources on the level of social and sexual functioning. Specifically, they examined the nature of behaviours that the older individuals who were autistic used in their attempts to initiate social and intimate relationships. The sample in the study comprised parental reports for 25 autistic adolescents and adults (aged 13–36, 16 males and 9 females) and 38 typical adolescents and adults (aged 13–30, 32 males and 6 females). Parents completed a number of questionnaires including the Courting Behaviour Scale, which was developed by the authors (and included in the appendix of their paper). Their Courting Behaviour Scale explored the parents' reports of their child's knowledge and behaviours related to social and intimate relationships.

The first section of the questionnaire involved basic demographic questions such as gender, age and diagnosis. The second section included items exploring social relationship issues. The third section of the questionnaire explored intimate romantic relationship issues, and formed the social and intimate behaviour subscales. These items looked at 20 behaviours that the individual may use in the following areas:

- In their attempt to initiate or pursue a social or romantic interest
- In relation to the type of person targeted (e.g., stranger, friend, colleague)
- The frequency with which the behaviours occurred.

The completion of the final section of the scale was optional for parents as it included sensitive issues that some parents might feel uncomfortable sharing (e.g., contact with the criminal justice system in relation to courtship behaviours). Findings from the study showed that autistic adolescents and adults were more likely to engage in inappropriate courting behaviours, including:

- Touching the person of interest inappropriately
- Believing that the target must reciprocate their feelings
- Showing obsessional interest
- Making inappropriate comments
- Monitoring the person's activities
- Following the person
- Pursuing them in a threatening manner
- Making threats against the person
- Threatening self-harm.

Stokes and colleagues (2007) found that autistic individuals exhibited most of the behaviours across all types of targets without any discrimination. Autistic individuals tended not to engage in behaviours involving interpersonal contact, such as asking the individual if they wanted to go on a date, which may be because of their lack of awareness of appropriate ways to initiate relationships or having little confidence with their impaired social competence. Findings also revealed that autistic individuals were more likely to focus their attention on celebrities, strangers, colleagues and ex-partners. Autistic adolescents and adults persisted for significantly longer in their relationship pursuits after the person had given a negative or 'no' response (or a negative or 'no' response had been given by one of their family members) compared to the typical adolescents and adults. Autistic individuals found it difficult to understand why the individual they were pursuing was not responding to them in the way they wanted. They also believed that they had not done anything wrong.

No learning about romantic skills from either their parents, siblings, observation, the media, sex education or peers was identified in the autistic individuals. Also, for the autistic individuals, the reported level of romantic functioning was significantly lower compared to their peers without autism (after being controlled for age). In the autistic individuals, level of social functioning was found to be the only significant predictor of romantic functioning. Parents of the autistic group reported that some of the factors that contributed to the relationship challenges experienced by their children included a 'lack of understanding in social contexts' and 'lack of empathy' in addition to a variety of other factors. Parents of children with autism also reported that when their child attempted to form a relationship, they struggled to know when to stop persisting (Stokes *et al.* 2007).

PRESENCE OF PARANOIA AND MISTRUST

In some contexts, higher levels of suspiciousness / tendencies to mistrust others are experienced by autistic individuals (as measured using the Paranoia Scale; see Fenigstein and Vanable 1992, for instance) when compared to individuals without an autism diagnosis (see, for example, Blackshaw *et al.* 2001; Maras and Bowler 2012; North, Russell and Gudjonsson 2008). Freckelton and List (2009) have also discussed how, compared to individuals without autism, autistic individuals can be more mistrustful of others to a degree that can border on paranoia. There are a variety of explanations for why this may happen, including:

- Being significantly interpersonally isolated, confused or perplexed about social rules
- Being limited in their appreciation of some matters that take place around them (e.g., being unable to recognise and appreciate expressions of emotions)
- Having difficulties in making causal attributions to others' mental states
- Having a limited understanding and recognition of social cues (see, for example, Blackshaw *et al.* 2001; Freckelton and List 2009; Maras and Bowler 2012).

It has also been suggested by Maras and Bowler (2012) that autistic individuals can be more mistrustful of others to a point bordering on paranoia, which is understandable when you consider how the social and change-coping difficulties that they can experience in their life might result in them being more inherently anxious (see, for example, Kuusikko *et al.* 2008). The increased mistrustfulness may present as a challenge when legal and clinical professionals are attempting to build rapport prior to questioning in forensic contexts.

ISSUES WITH TIME TO RESPOND

There can often be significant mental processing speed weaknesses in autistic individuals. When asked a question, additional time may be needed in order to allow them to process verbal information and to provide an answer (Crane and Maras 2018; Murphy 2018) – sometimes called 'Asperger time' (see, for example, Jacobsen 2003; Myles *et al.* 2005). This is irrespective of intellectual ability. Autistic individuals are more likely to process things even more slowly and have greater difficulty in expressing themselves and communicating, particularly in stressful situations (Kroncke, Willard and Huckabee 2016).

> **CASE STUDY THREE**: Harmful sexual behaviour
> Pritchard and colleagues (2016) describe the treatment of problem behaviour presented by Osian, a white, British, 16-year-old male diagnosed with autism. On four different occasions, Osian was placed in secure accommodation prior to his current placement, due to persistent and serious problem behaviour, including harmful sexual behaviour, aggression and absconding. Findings from the Wechsler Intelligence Scale for Children, Fourth Edition (WISC-IV) found his verbal reasoning skills to be relatively better developed when compared to his non-verbal reasoning skills. He had a significantly low 'processing speed index' score, which is a measure of skills in problem solving, attention and hand–eye coordination.
>
> When he was 4 years old, Osian's parents had separated and then divorced. Osian disclosed that when he was 8 years old, his father and a paternal uncle had abused him, but no charges were brought due to lack of evidence. It was reported that Osian regularly engaged in aggressive and sexualised behaviour towards other children aged between 8 and 11. After he made sexualised threats towards another pupil at primary school, Osian was excluded permanently. When he was still at home he told his family that when he was 11 years old he had sexually abused his sister, who was 8 at the time. Osian's mother went to social services following this disclosure, and Osian

was required to live away from the family in numerous children's homes when his sister confirmed that the abuse had occurred.

Osian told one of the staff at one of the children's homes he was at that there was a time when he had stalked two young girls with the plan to sexually assault them before 'murdering them so there were no witnesses'. This was investigated, but due to lack of evidence, no charges were made. During this period, Osian was reported to have received play therapy, but no impact on his sexually preoccupied behaviours was found despite getting two-to-one staff support.

Osian was transferred to a secure children's home where he was detained for 18 months to receive an intensive intervention to address his harmful sexual behaviour, which was deemed to pose significant risk to others. At 17 Osian perpetrated a sexual assault of a male child with a learning disability (who had also been detained at the children's home) in this placement, and he was charged and convicted of a sexual offence (following a review of closed-circuit television recordings). Alongside the harmful sexual behaviour, practitioners identified the following behavioural issues within their risk and intervention planning and assessment that required a response:

- Aggression (e.g., punching, head butting, kicking, spitting, using weapons including kettles full of hot water and biting).

  Intervention: Pritchard carried out a functional behavioural assessment (FBA) based on document review and interviews with Osian, Osian's mother as well as staff from his previous placement, a secure children's home. The findings from the FBA noted that Osian would act aggressively towards staff. This would be followed by him breaking doors and windows in an attempt to escape. He would do this in situations he found socially aversive. With regards to his verbal sexual behaviour towards residential staff, such as threatening to sexually abuse others, he told the therapist that he enjoyed shocking some of the staff and seeing their reactions to his episodes of verbal outbursts, which were sexually explicit. Therapy involved teaching Osian more socially appropriate ways to get the staff's attention, and helping him to understand the impact that his verbal behaviour had on others (Pritchard et al. 2016).

- Harmful sexual behaviour (e.g., sexual touching, gestures, comments and threats).

Intervention: The secure environment offered Osian an opportunity to address and regulate the suspected unrelated trauma he had experienced in his younger years that may have been contributing to his dysfunctional and harmful sexual behaviour. Prior to undertaking a harmful sexual behaviour-focused intervention, practitioners focused the intervention on the trauma and adversity in Osian's life, acknowledging that his sexual education had mostly been informed via adult sexual behaviour and abuse. Practitioners needed to re-educate and correct Osian's thinking and beliefs about sex, consent and sexuality, which was incredibly distorted.

Given the limitations of Osian's communication skills and IQ, practitioners were required to explore the key themes of sex education, translating it into a style that would meet Osian's learning and cognitive ability, using existing communication methods in his life that were deemed responsive, including visual aids such as timetables and Picture Exchange Communication Systems (PECS). The intervention team was acutely aware that the harmful sexual behaviour that posed a significant risk to others immediately stopped. This was instigated by using visual demonstrations of how to avoid invading others' spaces, such as drawing with chalk on the floor, showing Osian how people's bodies were their own, and the need to avoid unwanted touch or threats and how these could impact people, physically and emotionally.

It was noted that Osian used sexualised and violent language during times of frustration, anger or distress. It was repeatedly noted that practitioners felt Osian's understanding of the language was often limited, and was usually utilised to gain a reaction. The intervention team used a range of methods in response to this, specifically distraction techniques, and at times ignored language during a planned distraction to support a reduction in the reaction in the hope that Osian would begin to acknowledge the ineffectiveness of said language in social situations. Given Osian's level of communication and low IQ (compared to IQ norms), the intervention team highlighted the likelihood that Osian would require life-long support and supervision, not just in relation to harmful sexual behaviour, but also in other aspects of his life, including his general functioning and socialisation.

- Self-harm (e.g., banging his head against walls, tying an electrical cable around his neck).

   Intervention: Osian's self-harm was noted during similar times such as 'property damage', where he would appear to become overwhelmed or stimulated in the current environment. A painting exercise was encouraged during times of apparent depressive mood alongside an intense two-to-one staff ratio, to prevent Osian from causing himself significant harm. This often included removing items that Osian could hurt himself with, but carefully ensuring items such as paint, sponges and support blankets were continually available to avoid further distress. Osian also displayed symptoms of trichotillomania (compulsive hair pulling), which appeared to be another coping strategy during times of distress. It was noted that Osian only appeared to pull hair from his head. Practitioners supported Osian to divert this behaviour from himself onto a small doll that Osian could twist the hair off and pull, reducing the physical impact on his own body.

CONCLUSION

Interpersonal factors are variable, with many being static factors in a child or young person's life, either influenced or formed through varying environmental and relational circumstances. As we start to progress through the ASEM, prevention will begin to become a pertinent theme. Prevention, arguably, is influenced by wider factors often outwith the child's control, echoing the important role families and wider society have in promoting a child or young person's wellbeing, which can be instrumental throughout their lives, often influencing outcomes and goals for children, young people and families. The interpersonal domain highlights the importance of family engagement within any harmful sexual behaviour intervention, and the need for professionals to promote whole-family engagement.

CHAPTER FIVE

Community Factors

OVERVIEW OF THE COMMUNITY DOMAIN

This chapter explores the aspects of harmful sexual behaviour in autistic children and young people that relate to the community domain set out by the ASEM (Russell *et al*. 2025) (see Figure 6).

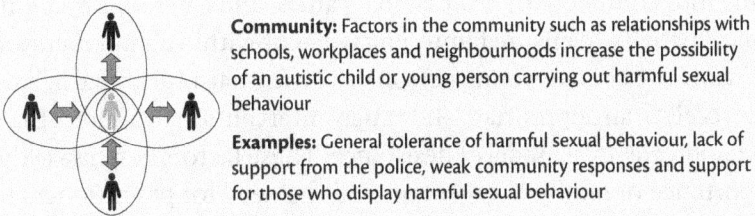

Community: Factors in the community such as relationships with schools, workplaces and neighbourhoods increase the possibility of an autistic child or young person carrying out harmful sexual behaviour

Examples: General tolerance of harmful sexual behaviour, lack of support from the police, weak community responses and support for those who display harmful sexual behaviour

Figure 6. Community factors of the autism socio-ecological model
Source: Russell et al. (2025)

A strengths-based approach exploring prosocial aspects of a child or young person's life can often support an intervention's success and shape outcomes. Decisions may be made to restrict the child or young person's movement and engagement with particular activities. Restrictions may be put in place to ensure the safety of others or at times to remove opportunistic harmful sexual behaviour. However, hobbies and leisure activities are often considered to be a prosocial factor, and can provide children and young people with healthy coping mechanisms to respond to periods of stress or trauma (Pressman *et al*. 2009). An example of this becoming problematic could be if a young person has a weekly structured routine that includes going swimming at the local leisure centre. For an autistic child or young person this space may provide a productive sensory coping strategy embedded within a predictable and structured time. However, if, in this instance, the harmful sexual behaviour took place in this environment, an immediate response may be to remove the young person. Depending on the severity of the behaviour, consideration should be given to wider factors that may allow this environment to remain a factor in the young person's life in a safe way. An initial screening exercise may find that opportunistic elements could be managed with higher levels of supervision, allowing the young person to remain active in a prosocial activity.

Religion can be a critical component to consider within any intervention with children, young people and families. This is more apparent, particularly when exploring interventions around sexual behaviour, with some religious beliefs holding strong gender and behavioural expectations, such as views on LGBTQI+, masturbation, premarital intimacy and sexual health. At times, these beliefs may come into conflict with professional values, and can require significant sensitivity to ensure family engagement within an intervention to ensure the child or young person displaying harmful sexual behaviour receives an appropriate and timely intervention to address their needs and ensure a model of desistance. These factors emphasise the importance of family engagement and the need for practitioners to support a child-centred and individualised approach.

Alongside the ASEM it is critical to give consideration to key factors that are often prevalent within autistic populations. These can contribute to the social communication styles and wider community expectations of how people interact on a social and emotional level.

MORAL OR LEGAL BOUNDARIES

The autistic young person who is socially isolated and sexually naïve may be completely unaware of any moral or legal boundaries when it comes to looking at CSAM: 'The lack of socio-sexual knowledge is always the major issue' (Hénault 2014, as cited in Mahoney 2021, p.13).

It is common for autistic individuals who are charged with viewing CSAM to state that one of the reasons why they recognised or understood that what they were doing was illegal was that they were freely able to access the material online. Given the literal view of the world or black-and-white thinking (also sometimes referred to as inflexibility of thought or cognitive rigidity) common in autistic individuals, they may think that the mere presence of CSAM on the internet gives the message of legality of the material (Mesibov and Sreckovic 2017).

IMPAIRED THEORY OF MIND (TOM)

It is well established that autistic individuals are commonly impaired in tasks involving ToM. ToM is someone's ability to understand and recognise that other people have different thoughts, desires, beliefs and intentions to them (understanding something from another person's perspective). There may be a genuine lack of awareness or understanding in some autistic individuals of the broader contextual issues relating to CSAM – for instance, where and how they got the CSAM, who else might be able to gain access to it, and the implications and consequences for the minors in the material they are looking at (Mesibov and Sreckovic 2017) – as a result of their impaired ToM.

SYSTEMIC APPROACHES: WORKING WITH SCHOOLS

Education professionals play a vital part in supporting community integration and a child or young person's skills in developing a range of community affiliations. Within a school environment, communities may vary, and so the expectations of each may hold differing expected nuances – for example, the different expectations from a classroom environment to that of a school trip, where although some aspects of a regular community association are present, the environment changes, and exposure to different community expectations can appear. For a child or young person who is autistic, this can require additional support strategies to ensure that their understanding of wider community expectations can be met, and this may, at times, cause difficulty in relation to unpredictability. In relation to harmful sexual behaviour it is important that when addressing this issue in a school environment, professionals are consistent in their approach, ensuring that children and young people feel supported and that their prosocial community interactions are upheld, where safe and appropriate to do so.

There are two key drivers behind the increasing focus on the role schools have to play in tackling harmful sexual behaviour in childhood and adolescence. The first is increased recognition of how the social ecology of extended family, neighbourhood, school and other contexts directly impacts the emergence, maintenance and cessation of adolescent harmful sexual behaviours (Letourneau *et al.* 2009). The second driver is the increasing recognition that a significant proportion of harmful sexual behaviour occurs in school-based contexts. Across a continuum, from sexist name-calling through to unwanted touching, coercion into sharing sexual images, rape and other forms of sexual assault, young people display, and experience, sexual abuse in their peer relationships at school. Surveys examining this issue (Letourneau and Shields 2017) all indicate that a significant minority of young people will experience a sexual assault at school, and far more will be exposed to sexist language and non-consensual sharing of sexual images.

Many children and young people who have displayed harmful sexual behaviours have had positive educational experiences prior to the onset of harmful behaviours. Fanniff and colleagues (2017), in a study of 127 young people who had committed sexual offences, compared them to a sample of more delinquently orientated youth. They found the former group more likely to be engaged at school and have more positive prosocial relationships. Other studies suggest that this picture is complicated by a more delinquently orientated group who may be more involved in peer-on-peer sexual abuse, often in school contexts. In a small study comparing 9 young people who had only been involved with sexual offending and 29 involved with sexual offending and delinquency, they found that the 'sex only' group had no identified school issues prior to offending (Schoeneberg *et al.* 2020).

The school environment has traditionally not been considered a protective factor for young people who have displayed harmful sexual behaviour. Yoder and colleagues (2016) argue that the literature has generally looked at psychological risk and protective factors and rarely explored external protective factors such as the school environment, or more specifically, risk and protective factors within school environments. However, van der Put and Asscher (2015) found that in a large study of more than 500 young people who had committed sexual offences, dynamic protective factors, such as school involvement (as well as relationships, substance use and aggression) were more accurately predictive of sexual recidivism than dynamic risk factors for young people with a history of harmful sexual behaviour.

Yoder *et al.* (2016), in trying to identify school-based risk and protective factors, retrospectively looked at treatment provider records of 85 young people in the US who had been adjudicated for sexual offences. All were males, with a mean age of 14. One finding identified that disruptions to the school environment or more school changes led to reduced likelihood for treatment success, including treatment dropout. Low attachment to a new school environment and displacement from a peer group were noted as issues for those required to move school. If moving to a different school is necessary, attention to transitions is key. Unfortunately, our experience as practitioners tells us that school exclusion is far too common for many young people who have displayed harmful sexual behaviour, and will be particularly disruptive for those who have positive relationships with peers at school and who are progressing well educationally.

Conversely, the results showed treatment success, measured by both treatment completion and specific outcomes, was positively associated with school-based protective factors. This was particularly true where young people engaged in extracurricular activities and when there was a member of a multidisciplinary team connected to the school. They concluded that as young people are embedded in many ecological systems, school representatives – much like family members or carers – should be included in the active planning, communication and supervision of those who have displayed harmful sexual behaviours. This not only demonstrates that the school is committed to the success of the young person in moving on from harm, but also provides continuity in developing safety plans, identifying risk-taking behaviours and granting privileges.

The challenges here cannot be underestimated, as a range of studies have also shown how ill equipped educational staff feel in relation to supporting young people who have displayed harmful sexual behaviour. A recent Norwegian survey of 159 primary school teachers (Sandvik *et al.* 2017) showed a lack of knowledge about children who display problematic and harmful sexual behaviour, and teachers struggling to find an appropriate response towards the behaviour when observed in school. This finding was replicated by an Australian study involving interviews with 20 primary school teachers and 3 social workers, identifying the need for better support regarding how to respond to sexual behaviours and appropriate referral pathways (Philander 2018). Similar findings concerning teachers' lack of confidence and skills in this area were found in McInnes and Ey (2020) and, in relation to educational psychologists and school counsellors, Waters (2019) and Morgan *et al.* (2016), respectively. Quadara *et al.* (2020) noted that in the Australian education system, knowledge of harmful sexual behaviour varied between school communities, affecting how schools responded to cases of young people engaging in harmful sexual behaviour and their preparedness to support care and safety plans. It was also acknowledged that schools particularly struggled with the challenge of balancing a duty of care for both the harmed child and the young person engaging in harmful sexual behaviour.

There are clear needs for training and additional support for teachers and for specialist services to work more closely with schools if they are to be placed where we can promote protective factors for young people who have displayed harmful sexual behaviour. However, there may be some clues from recent research about contextual safeguarding as to how this could be achieved. Firmin (2020), in a study using focus groups with students and staff in seven high schools looking at how education settings can tackle peer-on-peer sexual violence, found four factors that were key:

- The language staff and students used and heard
- Staff and student attitudes to disclosure
- Levels of exposure to harmful sexual behaviour in schools
- Staff and student approaches to addressing non-consensual sharing of sexually explicit photographs.

Research into contextual safeguarding in school settings has specifically focused on Beyond Referrals (Firmin, Lloyd and Walker 2019; Lloyd 2019). Contextual safeguarding is an approach that focuses on understanding extra-familial harm experienced by adolescents through paying particular attention to environmental factors such as location and peer relations. It extends the remit of traditional child protection services into locations such as schools, to consider ways to respond to harmful sexual behaviour as part of a strategic, joined-up multi-agency approach. However, this ecological environment – where policies, place-based situational prevention, staff training and support, high standards in identification and response to concerns as well as a focus on problematic attitudes and values – would integrate some of the school-based protective factors described by Yoder *et al.* (2016).

The key challenge is whether schools that employ a whole-school perspective to preventing harmful sexual behaviour are suited to support young people who have displayed harmful sexual behaviour. We would suggest it is highly likely that the emphasis on challenging attitudes, values and triggers that promote the normalisation of sexual violence makes schools using this methodology particularly suited to supporting the complex needs of young people who have displayed harmful sexual behaviour.

CASE STUDY FOUR: Possession of child sexual abuse material (Aral *et al.* 2018)

BA, a 15-year-old girl, was referred to a specialist harmful sexual behaviour service by social services due to a legal case in which she was charged with possessing CSAM on her computer and distributing them on social media. The practitioners assessed if BA presented symptoms of autism and / or obsessive-compulsive disorder (OCD). Based on the history they received, BA had been on social media talking with an unknown person. Using a fake account, the unknown person started the discussion about naked people, and kept the conversation highly focused on this topic. They then asked BA to send pictures of naked people, which BA did without questioning.

BA mentioned nude images of children and famous children. BA reported that the stranger then wanted her to send nude images of children. On the internet she searched for 'naked child pictures, visuals' and sent some of them to the stranger as a link. Her lack of reservations in talking about the issue of CSAM in an internet conversation with an unknown person can be considered evidence of poor social judgement and understanding. BA also sent the stranger some nude images of children she had got on the internet and had saved on her computer previously. She said to the practitioners during the assessment that for a number of years she had been researching and engaging in internet searches of famous children, and believed that everybody shared this need and curiosity. She was asked if it was legal to watch, download and share the naked pictures she had downloaded. She believed that they were legal because they were freely available online, and she also believed that the photographs taken of the children had not been taken against their will.

BA's knowledge about sexuality was found to be at an age-appropriate level, along with her sexual physical development. She stated that she had not engaged in masturbation and no sexual phobias were evident. She said she felt a sexual interest in men. Retrospective information from her family and medical files showed that BA had a history of changing circumscribed interests – for instance, collecting images of famous children from the internet, watching 'baby bath' videos, sending her friends images of children, asking every person she met their weight and size, and researching Egyptian history and the pharaohs. Her family started to notice her circumscribed interests during her fourth grade of elementary school.

Following assessment, BA was diagnosed with autism. Some of the key features relating to her autism included:

- Circumscribed interests (e.g., images of famous children on the internet)
- Long hours spent on the internet
- Failure to make friends.

On the final consultation, BA received a diagnosis of major depressive disorder as she was exhibiting a number of features associated with this (e.g., loss of interest, loss of motivation, low energy, low appetite, low mood and an increased desire to sleep). Although she was able to answer questions adequately, she had a tendency to talk around the topics. She exhibited a depressed mood and inappropriate affect. Her perception and memory abilities were unremarkable.

Following the consultation, practitioners concluded that BA lacked an understanding of the judicial significance and consequences of her action as an apparent result of her diagnosis of autism, and was unable to regulate her behaviour. The intervention team stated that they believed BA had not felt any arousal or pleasure watching pornographic material or CSAM, and did not appear to have any sexual urge or action towards either children or infants. The overall assessment did not consider BA's behaviour paedophiliac. To make the distinction between circumscribed behaviour associated with autism from harmful sexual behaviour, the intervention team recommended obtaining a detailed history of BA's sexual development, the motives of her actions and her social-sexual knowledge.

CONCLUSION
A number of predisposing factors must be considered when taking into account the role of communities within the prevention of harmful sexual behaviour. For many autistic children and young people, various social nuances and discourses can impact on their own community integration, often dependent on their wider interpersonal support, such as parents or carers. As noted, at times, many autistic children and young people can experience community rejection across their life, often due to what is perceived as a lack of socially expected behaviour and communication styles. To conclude, it is worth considering how practitioners consider the importance of early socialisation within these populations and avoid restrictive practices that may further remove a child or young person from opportunities to gain prosocial experiences, and therefore further isolate them from communities.

Communities often vary within a child or young person's life, and the expectations differ and are interchangeable. It is important to consider community factors as a dynamic theme and to appreciate social discourses that may hold different expectations for children and young people. If a child is in full-time education, attends social clubs outwith school and / or comes from a religious family environment, it is evident that these individual expectations will uphold different values and therefore expectations of the child. When supporting an autistic child or young person displaying harmful sexual behaviour, we should give significant consideration to how these individual communities influence a child, and explore the prosocial but also social detriments they may be having.

CHAPTER SIX

Societal and Risk Management Factors

OVERVIEW OF THE SOCIETAL DOMAIN

This chapter explores the aspects of harmful sexual behaviour in autistic children and young people that relate to the societal domain set out by the ASEM (Russell *et al.* 2025) (see Figure 7).

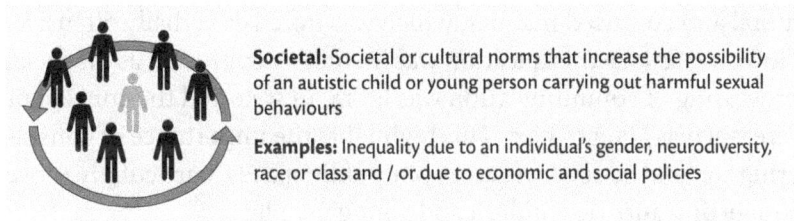

Societal: Societal or cultural norms that increase the possibility of an autistic child or young person carrying out harmful sexual behaviours

Examples: Inequality due to an individual's gender, neurodiversity, race or class and / or due to economic and social policies

Figure 7. Societal factors of the autism socio-ecological model
Source: Russell et al. (2025)

Children and young people who have displayed harmful sexual behaviour often face significant stigmatisation within wider society and at times social discourses. Practitioners must balance public safety and the rights of the child to ensure a contextual approach is upheld. This section will highlight a range of aspects professionals, parents or carers should consider in relation to intervention, but also prevention of harmful sexual behaviour, taking into account the wider issues autistic children and young people may have to navigate within wider society. Society often holds specific and static expectations as to how people interact and behave across public and social situations. It is important to consider how wider societal environments perceive harmful sexual behaviour, but also autism in its broader sense.

In our shopping centres and leisure centres a variety of people interact on a daily basis. However, are staff and the general public aware of the nuances often present within autism, and the ways in which social environments and interactions can impact an autistic person? When individuals in social environments display an association of a learning disability, for example, society often views them in a protective lens. However, when we consider autism, many individuals may mask or not conform to the general public's stigmatising perceptions of autism, highlighting the need for public awareness.

Jake, a 15-year-old autistic male in mainstream education, came to the attention of teaching staff on a regular basis due to what was frequently described by staff as 'verbal altercations and defiant behaviour'. An example of this was when a teacher asked Jake on one occasion, 'Is it raining in here?' This question was in relation to Jake sitting in class wearing a raincoat with his hood up. Jake replied in a literal and confused manner, which was noted as verbally offensive. However, to Jake this question was incredibly confusing as his social processing of communication was literal in style and the concept of sarcasm was alien to him. This highlights the importance of considering societal education across our public spaces, particularly those supporting autistic children and young people.

This section will highlight specifically factors that practitioners should give significant consideration to in responding to autistic children and young people displaying harmful sexual behaviour, and ensuring a whole-child approach is upheld to support outcomes.

CONFIDENTIALITY
The matter of confidentiality can often raise a range of ethical and legal debates based on nuanced legislation around the subject of children and young people. Getting it right for every child (GIRFEC[1]) suggests practitioners' insight is often required in making decisions regarding breaches of confidentiality outwith a child protection

---

1   www.gov.scot/policies/girfec?

context. Although there is a duty of care and legal responsibility in sharing information with external parties when a child or others are at risk of harm, within the context of a harmful sexual behaviour intervention, the balance can be complex to define.

Practitioners are often required to establish and maintain trusting and professional relationships with the children and young people they support, which requires significant skill and time. During an intervention it is likely children and young people will disclose developmentally expected or, in some instances with adolescents, normative sexual behaviours alongside harmful sexual behaviour. It may be that some of these behaviours coincide or contribute to the harmful sexual behaviour such as pornography use, which may be causing the young person distress or misinforming them on matters relating to consent or sex. However, practitioners should carefully consider the implications of escalating themes considered normative, and acknowledge the impact on the professional relationship an unnecessary disclosure to parents may have on the overall quality and engagement of an intervention.

For autistic children and young people, this may at times raise further issues for practitioners given that parents or carers will often have a significant supervisory role in their child or young person's life. However, practitioners should be mindful not to marginalise this group, and uphold the child's rights to confidentiality when and where possible. It may be that in some instances parents or carers will be required to be informed of behaviours that may be of an inappropriate or problematic nature, and must acknowledge the role parents or carers can play in supporting their child or young person within the home environment. If, for example, a young person is struggling to control urges relating to the viewing of pornographic material, and this is having an impact on their health or social skills, parents or carers can be a supportive network to help establish boundaries and support regulation of behaviours. In these instances, it may be helpful for the practitioner to support parental understanding of the behaviour that their young person is struggling with, and reiterate the need to avoid punitive measures that may impact them further.

It is essential that the voice of the young person is heard within this process, and where practitioners feel it is necessary to involve or inform parents or carers, they can consider the following:

- How is the child or young person involved in informing parents or carers?
- Are there any cultural or religious attributes to consider that may impact the discussion or response to the child or young person from parents or carers?
- How will parents or carers being informed support the child or young person?
- How will this impact the child or young person's home environment?
- How does the young person feel their parents or carers will respond to this?
- What support or safety plans could benefit both the young person and their parents or carers, including psycho-educational work with parents or carers in relation to expected sexual development among children and young people?

SAFEGUARDING

A child or young person displaying harmful sexual behaviour should always be considered under a safeguarding and child protection process, acknowledging developmental factors that may have contributed to the child or young person's harmful sexual behaviour (Allardyce *et al.* 2021; Scottish Government 2020). Education professionals often have greater contact with children and young people, and for autistic children, adult supervision is often greater again (Orsmond *et al.* 2013). Therefore harmful sexual behaviour being displayed may be identified within an education establishment where greater contact with peers is more prevalent. This contact may increase factors of risk but also the need for appropriate and child-centred interventions, both within the education establishment and the child or young person's wider environment.

It is important that harmful sexual behaviour is reported via child protection processes that involve the child or young person and their family (Scottish Government 2020). Although we must ensure a victim-centred approach in responding to harmful sexual behaviour, we must avoid inaccurately labelling children. At times, the justice system some children and young people access due to harmful sexual behaviour can lose sight of the child, due to a lack of professional understanding and a lost focus on the rights of the child. In ensuring a child protection focus is undertaken, this will increase the statutory support provision and should model a multi-agency support mechanism around the child or young person, holding them central to decision making.

RISK MANAGEMENT

Consideration of risk factors associated with harmful sexual behaviour should be given to aspects of vulnerability impacting the young person and their static or dynamic presence (Creeden 2013). The sexual behaviour identified is often reflective of an incident or instance that has alerted a child protection process or statutory attention; however, a focus on prevention should be given to consider factors that may influence recurring instances of the behaviour. A multi-agency approach to risk should be utilised ensuring developmental factors are well informed by relevant professionals or family members. This may include the concept of the child or young person's autism, and provide routes to distraction or disruption techniques that may be effective based on the child or young person's social and emotional functioning. The pertinent theme held within risk management should be the risk the child or young person poses to others and self (Allardyce and Yates 2013), and immediate interventions put in place to ensure safety.

At initial stages, a safety plan should be established (Allardyce and Yates 2018) that includes the child, their family and professionals, to establish an immediate response to the harmful sexual behaviour. It should be based on the child or young person's needs and involve relevant professionals to embed a response and intervention within the plan, outlining a frequent review schedule. The reviewing of safety plans should be established at the initial discussion and embedded within the framework of the multi-agency group, ensuring punitive measures are interim, and that the young person is given the opportunity to thrive and desist from further harmful sexual behaviour.

This may be most prevalent in supporting children under 12 in which their safety plan was collated during pre-pubescent stages.

In this instance it is important that the plan is reviewed in line with the young person's progress with it, but that it also aligns with their current age and stage of sexual and physical development. Safety plans will often initiate restrictive measures in which a balance has had to be achieved to ensure others remain safe. These measures may include factors such as restricted contact with peers, adult supervision, temporary removal of hobbies and leisure activities and removal of technology and access to social media – factors that, if prolonged, can be to the detriment of the child or young person's own wellbeing. Consideration should be given to the impact of these factors, in particular for autistic children and young people.

RECOGNISING AND UNDERSTANDING POTENTIAL INNATE VULNERABILITIES

In autistic individuals, having an interest in CSAM is not an anticipated characteristic (Mahoney 2021). However, as increasingly highlighted in the literature (see, for example, Allely 2022; Mahoney 2021), there are clear ways the features of autism in an adolescent or adult can provide the context of vulnerability for engaging with CSAM and / or failing to recognise or appreciate that such behaviour is illegal. Mahoney (2021) (who dedicates his practice almost exclusively to representing those with autism) has described how his experience with many of these cases as an attorney in North America shows that for those who are autistic, the pathway to engaging in CSAM does not typically start with the aim of looking at sexual images of children online, unless they started looking for naked pictures of other children when they themselves were children. Instead, he argues that, in many cases, the autistic child or adolescent (for example) has been lured by someone who is older with these curious images that may seem fascinating as opposed to being inappropriate or disturbing. Or images might be posted in chat rooms about computer games or topics that are appealing to many autistic individuals, such as Japanese-style animations (anime, hentai, manga), 'furries', My Little Pony, etc.

It is important in criminal law that there is an understanding and recognition of the innate vulnerabilities associated with autism that can contribute to the viewing of CSAM (Allely and Dubin 2018; Allely, Kennedy and Warren 2019; Freckelton 2011a, 2011b, 2013; Freckelton

and List 2009). Currently, there is limited understanding and recognition of how certain features of autism may provide the context
of vulnerability to engaging in CSAM, although the knowledge gap
has been raised in recent years (Allely and Dubin 2018; Allely *et al.*
2019; Dubin and Horowitz 2017). Early recognition and diagnosis of
autism is imperative in order to ensure that the individual receives
a fair trial (see also Cooper and Allely 2017).

It has been highlighted in the literature (see, for example, Allely
2020b; Allely and Dubin 2018; Allely *et al.* 2019; Mahoney 2009) that
there are a number of possible innate vulnerabilities in some autistic
individuals who are charged with viewing CSAM, as noted:

- Counterfeit deviance
- Social maturity
- Unaware of any moral or legal boundaries
- Literal thinking
- Impaired theory of mind (ToM)
- Impaired ability to correctly guess age
- Impaired ability to recognise negative facial expressions in
  CSAM
- Importance of considering the ritualistic nature of collecting
  CSAM in autistic individuals.

COUNTERFEIT DEVIANCE

In terms of the societal model, the concept of counterfeit deviance
underpins the role of a societal response to autism and how, at times,
autistic people can be mislabelled due to societal naivety or the
stigmatisation that is often associated with being involved with the
criminal justice system. 'Counterfeit deviance' is a term first coined
by Dorothy Griffiths (see Griffiths *et al.* 2013). The viewing of sexual
material that is extreme does not always indicate the presence of
harmful sexuality. In some cases, it may be 'counterfeit deviance'
rather than deviant sexuality (Hingsburger, Griffiths and Quinsey
1991; Mahoney 2009, 2017). Counterfeit deviance is when there is
a misperception of intention and an individual's motivations are
perceived as sexual when they are not. Mahoney incorporates the
concept of 'counterfeit deviance' in understanding what may appear

on the surface to be acts of deviant or offending behaviour, but the individual 'lacks the culpable mental state or blameworthiness which would normally attend such actions by persons who are typically developed' (Mahoney 2017, p.6). What appears to be malicious intent is frequently associated with the social misunderstandings of the autistic individual (Kumar *et al.* 2017).

AUTISM AND THE CRIMINAL JUSTICE SYSTEM

Although not all children and young people who have displayed harmful sexual behaviour are involved with the criminal justice system, some find themselves navigating this complex landscape. For autistic children and young people, there are significant factors we must consider in supporting them through this experience. This domain will look at the experiences and challenges for many autistic young people who become involved in the criminal justice system. It will take a whole-systems approach, including how certain features of autism may provide the context of vulnerability to engaging in offending behaviour and autistic young people and their interactions with the police, courts and custody. It will explore some of the procedural court adaptations that could be implemented to enable the autistic young person to more effectively participate in their own trial. We will highlight the benefits of predictability for an autistic young person and echo the importance of a health approach being considered alongside legal processes.

It is important to include expert insights regarding the nature of autism and the specific features of the disorder when appropriate (Berryessa 2017). Many courts decide not to include the evidence of psychiatric experts involving autism (in particular, Asperger's syndrome and high-functioning autism) because they believe that any probative value would be markedly outweighed by the potential for jury confusion. However, not providing the jury with information regarding the defendant's autism diagnosis may, in fact, *increase* juror confusion because many of the social mannerisms, expressions and behaviours the autism defendant may exhibit can often be similar to those displayed by a guilty party (Foster 2015).

Experts can provide helpful suggestions regarding areas of inquiry.

Putting the particular referral questions in writing can also be useful. Some examples of referral questions in an autism case include: What is the client's diagnosis? Did the client's diagnosis play a causal role in the charged offence? Did the client's diagnosis play a contributing role in the charged offence? What is the client's probable level of success in psychological treatment / intervention and / or probation supervision?

The effects of incarceration on the autistic individual should also be explored as the literature has indicated that autistic individuals tend to find incarceration far more burdensome, when compared to non-autistic individuals overall. Autistic individuals are also more vulnerable to being victimised as a result of certain features of their autism, including their social-emotional immaturity, naïveté and gullibility (Allely 2015).

Autism and offending behaviour

Autistic individuals are no more likely to engage in offending behaviours compared to the general population (see, for example, Mouridsen et al. 2008). In fact, studies have found that autistic individuals may be less likely to offend when compared to individuals without autism. The majority of autistic individuals are law-abiding (see, for example, Cederlund et al. 2008; Mouridsen et al. 2008). Gralton (2013, pp.112–113) outlined some of the potential reasons for offending by autistic individuals, modified for adolescents from earlier authors (Berney 2004; Wing 1997):

- Aggression resulting from the disruption of routines (this includes a lack of motivation to change or adapt behaviour)
- Crimes resulting from social naivety (including various types of sexual offending)
- Pursuit of a special interest, such as weapons, militaria, poisons, fire, sadistic interests
- Experiences of bullying, teasing, rejection and a desire for revenge (this may lead to an assault on the perpetrator or displacement onto another, often completely innocent, person)
- Hostility towards family members (often parents) representing long-standing complex dynamics due to the dependency of the autistic individual

- Sensory sensitivities leading to high levels of arousal and violent behaviour, including aggression to remain in low stimulus settings such as seclusion
- Passively following the lead of a stronger personality and committing an offence under their direction (more commonly in adolescents this takes the form of wanting to maintain membership of an anti-social peer group and being prepared to do anything to achieve this)
- A 'cry for help' in which violence is seen as the only way to obtain appropriate intervention
- A lack of awareness of wrongdoing, or an assumption that the individual's own needs supersede all other considerations
- Impairment in empathy (specifically cognitive empathy as opposed to emotional empathy) or lack of recognition of fearful emotions in others may lead to indifference to the wider consequences of actions on others
- An inability to see the consequences of actions due to poor central coherence or executive function impairment
- Co-occurring mental health conditions, including affective and psychotic illness
- Any combinations of the above.

It is also important to note that a 'pure' diagnosis of autism (that is, just a single diagnosis of autism) is the exception as opposed to being the norm. Most autistic individuals have other co-occurring mental health conditions or other neurodevelopmental disorders. Some of the most common co-occurring mental health conditions include depression, anxiety and other neurodevelopmental disorders such as attention deficit hyperactivity disorder (ADHD). Additionally, research has also found that there are significantly increased rates of all major psychiatric disorders in adults with a diagnosis of autism. It is therefore important that the presence of any co-occurring psychiatric disorders in autistic individuals is recognised and identified as early as possible when they come into contact with the justice system. These co-occurring mental health disorders or conditions can have a significant role in contributing to offending behaviour or providing the context of vulnerability to engaging in that offending behaviour.

THE IMPORTANT ROLE THAT CO-OCCURRING MENTAL HEALTH DISORDERS PLAY IN OFFENDING BEHAVIOUR IN AUTISTIC INDIVIDUALS

It is now well recognised that co-occurring mental health disorders or conditions are a likely factor when autistic individuals engage in offending or harmful behaviour (see, for example, Im 2016a, 2016b; Wachtel and Shorter 2013). A landmark review by Newman and Ghaziuddin (2008) supports this. They identified studies that explored the potential role that psychiatric factors played in contributing to offending behaviour in autistic individuals. Most of the identified 17 publications in their review were single case reports, with a total of 37 cases described across the 17 publications. A definite psychiatric disorder at the time of the offence was described in 11 of these 37 cases (29.7 per cent). In 20 of the 37 cases (54 per cent), probable psychiatric disorder was found. Newman and Ghaziuddin highlight that these individuals also had a number of co-occurring conditions, such as conduct disorder, depression or schizoaffective disorder.

These psychiatric disorders (with conduct disorder being an exception; see Hodgins *et al.* 2008) by themselves are not sufficient to cause a significant additional risk for violence or offending behaviour more generally. However, research has suggested that certain features of autism can provide the context of vulnerability to engaging in offending behaviour (see, for example, Allely 2019; Allely & Creaby-Attwood 2016; Allely and Faccini 2019; Baron-Cohen 1988; Barry-Walsh and Mullen 2004; Chesterman and Rutter 1993; Everall and Lecouteur 1990; Lazaratou *et al.* 2016; Ledingham and Mills 2015; Mouridsen *et al.* 2008; Schwartz-Watts 2005; Siponmaa *et al.* 2001).

DISPROPORTIONATELY HIGHER RISK OF AUTISTIC INDIVIDUALS EXPERIENCING ABUSE AND VICTIMISATION

Autistic individuals are more likely to be the victims of crime rather than the instigators. It is now well established that autistic individuals are at a disproportionately higher risk of experiencing abuse and victimisation (Brown-Lavoie *et al.* 2014; Sevlever *et al.* 2013). A considerable risk of interpersonal violence victimisation has also been found in adults with a diagnosis of autism. Interpersonal violence victimisation refers to violence and abuse that take place between people, including child maltreatment, intimate partner violence, adolescent dating violence and bullying (Brown-Lavoie *et al.* 2014; Cappadocia, Weiss and Pepler 2012; Weiss and Fardella 2018). Studies have also found evidence of increased risks of bullying and physical and emotional abuse in autistic adults (Fisher, Moskowitz and Hodapp 2013; Jawaid *et al.* 2012; Weiss and Fardella 2018).

Weiss and Fardella (2018) carried out a study that explored the self-reported experiences of childhood and adult victimisation and perpetration. They also examined how victimisation and perpetration were related to autism-related impairments. Their study included a sample of 45 autistic adults (age range = 18–53, mean age = 30.00, SD (standard deviation) = 1.48), and this group was compared with a matched sample of 42 adults without a diagnosis of autism who were matched on mean chronological age (age range = 19–54 years, mean age = 32.12, SD = 8.62). The two groups were not significantly different with regards to the percentage of men or on self-identified minority status (ethnicity status).

The autism group reported experiencing more overall victimisation during childhood compared to the participants without autism. They reported experiencing more property crime, maltreatment, teasing / emotional bullying and sexual assault by peers. More teasing / emotional bullying in adulthood and greater sexual contact victimisation were reported by the autistic participants compared to the participants without autism. No significant differences were found between the groups with regards to perpetration. Socio-communicative ability and emotion regulation impairments could not explain the increased risk of victimisation in the autism group (Weiss and Fardella 2018).

There may also be increased susceptibility and vulnerability to becoming accessories to crimes due to targeted 'befriending and mate crimes' in autistic individuals (Dickie, Reveley and Dorrity 2018; Dubin 2017; Mesibov and Sreckovic 2017). Some autistic individuals can be exploited when they mistake invitations to participate in performing malevolent intentions with friendship. One of the potential reasons for this can be the challenge they experience in making and maintaining friends.

AUTISTIC YOUNG PEOPLE AND POLICE INTERACTIONS

A study carried out in the US by Rava and colleagues (2017), based on a nationally representative sample of autistic young people, aimed to explore the prevalence and correlates of involvement in the criminal justice system. The study investigated whether young people, at 14–15 years old, and also at 21–22 years old, had been stopped and questioned by the police or arrested – 11,270 young people nationwide were enrolled. A total of 920 out of 11,270 were on the autism spectrum. The autistic young people were primarily white males (83.1 per cent), aged between 15 and 19, from middle-income households. Findings showed that by age 21, 19.5 per cent of autistic young people had been stopped and questioned by the police, and nearly a quarter of those who said they had been stopped and questioned had previously been arrested (4.7 per cent). Almost 50 per cent of all those who had ever been stopped and questioned by the police said that this had happened by the time they had reached 15 years of age. Young people were also more likely to be involved in the criminal justice system if they displayed externalising behaviours (Rava *et al.* 2017). These findings regarding arrest rates are consistent with previous studies (see, for example, Brookman-Frazee *et al.* 2009; Cheely *et al.* 2012; Tint *et al.* 2017).

A prospective Canadian study followed a sample of 284 autistic adolescents and adults over the course of 12 to 18 months. Findings showed that during this time about 16 per cent of participants were reported to have had some form of police involvement (Tint *et al.* 2017). Findings from a study based on a survey of 35 Canadian adults aged between 18 and 65 showed that having experienced at least one interaction with the police in their lifetime was reported in just over 80 per cent (N = 29) (Salerno and Schuller 2019). Findings showed that of those who indicated they had had an interaction with the police:

- 46.4 per cent (N = 13) reported between one and three interactions
- 39.3 per cent (N = 11) reported between four and nine interactions
- 14.3 per cent (N = 4) reported 10 or more interactions (one

respondent did not provide information as to the frequency of their police interactions).

Other surveys of police officers have also found frequent interactions with autistic individuals in the UK (Crane *et al.* 2016) and the US (Gardner, Campbell and Westdal 2019). An online survey collected the experiences and views of 394 police officers (from England and Wales) regarding autism (Crane *et al.* 2016). Only 42 per cent of police officers reported that they felt satisfied with how they had worked with autistic individuals (Crane *et al.* 2016). An increasing number of studies emphasise the need for formalised training in autism for police officers and other law enforcement professionals (see, for example, Gardner *et al.* 2019; see also, Gibbs and Haas 2020; Haas and Gibbs 2021; Holloway *et al.* 2020; Young and Brewer 2020).

One study conducted an analysis of media reports involving law enforcement officers' (LEOs) interactions with autistic individuals (Copenhaver and Tewksbury 2019). Findings showed that the most frequent interactions included elopement (e.g., wandering), being a victim of crime and positive accounts of interactions between LEOs and autistic individuals. The study also highlighted that there were a number of features of autism that might appear 'odd' and be misinterpreted as threatening by others, potentially causing LEOs to respond to calls even though there was no criminal element to the behaviour / actions. Some examples of such behaviours may include:

- Inappropriately intruding on the social boundaries of others (e.g., standing in the personal space of others or touching other people without their permission)
- Being considered to be under the influence of substances due to repetitive behaviours such as hand flapping, head banging, etc.
- Causing alarm to members of the public because of sudden mood changes or panic when faced with an unexpected change (Gardner *et al.* 2022).

In a national birth cohort study conducted in New Zealand, Bowden and colleagues (2022) investigated the prevalence of criminal justice system interactions among young adults with and without autistic presentations. They also examined whether there were any differences in offence types between the two groups. The data used for this study comprised 1197 autistic individuals and 147,879 individuals without autism. Findings revealed that, when compared to those without autism, autistic young people were at lower risk of being proceeded against by the police (37.6 per cent lower), as well as being charged (40.3 per cent lower) or convicted in court (43.6 per cent lower). This was even after controlling statistically for a number of key demographic factors. In contrast, the risk of being incarcerated was not significantly different between those with and without autism. It was found that conditional on being charged with an offence, autistic young people had higher rates of incarceration when compared to those without autism (13 per cent versus 8 per cent, respectively). The autistic young people who were charged with offences had higher numbers of total charges and were more likely to be charged with a serious offence (offences punishable by a minimum of two years in prison) compared to those without autism. For those charged with at least one offence, there was an increased risk of being charged with offences against a person, violent offences and offences against property, and they were at lower risk of offences against organisations, the government and the community (Brewer and Young 2015).

IMPORTANT CONSIDERATION FOR AUTISTIC YOUNG PEOPLE IN POLICE INVESTIGATIVE INTERVIEWS AND DURING COURTROOM PROCEEDINGS

A range of features of autism can be displayed by those with this disorder during court proceedings that can make them be perceived by jurors (who might have little understanding of autism) as being aloof, disinterested, remorseless or even imperious (Allely 2022; Berryessa 2021; O'Sullivan 2018). An autistic defendant, due to certain features of their autism, can appear evasive, remorseless, lacking in empathy and guilty, with memory impairments, lack of outward emotional expression, unusual ways of speaking, inappropriate expressions or behaviours, difficulty making or maintaining eye contact, literal cognitive style or interpretation of information (cognitive rigidity or inflexibility of thought), issues with compliance, misinterpretation or lack of understanding of repetitive interests or behaviours, presence of paranoia and mistrust, impaired social communication and interaction, issues with time to respond and echolalia or repetitive vocalisations (see Allely 2022).

Memory impairments

Research has found that memory impairments are common in autistic individuals, which may make them more vulnerable during forensic contexts (see, for example, Bigham *et al.* 2010; Boucher, Mayes and Bigham 2012; Bowler, Matthews and Gardiner 1997; Maister, Simons and Plaisted-Grant 2013). Autistic individuals, when compared to individuals without autism, are often impaired in their ability to recollect or remember past personally experienced events. They also tend to remember fewer of them and need more time in order to do so (Crane and Goddard 2008; Crane *et al.* 2012; Crane and Maras 2018; Goddard *et al.* 2007). Details of the event may be remembered but not when it happened, and research has also found that there can be difficulty in consciously recollecting events. The tendency to rely on feelings of familiarity to guide their memory has also been found in autistic individuals (see, for example, Bowler, Gardiner and Grice 2000; see also Bowler, Gardiner and Gaigg 2007; Johnson, Goodman and Mundy 2018; Maras and Bowler 2012). Although most people know that the capital of England is London, only a small number would be able to remember when or where they acquired this knowledge. These two instances form two types of memory. One is knowledge-based information (e.g., names of capital cities), which is called semantic memory, and the other is memory for an event or a specific episode, which is called episodic memory.

Research indicates that autistic individuals are typically unimpaired in their memory for semantic and general information (knowledge-based information). However, there is a tendency for much more prompting being required in order to retrieve specific episodes (memory for specific events / episodic memory) (Bigham *et al.* 2010; Crane and Goddard 2008; Crane and Maras 2018). For example, they may be able to remember that their younger brother usually throws things at them when he gets angry (semantic memory) but are unable to remember a specific example of this, such as the time their younger brother came home from work and was really angry because he had found out that someone had scratched his car (episodic memory). Additionally, they may be able to remember the details of the event but not when it happened. Such a memory profile may be considered as indicative of guilt in forensic contexts (Allely 2022).

Quantity and accuracy of free-recall narratives

The recommendation of best practice interviewing guidelines (see, for example, Ministry of Justice 2011) is that an individual's free-recall memory is first obtained using a narrative account. However, it is now well established that autistic children have difficulty with free recall, and their narratives are different when compared to their typically developing peers – autistic children may provide fewer event details (Malloy, Mugno and Arndorfer 2018). Bruck and colleagues (2007) carried out a study investigating data on numerous autobiographical memories of children aged between 5 and 10 (Bruck *et al.* 2007). The 5- to 10-year-old autistic children, when compared to the children with no autism diagnosis, displayed less correct autobiographical recall relevant to current life circumstances (e.g., a teacher's name). Autistic children displayed higher error rates to improbable autobiographical event questions. When compared to the children without autism, the autistic children, when asked for their open-ended recall of a number of distant autobiographical events that were confirmed by a parent and one specific event (e.g., going to the hospital) confirmed by a parent, recalled less confirmed information. Forty-four per cent of autistic children were unable to recall a time when they had to go to the hospital (which would typically be considered an emotional event). This was much higher than the children without autism, where only 4 per cent were unable to recall a time when they had to go to the hospital.

In their study, Bruck and colleagues (2007) also looked at suggestibility in the sample of autistic children aged between 5 and 10. In the first interview about a magic show that the children in the study had experienced about eight days earlier, researchers infused suggestive information into the event representations for the children by providing statements about non-occurring event components, followed by asking option-posing questions about the non-occurring event components. These suggestive interviewing techniques were coupled with the interviewer putting pressure on the child to select a response if they did not reply. If a non-occurring event option was selected by the child, the research assistant would then restate the option (e.g., 'You told me that...'; Bruck *et al.* 2007, p.86).

Throughout the duration of the interview, the children received compliments. However, the compliments were not necessarily tied to the child selecting non-occurring event options. The likelihood of selecting one of the two non-occurring event components was not significantly different between the two groups (autistic children, 67 per cent, and children without autism, 55 per cent). About four days later, the children took part in a second interview in order to assess the incorporation of false information presented during Interview 1 into their event representations. The children's open-ended recall and their responses to the yes-no questions was how the researchers measured the incorporation of false information. No significant differences in the children's incorporation of false information into open-ended recall was found (20 per cent for the autistic children vs. 17 per cent for the comparison children). However, the autistic children were found to be more susceptible to misleading questions that were asked in a yes-no format about the previously suggested non-occurring event components – but only if the misleading question consisted of information that was restated by the research assistant. The findings from this study would suggest that, compared to the children without autism, autistic children may only be more suggestible when certain highly coercive interviewing techniques are employed (Bruck *et al.* 2007).

Findings by Mattison, Dando and Ormerod (2015) also showed that free-recall performance was impaired in autistic children (mean age = 14 years, 6 months) when compared to their typically developing peers (mean age = 10 years, 2 months) who were matched on verbal mental age. Findings showed that the typically developing children were able to recall significantly more correct information when compared to the autistic children about a brief crime video after a one-hour delay. Mattison and colleagues found that 'articulated sketching' (which involves asking the child to sketch anything they feel would aid them in their ability to remember what they saw) in order to reinstate the context does appear to be useful for recalling an event in autistic children.

It increased the amount of information they could recall without increasing the number of details that were inaccurate. Interestingly, when compared to the other autistic children who were in the control and mental context reinstatement conditions, the autistic children who were in the condition where they sketched while narrating were also found to be more accurate when reporting about 'person' information and reported more correct 'action' details.

A tendency to focus on peripheral event details (such as the description of a bystander at a crime scene rather than the perpetrator) and difficulty extracting the greater meaning or gist of an event is also found in autistic children (Happé and Frith 2006; McCrory, Henry and Happé 2007). Compared to their typically developing peers, autistic children may supply narratives that are less social in nature. For instance, the narratives will be missing information regarding emotions, social relationships and conversations with others. Instead, there is a tendency for their narratives to focus on factual information (Malloy et al. 2018). There is also a tendency for a lack of coherence, organisation around central themes, evaluative devices (e.g., character dialogue), and causal and mental state details in the narratives provided by autistic children (see, for example, Capps, Losh and Thurber 2000; Diehl, Bennetto and Young 2006). The narratives of autistic children are also likely to include details that are bizarre or even inappropriate (Loveland et al. 1990).

Time segmentation prompts can be used in order to inquire about events that the child had stated previously. An example of this would be: 'Think back to that day and tell me everything that happened from the time you left school until the time your friend came over.' Such an approach could assist autistic children to produce more coherent and logical narratives.

Impairment in ability to recall events in a sequential manner

Some autistic individuals may also have impairments in their ability to recall events in a sequential manner and with sufficient detail (Kroncke et al. 2016). Autistic individuals can be perceived erroneously as being uncooperative and non-responsive when under cross examination or during investigative interviews as they frequently display difficulty in recalling events in a sequential manner and with sufficient detail. They are impaired in their ability to recall a clearly sequenced narrative of events (see also Kroncke *et al.* 2016). Autism may also impact on an individual's perception of time, and they can find it difficult to estimate 'how long' specific events were (The Advocate's Gateway 2016). Research has suggested that disorders in timing and / or time perception may be a key feature (or aetiology of) some of the behavioural and cognitive impairments found in autism (see, for example, Allman 2011; Allman and DeLeon 2009; Allman, DeLeon and Wearden 2011; Jurek *et al.* 2019). Having difficulty with determining how long specific events lasted for and ordering or sequence of events can make an individual appear as if they are guilty or evasive (Allely 2022).

Toolkit 14: *Using Communication Aids in the Criminal Justice System* from the Advocate's Gateway (2015) suggests the use of Post-it® notes and visual timelines that may assist the autistic individual with respect to issues with temporal questions (e.g., sequencing events and details in order) and help them narrate events in chronological order and whether an event took place before or after another. They can also support questions about categories of information (e.g., event locations, dates, times). They are especially effective in the case of multiple events. Different-coloured pens and Post-it® notes can be used for the different events, which can help the individual when being verbally questioned about different events.

Mattison and Allely (2022, p.61) also recommend the following:

- Be aware of the challenges that an autistic person may have when trying to recall information about past events – some details may be easier to recall, and others challenging.
- Allow additional time for recall.
- Support recall by providing additional prompts with careful questioning.
- Prior to questioning, explore the use of appropriate visual aids. For some autistic people, these can scaffold recall and reduce anxiety.

Odd or pedantic manner of speaking
Some autistic individuals may have an odd or pedantic manner of speaking. They may unexpectedly speak at an increased volume or

at a very low volume, or suddenly and unexpectedly shout out unrelated words or phrases. This can be seen as rude and / or aggressive when this might not be the case, as outward display is not necessarily reflective of what they are feeling inside. An unusual or odd-sounding prosody can also be exhibited. A monotonous voice, with little or no emotional intonation or variation in prosodic elements (e.g., speech rate and rhythm, loudness, pitch / fundamental frequency, intensity, duration and pause/silence), is also often found in autistic individuals (McCann and Peppé 2003). If an autistic individual talks in a monotonous tone of voice, with no emotional intonation and a lack of emotional expressions, they may be viewed in forensic contexts as being cold or standoffish, which can have adverse implications (Allely and Cooper 2017).

Exaggerated levels of compliance, eagerness to please and avoidance of confrontation

Exaggerated levels of compliance, eagerness to please and avoidance of confrontation is frequently found in autistic individuals in certain situations (see, for example, Chandler, Russell and Maras 2019; North *et al.* 2008). Compared to individuals without autism, autistic individuals are often more compliant, fearful and deferential when they are asked questions, particularly by those in authority (Freckelton 2013), which may increase their risk of complying with interrogative pressures. This feature can lead some autistic individuals to make statements that are erroneous and self-incriminating in forensic contexts (Gudjonsson 2003), or respond compliantly to any requests and demands (Maras and Bowler 2012). Autistic individuals may also be particularly fearful of authority figures who place them under what they experience as pressure because of their authoritarian manner and questioning style (Freckelton 2011a, 2011b; Freckelton and Selby 2009). In a criminal justice setting autistic individuals who have higher levels of compliance may be more likely to feel pressured into agreeing to a statement (even if it is not accurate) just to terminate the interview as soon as possible (Gudjonsson 2003). Increased compliance may also lead to an autistic individual being less likely to ask for a break when they need it or to ask questions when they do not understand something (Allely 2022).

KEY RECOMMENDATIONS WHEN QUESTIONING AN AUTISTIC INDIVIDUAL IN FORENSIC CONTEXTS

Walsh and colleagues (2023) outlined a number of recommendations that the police could adopt when questioning autistic individuals and trying to build rapport. These include:

- Maintain a safe distance from the individual.
- Avoid invading the personal space of the individual.
- Model behaviours as an example for the individual to emulate.
- Adopt a calm disposition and voice.
- Use simple language.
- Avoid touching the individual.
- Accommodate a delayed response to questions and instructions (Allely 2015).

Murphy (2018) developed a checklist of areas that need to be taken into consideration when interviewing individuals with a diagnosis of autism in a forensic setting, including personal safety, sensory issues, difficulties with reciprocal social communication, cognitive style, and neurodevelopmental disorder and psychiatric co-morbidity.

Personal safety

The interviewer should obtain any formal risk assessments and available case notes that have previously been carried out. It can be helpful to speak to a family member or member of staff who may have an insight or information regarding any specific triggers to violence that the individual may have. Information could also be obtained regarding any history of making false accusations. Having an appropriate member of staff (e.g., a prison officer) to observe may also be useful. It is also recommended that the interviewer / assessor is explicitly clear about the purpose of the interview. Having short duration meetings / interviews is also suggested. Such actions may reduce the risk of the individual acting on any violent impulses (which is particularly important for individuals with emotional regulation difficulties or limited tolerance for frustration). It might also be helpful for the interviewer to arrange the meeting / interview to occur at a time when it is not likely to cause any disruption to the individual's routines or rituals (Murphy 2018).

Sensory issues

In the courtroom environment, autistic defendants may have more difficulty (and may even have feelings of distress) due to being over-stimulated by the sensory environment (the sights, sounds, etc.) (Taylor, Mesibov and Debbaudt 2009). The interviewer should seek information regarding any sensory functioning or any hypersensitivities. This could be obtained by asking relatives or other people who know the individual. Additionally, before the interview, it would be useful to ask the individual themself if they have any sensory sensitivities. They could be asked if there is anything in the room that is causing any discomfort, impacting on their ability to engage in the interview (e.g., fans, strip lights, direct eye contact). Certain times of day may be quieter for an interview. The sensory profile checklist, which is a self-report measure, may be completed by the individual. When meeting the individual for the first time, any initial body contact should be avoided (e.g., a handshake, unless this is offered by the individual first, and safety permits). An even and calm tone of voice should be maintained by the interviewer (Murphy 2018).

The implementation of accommodations to the sensory environment for autistic individuals has also previously been recommended by Taylor and colleagues (2009), who suggested keeping the lighting low, using subdued colours, limiting distracting images or pictures, avoiding the presence of personnel who are not essential, avoiding using perfume, aftershave or scented soap and avoiding touching the individual (Taylor *et al.* 2009). Mattison and Allely (2022) have also made some recommendations regarding sensory processing:

- Carefully consider the environment where questioning will take place.
- Gather information about any hypersensitivities that the individual may have.
- Ask the person themselves or someone who knows them (e.g., friends, relatives).
- Where possible, arrange for pre-interview visits to the interview venue and/or pre-trial visits to the court.
- Ask if anything in the room is causing any discomfort (e.g., fans, strip lights, direct eye contact) or distracting with their ability to focus.

- When possible, make appropriate adaptations to settings.
- Allow the individual to bring an appropriate sensory comfort item to reduce anxiety and manage hypersensitivity. (Mattison and Allely 2022, p.61)

Difficulties with reciprocal social communication

As much information as possible should be obtained from others about the individual's difficulties with reciprocal social interaction (e.g., difficulties with turn-taking during conversations). If safety allows, an autistic individual who has verbal communication impairments might find the use of a laptop or pen and paper to respond to questions. With some autistic individuals it might be very difficult to interrupt them when they are talking, hindering their ability to engage in a meaningful exchange. At the start of the interview, the interviewer should set out the 'rules' of discussion, such as no interrupting when others are talking, clearly specifying the start and end times of the interview and having a fixed length of time to talk (e.g., 2-minute intervals) (Murphy 2018). Consistency is also important, as inconsistency can be particularly confusing for some autistic individuals. For example, if the autistic individual interrupts when someone else is talking, this needs to be stopped the first time it happens (and explained to the individual exactly why) or allow the interruptions to continue throughout to ensure consistent communication dialogue and expectations are upheld (Judicial College 2021).

Adding to this, others have also highlighted that an autistic client, during their consultation with their lawyer or during court proceedings, may display marked indications of their impairments associated with their autism (e.g., being overly withdrawn and not being able to engage in reciprocal social interactions). On the other hand, some autistic individuals can engage in a reciprocal conversation and appear to be able to read social cues. This apparent ability is possibly due to intellectual analysis rather than intuition. The individual is 'acting' or 'mimicking' what they consider to be 'normal' neurotypical behaviour, which can actually lead others to not suspect autism – that they are completely unimpaired with respect to social communication and interaction (Stokes and Attwood 2020). Even though the individual gives the appearance of social engagement and understanding, this does not automatically mean that they actually understand the specific circumstances of the situation or context they are in (Berryessa 2021). Much of the meaning of communication, including crucial details and salient points, may actually be missed. One of the explanations for this is that they may only have an understanding of the specific words that are said, but they may have little or no understanding of the 'broader meaning' of the communication (Freckelton 2021; Sperry, Hughes and Forsee 2020).

The *Equal Treatment Bench Book* (Judicial College 2021) also provides some useful recommendations. For instance, the interviewer should not rely on intonation, gestures, facial expressions or context in order to convey meaning. Some autistic individuals find it challenging to make and maintain direct eye contact (although not all autistic individuals have difficulty doing this). For autistic individuals who have difficulty making eye contact, it is suggested that the questioner tells the individual that they do not need to make direct eye contact (e.g., 'I do not expect eye contact. You can look wherever you need to look to make you feel comfortable and concentrate') (Judicial College 2021).

Cognitive style

Information should be obtained on previous neuropsychological assessments. These might inform an understanding of the individual's general intellectual functioning and cognitive style (e.g., literal thinking, memory functioning) as well as any potential vulnerability to suggestibility. Regarding appropriate questioning of an autistic individual in a forensic setting, Murphy (2018) outlined a number of recommendations:

- There is a need to keep questions concise.
- The individual should be given more time in order to process and comprehend questions and should also be given more time to provide answers.
- Avoid questions which may be leading and ambiguous in interpretation.
- The use of metaphor or sarcasm in questions should be avoided.
- Avoid questions that are non-literal and require any amount of inference, insinuation, deduction, or abstractive extrapolation.

- Questions should be direct and avoid the use of 'tags'. An example of a tag question is 'You went to the concert, didn't you?'
- Questions should also not include negatives and double negatives. Some examples of questions that include negative and double negatives are: 'You would not disagree with that interpretation, Jeffrey, would you?' or 'Is it not the case that he did not go outside?'
- In autistic individuals, an impaired autobiographical memory is common. Therefore, it is important that the interviewer asks questions which are framed in the correct tense and not make reference to a past event as if in the present. An example of a question which is not framed in the correct tense is: 'Now you are in the garden and looking at the house?'
- Questions which are comprised of multiple parts should be avoided. An example of this type of question is, 'On the evening of the 30th of January were you in the park, and on the following morning did you see Hamish?'
- Questions should be avoided which are phrased as statements. An example of this type of question would be: 'So you saw her leave the restaurant?' These types of questions may not be recognised by an autistic individual as being something that can be disagreed with. Instead, the example question above should be rephrased as a clear question: 'Did you see him enter the shop?' (Murphy 2018)

Recommendations regarding appropriate questioning for autistic individuals have also been suggested by the *Equal Treatment Bench Book* (Judicial College 2021):

- Autistic individuals tend to have difficulty with answering hypothetical questions. This would also include difficulty with answering questions such as 'What adjustments would you find helpful?' They may find it difficult to imagine how they would feel if certain adjustments were implemented. Overall, autistic individuals tend to have difficulty with hypothetical thinking: specifically, the ability to accurately interpret and make a decision based on something which has not happened yet.

- It is also recommended to ask additional questions in order to check the individual's understanding of longer explanations (e.g., their understanding of court processes). It may not be sufficient to ask questions such as 'Do you understand?' The individual may think that they understand when actually they do not or they may find it challenging to let someone know that they do not understand. Misunderstandings may be avoided by careful questioning which is based on the content of the previous explanation, such as 'What will happen next?'

- Questions which are phrased as statements. For instance, the question, 'So you saw her enter the house?' may not be recognised as something that the individual can disagree with. It would be clearer to ask the question, 'Did you see him enter the building?'

- It is recommended to plan questions in topics. The questioner should start by introducing the topic and then clearly indicate when the topic changes by saying, for example, 'Now we are going to talk about...'

- When asking questions, you need to follow a logical, chronological order.

- Questions and explanations should be used that are short and simply phrased, unambiguous and 'to the point'. It is important to say what you really mean and be clear and precise in questioning. Unless you explicitly ask, the individual may not know what you know or need to know (one of the explanations for this may be impaired theory of mind, the ability to understand and recognise that others have different beliefs, intentions, desire, etc., to yourself). Checking your questions for alternative meanings prior to asking them is also useful.

- Avoid very open-ended questions / instructions such as 'Tell me everything'. Ambiguity in questions can be reduced by setting out questions within more precise or narrow (but non-leading) parameters (Maras *et al.* 2013). For example, rather than ask 'Tell me what you saw yesterday', ask 'You told me that you went to a shopping centre yesterday…[pause] Tell me more about that.'

- Allow extra time for the individual to respond to your question.

- Use the individual's name at the start of a question as opposed to at the end of a question. Using the individual's name at the start of the question will help to cue them to know they are being addressed.

- Avoid figurative communication. For instance, rather than say 'Take a seat', say 'Sit down, please'.

Taylor *et al.* (2009) have also provided some further recommendations for the effective questioning of autistic individuals:

- Questions which are metaphorical should be avoided as they can result in confusion when they are taken literally. Some examples include: 'A hard time', 'Raining cats and dogs', 'Are you pulling my leg?', 'Cat got your tongue?', 'What's up your sleeve?'
- Understand the importance of repeating and rephrasing questions.
- Use simple and direct instructions.
- Allow for delayed responses to questions, directions and commands.

Neurodevelopmental disorder and psychiatric co-morbidity

It is the exception rather than the norm that an autistic individual has a 'pure' diagnosis of autism. The majority of autistic individuals will have at least one co-occurring condition or disorder. Murphy (2018) recommends conducting further assessments when there is a suspicion of co-occurring conditions or disorders such as ADHD, personality disorder or psychopathy, or seeking a psychiatric opinion regarding whether psychosis is present. When a co-occurring condition is identified, it is useful to determine how it may influence the individual's presentation.

PROCEDURAL COURT ADAPTIONS THAT COULD BE IMPLEMENTED TO ENABLE THE AUTISTIC YOUNG PERSON TO MORE EFFECTIVELY PARTICIPATE IN THEIR OWN TRIAL

Some of the common indications of heightened anxiety in autistic individuals may be speaking louder (they may even shout) and, more formally, dropping contractions (e.g., saying 'did not' instead of 'didn't') and swearing, and they may start to engage in stimming behaviour, which is a coping mechanism in order to self-regulate their feelings of anxiety. There is a range of 'stimming' behaviour, including fidgeting, flapping, scratching, picking, humming and coughing (Judicial College 2021). The individual should be asked what would help reduce their anxiety and strategies identified that would also help. Many strategies are likely to be possible to implement in the courtroom, for instance, allowing them to have quiet, calming objects in the dock to help them with their anxiety (like a plastic tangle chain or stress ball). Additionally, being allowed to have some time alone in a quiet place can help reduce anxiety.

Anxiety levels on the day can also be reduced by ensuring the individual has at least one court familiarisation visit. If the rooms change, another visit to the new room should be offered. A useful recommendation is to consider the use of visual aids in order to help the individual understand what will happen at court. Some examples of visual aids include the use of 'visual timetables' (see Toolkit 14, The Advocate's Gateway 2015). Regular breaks should also be allowed (e.g., 10 minutes after every 40 minutes in court). Regular breaks will help to prevent anxiety escalating, for instance.

Symbol cards to support rules or serve as prompts

Toolkit 14 (The Advocate's Gateway 2015) highlighted how symbol cards can be used to support rules or serve as prompts. They can assist with establishing and reinforcing communication 'rules'. They may also help decrease levels of anxiety by reducing cognitive load and / or transferring control to the individual.

Anxiety and emotions scale

Toolkit 14 (The Advocate's Gateway 2015) also highlighted how an anxiety and emotions scale can be used to monitor stress and anxiety.

The individual can communicate where they are on the scale at regular intervals. If they get too high on the scale, a break can be considered. Scales should be tailor-made in order to ensure that they have subjective meaning for the individual. An example could be an 'emotions thermometer', which is a gauge with calm / relax at the bottom and worried / rage / frustrated at the top. This can help an autistic individual to externalise their feelings and help them with emotional containment.

Visual timetables

Toolkit 14 (The Advocate's Gateway 2015) also recommends the use of visual aids that will help prepare the individual for interview or trial proceedings (they can predict / anticipate what will happen and when, which helps to reduce anxiety). A visual timetable is a pictorial representation of a series of events (with a simple explanation at each phase) in time.

RECOMMENDATIONS FOR CHANGES TO BETTER SUPPORT AUTISTIC INDIVIDUALS IN CUSTODY

Autistic young people and adults are at increased risk of being negatively affected when they are detained in police custody. Holloway and colleagues (2020) have highlighted that a variety of adjustments may be needed to the custody process and environment in order to support interactions between autistic individuals and police officers, and have a positive impact on the wellbeing of autistic individuals.

Custody environment

- Ask individuals directly whether they have any sensory sensitivities.
- Ask individuals if they would like the lights adjusting.
- Provide reading material and paper and pens, risk permitting.
- Reassure individuals they are not visible on CCTV using the toilet.
- Take individuals for regular exercise breaks.

Communication

- Ask direct questions (e.g., What is your full address?).
- Explain technical terminology (e.g., 'appropriate adult').
- Ask individuals whether they might have any difficulties in a specific process and how you can help (e.g., interview).
- Ask individuals directly whether they would like something (e.g., food / drink or a break).

Explain to individuals

- What will happen during each process.
- The order things will happen.
- Why something is being done.
- What will happen after.
- Keep individuals updated on the time of day.
- Give individuals updates on any changes and how long it might be until the next process.
- Check the individual has understood what has been said (Holloway *et al.* 2020, p.10).

DIVERSION FROM PROSECUTION IN RESPONSE TO HARMFUL SEXUAL BEHAVIOUR

According to the *Diversion from Prosecution Toolkit* (Scottish Government 2011, p.2):

Diversion from prosecution is a formal decision by the Procurator Fiscal. On receipt of a police report the Procurator Fiscal can choose to divert the young person to a local social work team or other service provider. The provider should have specific expertise in working with young people. The young person undertakes a programme and / or is directed to services tailored to their particular needs that are designed to deal with the underlying causes of their offending. Intervention in this way keeps young people away from the formal criminal justice process and gives them the opportunity to make positive changes at a crucial time in their lives.

Generally cases involving sexual, domestic or violent offences are not considered appropriate for diversion but should be given consideration on an individual basis and assessed carefully by the criminal justice system and other agencies to consider the benefits to wider society, the young person who has caused harm and the victim(s). In relation to autistic young people displaying harmful sexual behaviour on a varying scale, the use of diversion may be implemented to support an intensive and targeted intervention to address cognitive, intellectual and social impairments that may have contributed to the harmful sexual behaviour. Diversion can at times arguably be more beneficial to the young person and wider community safety, as often when prosecution is sought this can place limitations and barriers on the young person receiving a specialist intervention to address their harmful sexual behaviour due to concerns of legal implications and an impact on their defence.

CASE STUDY FIVE: Possession and distribution of child sexual abuse material

Noah, was diagnosed with autism and a mild learning disability at age 8. He found social interactions with peers and adults quite challenging and enjoyed collecting Pokémon cards. From the age of 13 his school had concerns about sexualised conversations he had with peers, often in disinhibited ways, when he would talk about extreme material he looked at on Reddit.

At age 15 Noah was charged with possession of sexual images of under-18s. He was referred to a harmful sexual behaviour project by his parents. They contacted the service directly following the police issuing an arrest warrant for his downloading sexual images of under-18s. Noah described himself as coming from a loving, supportive family. An only child, he felt that his parents had been overprotective of him when he was growing up.

Noah reported that he started using online pornography when he was 14. This was around the time of the first Covid-19 lockdown, and he said that he felt lonely, bored, isolated and quite sad, as he was not surrounded by his peers or being active in any way. He stated that he started to use legal pornography and view adult images online. He found this behaviour gratifying as he enjoyed the sexual imagery and also the sense of risk, as his parents were also at home at the time. He told his social worker that he found lots of advertisements for apps encouraging conversations with strangers online, and he started to use several of these apps frequently.

Noah stated that these initial chats online were with other males he assumed to be his own age. He then realised that they were adult males when the conversations became sexualised. They asked him questions like 'Do you have a girlfriend?' and 'Have you seen a naked woman before?', and they asked him if he would like to see sexual images. Noah reported that soon he was actively involved in sharing illegal images online with around 30–40 adult males. He liked the feeling of being the one in control and the one who had the images they wanted, and started to collect images for the purposes of sharing. He said that adults paying attention to him sexually was the first experience he had ever had of someone considering him as a sexual being. This sense of control and power in finding and sharing sexual images of children was exciting for him. He also stated that he found some, but not all, of the images sexually exciting. However, the act of sharing was more powerful for him than the images themselves. He also liked collecting the images and categorising them in folders on his laptop, and looking for missing images in 'sets' of photographs depicting abuse. He said that he knew this was illegal, but did not think it was 'very illegal' as lots of people shared images like this in the chat rooms he frequented, and the children were often smiling in the photographs and videos.

Noah completed a programme of work addressing concerns around his behaviour. He showed insight into his offending, was able to make clear steps in adhering to an internet safety plan, and is now addressing many of the issues underpinning his offending in positive ways with support from his family and school.

CHAPTER SEVEN

Prevention

A key theme within this book has been identifying sexual behaviour among autistic children and young people that has caused harm either to self or to others. Therefore, our focus has been on the proportionate identification of when sexual behaviour becomes a concern, and how we can assess the behaviour so we understand the psychological and contextual drivers that underpin both its emergence and persistence over time. Our focus has also been on interventions for young people and their families that flow from high-quality assessment, which can help nudge autistic young people away from behaviours that may cause distress to others around them. In addition, we have looked in detail at criminal and youth justice systems, and what may constitute best practice with respect to young people who come into conflict with the law because of their sexual behaviour.

All this focuses on what we do *after* behaviour becomes a concern. To conclude this book, we look at what can be done to prevent harmful sexual behaviour before it emerges as an issue, and how we can see the spectrum of prevention embedded across the autism socio-ecological framework.

There are several reasons why prevention is important. It is clear that there are significant economic savings to be made through preventing adolescent harmful sexual behaviour. If the behaviour is abusive, considerable costs are accrued by law enforcement agencies in detecting sexual crime, by legal processes in prosecuting those who commit sexual crimes, and by social work related to protecting the public from further harm and also rehabilitation. There are also significant costs relating to medical expenditure and the provision of appropriate therapeutic and mental healthcare for many trauma-tised by their experiences of sexual crime. Even when concerns are diverted from the criminal justice system, the cost of responses from education, health and social services can still be significant.

However, the principal reason to foreground prevention is not economics; rather, the rationale for prevention is a moral and humane one. As an issue that causes distress to those who experience harm and stigmatisation of those who cause the harm, it is morally imperative to develop initiatives and interventions that stop harm before it occurs, avoiding victimisation in the first place.

PUBLIC HEALTH APPROACHES TO PREVENTION

The idea of 'prevention' is incontrovertible. However, the term is underdefined in relation to harmful sexual behaviour displayed by children and young people. One way to better understand what prevention of harmful sexual behaviour among autistic children and young people is, is to look at this as a public health issue. Public health approaches usually involve strategies such as the use of vaccines and immunisation, sanitation of drinking water as well as disseminating health information to the general public to improve health outcomes across the population.

Over the last 50 years we have seen the successful application of public health models to social issues such as substance use and youth violence. Such approaches tend to follow a similar set of steps:

1. Identifying the problem – understanding the nature of the social problem through data collection and research. This often involves looking at how widespread the issue is, who it affects and what factors contribute to it.

2. Determining risk factors – analysing the social, environmen-tal and economic factors that increase the likelihood of the problem occurring. This could include factors such as poverty, access to education, housing, discrimination, etc.

3. Developing and implementing interventions – creating strat-egies that aim to reduce or eliminate risk factors and address

the root causes. These might include policy changes, public education campaigns, community-based programmes or social support systems.

4. Evaluating effectiveness – assessing the outcomes of interventions to see if they are working. Public health approaches rely on data and ongoing monitoring to ensure that strategies are reducing harm and improving conditions for the affected population.

Some proponents of public health models have argued that similar approaches targeted at raising public awareness of the impact of sexual violence and the practical steps adults can take to protect children could significantly reduce incidence rates of child sexual abuse in society (Brown, O'Donnell and Erooga 2011). This includes harmful sexual behaviour displayed by children and young people (Allardyce and Yates 2018).

Public health interventions can be primary (or universal), secondary (or selected) or tertiary (or indicated) in nature. Although there is no universal agreement about how these terms are defined, primary prevention strategies are generally targeted at a community or whole population, secondary prevention strategies focus on at-risk groups or on situations where problems are starting to emerge, and tertiary prevention strategies are designed for reducing harm and preventing the re-emergence of an issue after it has been identified.

When these terms are applied to harmful sexual behaviour, interventions may be directed to preventing incidents before they would otherwise first occur (primary or secondary prevention), as well as after their occurrence, to prevent further offending and victimisation (tertiary prevention) (Smallbone, Marshall and Wortley 2008). Most current service provision, including much of what is described in this book, focuses on tertiary prevention.

Prevention targets are generally identified by addressing underlying risk factors that increase the likelihood that an individual will become a victim or a perpetrator of harmful sexual behaviour. As Smallbone, Rayment-McHugh and Smith (2013, p.49) put it:

Without good theory, evidence based prevention strategies may inadvertently be directed towards managing its consequences, which are more readily observable, rather than targeting its causes. A clear theoretical framework is needed that organises and makes sense of the available evidence, and provides a firm basis for making empirically defensible inferences and causal mechanisms and processes.

AETIOLOGY OF HARMFUL SEXUAL BEHAVIOUR AMONG AUTISTIC YOUNG PEOPLE

It is critically important to have an ecological perspective about why some autistic young people display harmful sexual behaviour. This requires looking at behaviour at the individual, family, social and macro political level. Key factors can include some or all of the following (adapted from Radford, Allnock and Hynes 2015):

Individual factors – challenges for autistic children in understanding social contexts

- Fixations on particular individuals or situations
- Confusion about sexual identity and / or sexual development
- Pro offending values and attitudes, or values and attitudes that undermine women and girls
- Access to vulnerable children and peers
- Online activity (including access to pornography)
- Experiences of abuse, exploitation and maltreatment.

Interpersonal factors that may impact on sexual regulation (early puberty, chromosomal defects)

- Family and relationships (overprotectiveness of social and sexual development of autistic children by primary carers)
- Parenting problems (including disengaged parenting styles)
- Domestic violence
- Child maltreatment
- Peer bullying
- Social isolation
- Negative peer influence
- Extrafamilial harm (e.g., child sexual exploitation).

Community factors

- Limited social and sexual education for autistic children
- Victim blaming among peers
- Gender stereotyping and toxic values
- Community violence
- Tolerance of child sexual abuse and exploitation
- Poverty
- Weak sanctions in relation to concerning sexual behaviour.

Societal factors

- Social norms
- Male sexual entitlement
- Inequality
- Discrimination
- Weak legal sanctions.

Societal factors can also include more culturally specific issues such as child marriage, humanitarian crises and armed conflicts.

How some of these different risk factors interact in particular situations involving an autistic child or young person who has acted in a harmful sexual way is highly individualistic in nature. However, each of these risk factors can be paired with a mitigating protective factor or set of factors, which can, in turn, provide a blueprint for prevention targets and initiatives that derive from a clear evidence base. For example, for some boys experience of sexual abuse in childhood is coming to be recognised as a risk factor for sexual offending (Ogloff *et al.* 2012). Early interventions to reduce the impact of these childhood experiences might reduce the risk of future sexual offending, particularly when this may include input about healthy sexuality in childhood and adolescence, boundaries and consent.

An understanding of common aetiological risk factors allows us to consider how we could tackle this issue universally, or how we could intervene before harm has happened but where there are high risk factors and low levels of protective factors.

PREVENTION TARGETS

Smallbone *et al.* (2008) discuss public health approaches to the prevention of child sexual abuse outline, considering how we respond to situations after they have happened (tertiary prevention) as well as universal prevention messaging (primary prevention) and messaging when behaviour has not emerged as an issue or is at an early stage and where early help may be useful. They then consider what these three levels mean for those who harm others (or who are at risk of doing so), for victims and families, and for the social situations or contexts where harm emerges.

Adapting this for autistic children would look like:

	Primary prevention	Secondary prevention	Tertiary prevention
Autistic child who has displayed harmful sexual behaviour (or who may be at risk of doing so)	Developmental prevention by promoting healthy emotional, social and psychological development in children Deterrence messaging	Interventions with inappropriate or problematic sexual concerns (sometimes from early childhood onwards)	Early detection of harm Assessment and intervention Risk management, safety plan Relevant sanctions
Victims	Age- and stage-appropriate educational input about bodies, relationships, consent, healthy interactions and what to do if the behaviour of a peer or adult concerns them	Resilience building for at-risk children (e.g., children with disabilities or children who have already experienced sexual victimisation)	Ameliorating harm Preventing revictimisation
Families	Reduction in opportunities for harm Controlling precipitators (e.g., online pornography) Extended guardianship Nurture and attachment Parental education	Safety plans Situational prevention in the family home (recognising when higher levels of supervision and / or support are necessary)	Family-based interventions

Situations or contexts	Community capacity building	Responsible bystander training Enabling guardianship Interventions with at-risk communities	Interventions with families, peer groups, social or organisational contexts where harm has occurred

This list is not comprehensive and is meant to be a prompt for further thinking about harmful sexual behaviour prevention among autistic youth. Many of the prevention initiatives mentioned are not specific to autistic young people and are relevant for all children and young people. However, adaptations are needed to ensure general interventions are effective with autistic children. For example, key aspects of developmental prevention would include:

- Education and awareness. Teaching children about boundaries, consent and body autonomy in an age-appropriate manner is essential. This includes helping children understand that their bodies belong to them and that they have the right to say 'no' to unwanted touch.

- Safe environments – creating environments (home, school, community) that are safe and supportive, where children feel comfortable and confident in seeking help if they feel threatened or unsafe. This may involve ensuring that trusted adults are available and approachable.

- Positive role models. Having supportive, non-abusive adults in children's lives is crucial. Positive relationships with parents or carers and teachers help children develop self-esteem and the ability to navigate difficult situations.

- Social skills and emotional intelligence. Helping children develop social skills, emotional regulation and assertiveness can prevent them from being manipulated by abusers. Children who understand how to manage emotions and have healthy communication skills are less vulnerable to abuse.

However, as obvious as these goals are, adaptations are needed when working with autistic children. In talking with children about boundaries and bodily autonomy, the use of clear and concrete language is necessary. Visual aids or social stories can be especially helpful for autistic children, as they provide concrete examples of appropriate and inappropriate behaviour. Sensory sensitivity issues also need to be considered in groupwork. Understanding the child's sensory needs and providing alternatives, such as fidget toys or quiet time, can help prevent this behaviour.

It may also be necessary to provide additional support on themes, such as explaining which behaviours are appropriate in public (e.g., not touching private parts in public) and which behaviours are private, as well as consistent modelling in respecting others' personal space and asking for permission before touching someone.

INAPPROPRIATE AND PROBLEMATIC SEXUAL BEHAVIOUR

Of particular note from a prevention point of view is the importance of responding constructively to inappropriate or problematic sexual behaviour before it becomes abusive. By inappropriate and problematic sexual behaviour we mean behaviour that is concerning but that has not led to victimisation, abuse or exploitation. There are some conceptual complexities here – harmful sexual behaviour – but it is worth saying more on this.

Low-level sexual concerns will often be linked to contextual factors and concerning behaviours may naturally end, even without interventions, when contexts change or when natural maturation occurs. We should not assume that concerning sexual behaviour among autistic youth will always escalate and become abusive over time. Nonetheless, it is also often the case that abusive behaviour may have previously been inappropriate, with problematic sexual behaviour that was not effectively responded to, particularly in relation to young children in pre-pubescence.

Although the evidence base is limited in response to sexual behaviour problems with children under 12, a few key messages can be drawn from the literature. Caution should be drawn here, however, as the literature on younger children with sexual behaviour problems rarely discusses autism and other neurodevelopmental issues.

When behaviour is self-directed or involves mutual sexual behaviour without coercion, clear boundaries, redirection and input about healthy relationships will often be sufficient to ensure that the child is nudged on to a more positive developmental pathway (Friedrich 2007). Guidance for nursery and primary schools suggests that low-level problematic sexual behaviour should be responded to in line with other challenging behaviour, requiring adults to be specific about naming and describing the behaviour, pointing out to the child the impact on others, setting clear boundaries, and developing individualised strategies to reduce the likelihood of repetition (British Columbia Ministry of Education 1999). In home settings, explaining why the behaviour is inappropriate in a way that does not increase shame, setting boundaries, encouraging strategies around self-control and positive emotional expression, and establishing a plan to increase safety are often sufficient measures to modify behaviour (Bateman and Milner 2014).

Closing Remarks

The subject of preventing harmful sexual behaviour among autistic children could serve as a theme for an entire book. And it is clear that we lack good materials for working with autistic children with this goal of prevention in mind (with the exception of the wealth of guides for parents and for autistic children themselves on sexual development). However, one thing is particularly striking if we bring a social model to how we think about autism. Autistic children, along with all children, have the right to live a life where they are supported to become happy, healthy young adults who can make a significant contribution to society. This includes the right to positive social and sexual development.

But many autistic children live in disabling environments that do not provide them with the information and support to live a rewarding and balanced life. If we are serious about preventing harmful sexual behaviour among autistic children, key to this will be creating environments where children feel supported, understood and empowered to explore their potential. With the right resources, guidance and opportunities, autistic children can thrive in all aspects of life, from social interactions to personal development and future aspirations, including constructive and positive choices about sexuality and sexual expression. This focus on healthy relations and sexuality is key to supporting young people in their journey to independence and life fulfilment in young adulthood and beyond.

In tackling this growing issue, prevention must be implemented on a societal scale, with children and young people given fair and equal opportunities to access individualised and appropriate sex education, acknowledging a rights-respecting approach (King-Hill and

McCartan 2024a). This includes ensuring autistic children and young people whose learning, cognitive and emotional needs may vary are given a similar opportunity to their peers, to achieve prosocial and positive sexual behaviours over the discourse of their lives.

It is critical that greater consideration is given to a developmental and wider socio-environmental approach (Hackett *et al.* 2024), and that practice is not solely focused on static risk factors that arguably demonstrate a smaller impact on the life outcomes for children and young people. Exploring and encouraging socio-ecological change and tackling wider factors such as the impact of adversity and family dynamics may provide a greater impact and outcomes for young people, families and wider community safety. Specifically when supporting autistic children and young people, consideration must be given to the need for a multidisciplinary intervention that supports the ranging needs of a young person's life and the wider environment that may, at times, be influencing occurrences of harmful sexual behaviour.

References

Advocate's Gateway, The (2015) *Using Communication Aids in the Criminal Justice System. Toolkit 14.* 27 February. www.theadvocatesgateway.org/_files/ugd/1074f0_f5d07af401574f289401e2c0df981c4d.pdf

Advocate's Gateway, The (2016) *Planning to Question Someone with an Autism Spectrum Disorder Including Asperger Syndrome. Toolkit 3.* 1 December. www.theadvocatesgateway.org/_files/ugd/1074f0_aee057da809d412f88afd683dcc402e7.pdf

Aebi, M., Plattner, B., Ernest, M., Kaszynski, K. and Bessler, C. (2014) 'Criminal history and future offending of juveniles convicted of the possession of child pornography.' *Sexual Abuse 26,* 4, 375–390. https://doi.org/10.1177/1079063213492344

Allardyce, S. and Yates, P.M. (2013) 'Assessing risk of victim crossover with children and young people who display harmful sexual behaviours.' *Child Abuse Review 22,* 4, 255–267. https://doi.org/10.1002/car.2277

Allardyce, S. and Yates, P.M. (2018) *Working with Children and Young People Who Have Displayed Harmful Sexual Behaviour.* Edinburgh: Dunedin Academic Press.

Allardyce, S., Yates, P. and Gurpreet, K. (2021) *Working with Children and Young People Who Have Displayed Harmful Sexual Behaviour.* Centre of Expertise on Child Sexual Abuse.

Allely, C.S. (2019) 'Firesetting and arson in individuals with autism spectrum disorder: A systematic PRISMA review.' *Journal of Intellectual Disabilities and Offending Behaviour 10,* 4, 89–101. https://doi.org/10.1108/JIDOB-11-2018-0014

Allely, C.S. (2015) 'Experiences of prison inmates with autism spectrum disorders and the knowledge and understanding of the spectrum amongst prison staff: A review.' *Journal of Intellectual Disabilities and Offending Behaviour 6,* 2, 55–67. https://doi.org/10.1108/JIDOB-06-2015-0014

Allely, C.S. (2020a) 'Autism spectrum disorder, bestiality and zoophilia: A systematic PRISMA review.' *Journal of Intellectual Disabilities and Offending Behaviour 11,* 2, 75–91. https://doi.org/10.1108/JIDOB-06-2019-0012

Allely, C.S. (2020b) 'Contributory role of autism spectrum disorder symptomology to the viewing of indecent images of children (IIOC) and the experience of the criminal justice system.' *Journal of Intellectual Disabilities and Offending Behaviour 11,* 3, 171–189. https://doi.org/10.1108/JIDOB-11-2019-0026

Allely, C.S. (2022) *Autism Spectrum Disorder in the Criminal Justice System: A Guide to Understanding Suspects, Defendants and Offenders with Autism.* London: Routledge.

Allely, C.S. and Cooper, P. (2017) 'Jurors' and judges' evaluation of defendants with autism and the impact on sentencing: A systematic Preferred Reporting Items for Systematic Reviews and Meta-analyses (PRISMA) review of autism spectrum disorder in the courtroom.' *Journal of Law and Medicine 25*, 1, 105–123.

Allely, C.S. and Creaby-Attwood, A. (2016) 'Sexual offending and autism spectrum disorders.' *Journal of Intellectual Disabilities and Offending Behaviour 7*, 1, 35–51. https://doi.org/10.1108/JIDOB-09-2015-0029

Allely, C.S. and Dubin, L. (2018) 'The contributory role of autism symptomology in child pornography offending: Why there is an urgent need for empirical research in this area.' *Journal of Intellectual Disabilities and Offending Behaviour 9*, 4, 129–152. https://doi.org/10.1108/JIDOB-06-2018-0008

Allely, C.S. and Faccini, L. (2019) 'The importance of considering trauma in individuals with autism spectrum disorder: Considerations and clinical recommendations.' *The Journal of Forensic Practice 22*, 1, 23–28. https://doi.org/10.1108/JFP-11-2019-0049

Allely, C.S., Kennedy, S. and Warren, I. (2019) 'A legal analysis of Australian criminal cases involving defendants with autism spectrum disorder charged with online sexual offending.' *International Journal of Law and Psychiatry 66*, 101456. https://doi.org/10.1016/j.ijlp.2019.101456

Allman, M.J. (2011) 'Deficits in temporal processing associated with autistic disorder.' *Frontiers in Integrative Neuroscience 5*, 2. https://doi.org/10.3389/fnint.2011.00002

Allman, M.J. and DeLeon, I.G. (2009) '"No Time Like the Present": Time Perception in Autism.' In A.C. Giordano and V.A. Lombardi (eds) *Causes and Risks for Autism* (pp. 65–76). Hauppage, NY: Nova Science Publishers, Inc.

Allman, M.J., DeLeon, I.G. and Wearden, J.H. (2011) 'Psychophysical assessment of timing in individuals with autism.' *American Journal on Intellectual and Developmental Disabilities 116*, 2, 165–178. https://doi.org/10.1352/1944-7558-116.2.165

Álvarez-Guerrero, G., Fry, F., Lu, M. and Gaitis, K.K. (2024) 'Online Child Sexual Exploitation and Abuse of Children and Adolescents with Disabilities: A Systematic Review.' *Disabilities 4*, 2, 264–276. https://doi.org/10.3390/disabilities4020017

APA (American Psychiatric Association) (2013) *Diagnostic and Statistical Manual of Mental Disorders, Fifth Edition* (DSM-5). Washington, DC: American Psychiatric Association.

Aral, A., Say, G.N. and Usta, M.B. (2018) 'Distinguishing circumscribed behavior in an adolescent with Asperger syndrome from a pedophilic act: A case report.' *Dusunen Adam: The Journal of Psychiatry and Neurological Sciences 31*, 1, 102–106. https://doi.org/10.5350/DAJPN2018310111

Ariès, P. (1962) *Centuries of Childhood: A Social History of Family Life* [English translation]. New York: Knopf.

Arora, A. (2014) 'Staying safe online.' *Your Autism Magazine*, Winter.

Ashley, N., Jackson, J. and Davies, S. (2008) 'Sexual self-schemas of female child sexual abuse survivors: Relationships with risky sexual behavior and sexual assault in adolescence.' *Archive of Sexual Behaviour 39*, 6, 1359–1374. https://doi.org/10.1007/s10508-010-9600-9

Attwood, A., Hénault, I. and Dubin, N. (2014) *The Autism Spectrum, Sexuality and the Law: What Every Parent and Professional Needs to Know.* London: Jessica Kingsley Publishers.

Autism Speciality Group (2021) 'Understanding the importance of consistency in autism.' https://christoph-ronacher.squarespace.com/blog/importance-of-consistency-in-autism

Babchishin, K.M., Merdian, H.L., Bartels, R.M. and Perkins, D. (2018) 'Child sexual exploitation materials offenders: A review.' *European Psychologist 23*, 2, 130–143. https://doi.org/10.1027/1016-9040/a000326

Bagby, R.M., Parker, J.D. and Taylor, G.J. (1994) 'The twenty-item Toronto Alexithymia Scale – 1. Item selection and cross-validation of the factor structure.' *Journal of Psychosomatic Research 38*, 1, 23–32. https://doi.org/10.1016/0022-3999(94)90005-1

Ballan, M.S. (2012) 'Parental perspectives of communication about sexuality in families of children with autism spectrum disorders.' *Journal of Autism and Developmental Disorders 42*, 5, 676–684.

Barnett, J.P. and Maticka-Tyndale, E. (2015) 'Qualitative exploration of sexual experiences among adults on the autism spectrum: Implications for sex education.' *Perspectives on Sexual and Reproductive Health 47*, 4, 171–179. https://doi.org/10.1363/47e5715

Baron-Cohen, S. (1988) 'An assessment of violence in a young man with Asperger's syndrome.' *Journal of Child Psychology and Psychiatry 29*, 3, 351–360. https://doi.org/10.1111/j.1469-7610.1988.tb00723.x

Baron-Cohen, S., Leslie, A.M. and Frith, U. (1985) 'Does the autistic child have a "theory of mind"?' *Cognition 21*, 1, 37–46. https://doi.org/10.1016/0010-0277(85)90022-8

Barra, S., Bessler, C., Landolt, M.A. and Aebi, M. (2017) 'Patterns of adverse childhood experiences in juveniles who sexually offended.' *Sexual Abuse: A Journal of Research and Treatment 30*, 7, 803–827. https://doi.org/10.1177/1079063217697135

Barry-Walsh, J.B. and Mullen, P.E. (2004) 'Forensic aspects of Asperger's syndrome.' *The Journal of Forensic Psychiatry & Psychology 15*, 1, 96–107. https://doi.org/10.1080/14789940310001638628

Bateman, J. and Milner, J. (2014) *Children and Young People Whose Behaviour Is Sexually Concerning or Harmful: Assessing Risk and Developing Safety Plans.* London: Jessica Kingsley Publishers.

Beddows, N. and Brooks, R. (2015) 'Inappropriate sexual behaviour in adolescents with autism spectrum disorder: What education is recommended and why.' *Early Intervention in Psychiatry 10*, 4, 282–289. https://doi.org/10.1111/eip.12265

Beier, K.M., Oezdemir, U.C., Schlinzig, E., Groll, A., Hupp, E. and Hellenschmidt, T. (2016) '"Just dreaming of them": The Berlin project for primary prevention of child sexual abuse by Juveniles (PPJ).' *Child Abuse & Neglect 52*, 1–10. https://doi.org/10.1016/j.chiabu.2015.12.009

Belton, E. and Hollis, V. (2016) *A Review of the Research on Children and Young People Who Display Harmful Sexual Behaviour Online.* NSPCC Evaluation Department, Impact and Evidence series. London: NSPCC.

Bentley, H., Fellowes, A., Glenister, S., Mussen, N., *et al.* (2020) *How Safe Are Our Children? An Overview of Data on Adolescent Abuse.* London: NSPCC.

Berney, T. (2004) 'Asperger syndrome from childhood into adulthood.' *Advances in Psychiatric Treatment 10*, 5, 341–351. https://doi.org/10.1192/apt.10.5.341

Berryessa, C.M. (2017) 'Educator of the court: The role of the expert witness in cases involving autism spectrum disorder.' *Psychology, Crime and Law 23*, 6, 575–600. https://doi.org/10.1080/1068316X.2017.1284218

Berryessa, C.M. (2021) 'Defendants with autism spectrum disorder in criminal court: A judges' toolkit.' *Drexel Law Review 13*, 4, 841–868. https://ssrn.com/abstract=3730822

Berthoz, S. and Hill, E.L. (2005) 'The validity of using self-reports to assess emotion regulation abilities in adults with autism spectrum disorder.' *European Psychiatry 20*, 3, 291–298. https://doi.org/10.1016/j.eurpsy.2004.06.013

Bigham, S., Boucher, J., Mayes, A. and Anns, S. (2010) 'Assessing recollection and familiarity in autistic spectrum disorders: Methods and findings.' *Journal of Autism and Developmental Disorders 40*, 7, 878–889. https://doi.org/10.1007/s10803-010-0937-7

Bird, G. and Cook, R. (2013) 'Mixed emotions: The contribution of alexithymia to the emotional symptoms of autism.' *Translational Psychiatry 3*, 7, e285. https://doi.org/10.1038/tp.2013.61

Blackshaw, A.J., Kinderman, P., Hare, D.J. and Hatton, C. (2001) 'Theory of mind, causal attribution and paranoia in Asperger syndrome.' *Autism 5*, 2, 147–163. https://doi.org/10.1177/1362361301005002005

Blechman, E.A. and Vryan, K.D. (2000) 'Prosocial family therapy: A manualized prevention intervention for juvenile offenders.' *Aggression and Violent Behaviour 5*, 4, 343–378. https://doi.org/10.1016/S1359-1789(98)00013-5

Bondy, A.S. and Frost, L.A. (1994) 'The Picture Exchange Communication System.' *Focus on Autistic Behavior 9*, 3, 1–19. https://doi.org/10.1177/108835769400900301

Boucher, J., Mayes, A. and Bigham, S. (2012) 'Memory in autistic spectrum disorder.' *Psychological Bulletin 138*, 3, 458–496. https://doi.org/10.1037/a0026869

Bowden, N., Milne, B., Audas, R., Clasby, B., *et al.* (2022) 'Criminal justice system interactions among young adults with and without autism: A national birth cohort study in New Zealand.' *Autism 26*, 7, 1783–1794. https://doi.org/10.1177/13623613211065541

Bowlby, J. (1969) *Attachment and Loss, Volume I*. London: Penguin Books.

Bowler, C. and Collacott, R.A. (1993) 'Cross-dressing in men with learning disabilities.' *The British Journal of Psychiatry 162*, 4, 556–558. https://doi.org/10.1192/bjp.162.4.556

Bowler, D.M., Gardiner, J.M. and Gaigg, S.B. (2007) 'Factors affecting conscious awareness in the recollective experience of adults with Asperger's syndrome.' *Conscious Cognition 16*, 1, 124–143. https://doi.org/10.1016/j.concog.2005.12.001

Bowler, D.M., Gardiner, J.M. and Grice, S.J. (2000) 'Episodic memory and remembering in adults with Asperger syndrome.' *Journal of Autism and Developmental Disorders 30*, 4, 295–304. https://doi.org/10.1023/a:1005575216176

Bowler, D.M., Matthews, N.J. and Gardiner, J.M. (1997) 'Asperger's syndrome and memory: Similarity to autism but not amnesia.' *Neuropsychologia 35*, 1, 65–70. https://doi.org/10.1016/s0028-3932(96)00054-1

Boyd, B.A., McCarty, C.H. and Sethi, C. (2014) 'Families of children with autism: A synthesis of family routines literature.' *Journal of Occupational Science 21*, 3, 322–333. https://doi.org/10.1080/14427591.2014.908816

Boyer, D. and Fine, D. (1992) 'Sexual abuse as a factor in adolescent pregnancy and child maltreatment.' *Family Planning Perspectives 24*, 1, 4–11, 19.

Bragg, S., Ponsford, R., Meiksin, R., Lohan, M., *et al.* (2022) 'Enacting whole-school relationships and sexuality education in England: Context matters.' *British Educational Research Journal 48*, 4, 665–683. https://doi.org/10.1002/berj.3788

Bremer, J.F. (2001) *Protective Factors Scale*. St Paul, MN: Project Pathfinder, Inc.

Brewer, N. and Young, R.L. (2015) *Crime and Autism Spectrum Disorder: Myths and Mechanisms*. London: Jessica Kingsley Publishers.

Briggs, D., Hill, S. and Kennington, R. (2020) 'NOTA Individualised Treatment Programme.' https://ecsa.lucyfaithfull.org/nota-individualised-treatment-programme

British Columbia Ministry of Education (1999) *Responding to Children's Problem Sexual Behaviour in Elementary Schools: A Resource for Educators.*

Brookman-Frazee, L., Baker-Ericzén, M., Stahmer, A., Mandell, D., Haine, R.A. and Hough, R.L. (2009) 'Involvement of youths with autism spectrum disorders or intellectual disabilities in multiple public service systems.' *Journal of Mental Health Research in Intellectual Disabilities 2*, 3, 201–219. https://doi.org/10.1080/19315860902741542

Brown, J., O'Donnell, T. and Erooga, M. (2011) *Sexual Abuse: A Public Health Challenge*. London: NSPCC.

Brown-Lavoie, S.M., Viecili, M.A. and Weiss, J. (2014) 'Sexual knowledge and victimization in adults with autism spectrum disorders.' *Journal of Autism and Developmental
Disorders 44*, 9, 2185–2196. https://doi.org/10.1007/s10803-014-2093-y

Brownlow, C. and O'Dell, L. (2006) 'Constructing an autistic identity: AS voices online.'
Mental Retardation 44, 5, 315–321. https://doi.org/10.1352/0047-6765(2006)44[315:-
CAAIAV]2.0.CO;2

Bruck, M., London, K., Landa, R. and Goodman, J. (2007) 'Autobiographical memory
and suggestibility in children with autism spectrum disorder.' *Development and
Psychopathology 19*, 1, 73–95. https://doi.org/10.1017/S0954579407070058

Buss, D.M. (2002) 'Human mating strategies.' *Samfundsøkonomen 4*. https://labs.
la.utexas.edu/buss/files/2015/10/Buss-2002-human-mating-strategies.pdf

Byers, E.S., Nichols, S. and Voyer, S.D. (2013) 'Challenging stereotypes: Sexual functioning of single adults with high functioning autism spectrum disorder.' *Journal
of Autism and Developmental Disorders 43*, 11, 2617–2627. https://doi.org/10.1007/
s10803-013-1813-z

Caldwell, M.F. (2010) 'Study characteristics and recidivism base rates in juvenile sex
offender recidivism.' *International Journal of Offender Therapy and Comparative
Criminology 54*, 2, 197–212. https://doi.org/10.1177/0306624X08330016

Caldwell, M.F. (2016) 'Quantifying the decline in juvenile sexual recidivism rates.' *Psychology, Public Policy and Law 22*, 4, 414–426. https://doi.org/10.1037/law0000094

Cappadocia, M.C., Weiss, J.A. and Pepler, D. (2012) 'Bullying experiences among children
and youth with autism spectrum disorders.' *Journal of Autism and Developmental
Disorders 42*, 2, 266–277. https://doi.org/10.1007/s10803-011-1241-x

Capps, L., Losh, M. and Thurber, C. (2000) '"The frog ate the bug and made his mouth
sad": Narrative competence in children with autism.' *Journal of Abnormal Child
Psychology 28*, 2, 193–204. https://doi.org/10.1023/a:1005126915631

Cazalis, F., Reyes, E., Leduc, S. and Gourion, D. (2022) 'Evidence that nine autistic
women out of ten have been victims of sexual violence.' *Frontiers in Behavioral
Neuroscience 16*, 852203. https://doi.org/10.3389/fnbeh.2022.852203

Cederlund, M., Hagberg, B., Billstedt, E., Gillberg, I.C. and Gillberg, C. (2008) 'Asperger
syndrome and autism: A comparative longitudinal follow-up study more than 5
years after original diagnosis.' *Journal of Autism and Developmental Disorders 38*, 1,
72–85. https://doi.org/10.1007/s10803-007-0364-6

Chaffin, M., Letourneau, E. and Silovsky, J.F. (2002) 'Adults, Adolescents, and Children
Who Sexually Abuse Children: A Developmental Perspective.' In J.E.B. Myers, L.
Berliner, J. Briere, C.T. Hendrix, C. Jenny and T.A. Reid (eds) *The APSAC Handbook
on Child Maltreatment*, 2nd edn (pp.205–232). London: Sage Publications.

Chandler, R.J., Russell, A. and Maras, K.L. (2019) 'Compliance in autism: Self-report in
action.' *Autism 23*, 4, 1005–1017. https://doi.org/10.1177/1362361318795479

Cheely, C.A., Carpenter, L.A., Letourneau, E.J., Nicholas, J.S., Charles, J. and King, L.B.
(2012) 'The prevalence of youth with autism spectrum disorders in the criminal
justice system.' *Journal of Autism and Developmental Disorders 42*, 9, 1856–1862.
https://doi.org/10.1007/s10803-011-1427-2

Chesterman, P. and Rutter, S.C. (1993) 'Case report: Asperger's syndrome and sexual offending.' *The Journal of Forensic Psychiatry 4*, 3, 555–562. https://doi.
org/10.1080/09585189308408222

Chianese, A.A., Jackson, S.Z. and Souders, M.C. (2021) 'Psychosexual knowledge and education in autism spectrum disorder individuals.' *Journal of the American Association
of Nurse Practitioners 33*, 10, 776. https://doi.org/10.1097/JXX.0000000000000508

Children's Commissioner (2023) *Evidence on Pornography's Influence on Harmful Sexual Behaviour among Children*. Resources, 9 May. www.childrenscommissioner.gov.uk/resource/pornography-and-harmful-sexual-behaviour

Church, C., Alisanski, S. and Amanullah, S. (2000) 'The social, behavioral, and academic experiences of children with Asperger syndrome.' *Focus on Autism and Other Developmental Disabilities 15*, 1. https://doi.org/10.1177/108835760001500102

Clements, J. and Zarkowska, E. (2000) *Behavioural Concerns & Autistic Spectrum Disorders: Explanations and Strategies for Change*. London: Jessica Kingsley Publishers.

Cole, P.M. and Putnam, F.W. (1992) 'Effect of incest on self and social functioning: A developmental psychopathology perspective.' *Journal of Consulting and Clinical Psychology 60*, 2, 174–184. https://doi.org/10.1037//0022-006x.60.2.174

Collis, E., Gavin, J., Russell, A. and Brosnan, M. (2022) 'Autistic adults' experience of restricted repetitive behaviours.' *Research in Autism Spectrum Disorders 90*, 101895. https://doi.org/10.1016/j.rasd.2021.101895

Coogan, M. (2010) *God and Sex: What the Bible Really Says*. New York: Hachette Book Group.

Cooper, P. and Allely, C.S. (2017) 'You can't judge a book by its cover: Evolving professional responsibilities, liabilities and "judgecraft" when a party has Asperger's syndrome.' *Northern Ireland Legal Quarterly 68*, 1, 35–58. https://doi.org/10.53386/nilq.v68i1.21

Cooper, S.A., Mohamed, W.N. and Collacott, R.A. (1993) 'Possible Asperger's syndrome in a mentally handicapped transvestite offender.' *Journal of Intellectual Disability Research 37*, 2, 189–194. https://doi.org/10.1111/j.1365-2788.1993.tb00587.x

Copenhaver, A. and Tewksbury, R. (2019) 'Interactions between autistic individuals and law enforcement: A mixed-methods exploratory study.' *American Journal of Criminal Justice 44*, 309–333. https://doi.org/10.1007/s12103-018-9452-8

Coskun, M. and Mukaddes, N.M. (2008) 'Mirtazapine treatment in a subject with autistic disorder and fetishism.' *Journal of Child and Adolescent Psychopharmacology 18*, 2, 206–209. https://doi.org/10.1089/cap.2007.0014

Cousin, G. (2006) 'An introduction to threshold concepts.' *Planet*, No. 17, December. www.ee.ucl.ac.uk/mflanaga/Cousin Planet 17.pdf

Crane, L. and Goddard, L. (2008) 'Episodic and semantic autobiographical memory in adults with autism spectrum disorders.' *Journal of Autism and Developmental Disorders 38*, 3, 498–506. https://doi.org/10.1007/s10803-007-0420-2

Crane, L. and Maras, K. (2018) 'General Memory Abilities for Autobiographical Events in Adults with Autism Spectrum Disorder.' In J.L. Johnson, G.S. Goodman and P.C. Mundy (eds) *The Wiley Handbook of Memory, Autism Spectrum Disorder, and the Law* (pp.146–178). Oxford: Wiley Blackwell.

Crane, L., Pring, L., Jukes, K. and Goddard, L. (2012) 'Patterns of autobiographical memory in adults with autism spectrum disorder.' *Journal of Autism and Developmental Disorders 42*, 10, 2100–2112. https://doi.org/10.1007/s10803-012-1459-2

Crane, L., Chester, J.W., Goddard, L., Henry, L.A. and Hill, E. (2016) 'Experiences of autism diagnosis: A survey of over 1000 parents in the United Kingdom.' *Autism 20*, 2, 153–162. https://doi.org/10.1177/1362361315573636

Creaby-Attwood, A. and Allely, C.S. (2017) 'A psycho-legal perspective on sexual offending in individuals with Autism Spectrum Disorder.' *International Journal of Law and Psychiatry 55*, 72–80. https://doi.org/10.1016/j.ijlp.2017.10.009

Creeden, K. (2013) 'Taking a developmental approach to treating juvenile sexual behaviour problems.' *International Journal of Behavioural Consultation and Therapy 8*, 3–4, 12–16. https://doi.org/10.1037/h0100977

Cunningham, H. (2006) *The Invention of Childhood*. London: BBC Books.

Cutler, E. (2013) 'Autism and child pornography: A toxic combination.' http://sexof-fender-statistics.blogspot.com/2013/08/autism-and-child-pornography-toxic.html

Davidson, J. and Tamas, S. (2015) 'Autism and the ghost of gender.' *Emotion, Space and Society 19*, 59–65. https://doi.org/10.1016/j.emospa.2015.09.009

Davies, A.W.J., Balter, A.-S., van Rhijn, T., Spracklin, J., Maich, K. and Soud, R. (2022) 'Sexuality education for children and youth with autism spectrum disorder in Canada.' *Intervention in School and Clinic 58*, 2, 129–134. https://doi.org/10.1177/10534512211051068

Dekker, M. (2019) 'Community Contribution.' In S. Fletcher-Watson and F. Happé, *Autism: A New Introduction to Psychological Theory and Current Debate* (pp. 25–27). London: Routledge.

de la Cuesta, G. (2010) 'A selective review of offending behaviour in individuals with autism spectrum disorders.' *Journal of Learning Disabilities and Offending Behaviour 1*, 2, 47–58. https://doi.org/10.5042/jldob.2010.0419

Department for Education (2025) Relationships and sex education (RSE) and health education: Statutory guidance on relationships education, relationships and sex education (RSE) and health education. July. https://www.gov.uk/government/publications/relationships-education-relationships-and-sex-education-rse-and-health-education

de Vries, A.L.C., Noens, I.L.J., Cohen-Kettenis, P.T., van Berckelaer-Onnes, I.A. and Doreleijers, T.A. (2010) 'Autism spectrum disorders in gender dysphoric children and adolescents.' *Journal of Autism and Developmental Disorders 40*, 8, 930–936. https://doi.org/10.1007/s10803-010-0935-9

Dewinter, J., Vermeiren, R. and Vanwesenbeeck, I. (2013) 'Autism and normative sexual development: A narrative review.' *Journal of Clinical Nursing 22*, 23–24, 3467–3483.

Dewinter, J., Vermeiren, R., Vanwesenbeeck, I. and Van Nieuwenhuizen, Ch. (2016) 'Adolescent boys with autism spectrum disorder growing up: Follow-up of self-reported sexual experience.' *European Child & Adolescent Psychiatry 25*, 9, 969–978. https://doi.org/10.1007/s00787-016-0816-7

Dickie, I., Reveley, S. and Dorrity, A. (2018) 'The criminal justice system and people on the autism spectrum: Perspectives on awareness and identification.' *Journal of Applied Psychology and Social Sciences 4*, 1, 1–21.

Diehl, J.J., Bennetto, L. and Young, E.C. (2006) 'Story recall and narrative coherence of high-functioning children with autism spectrum disorders.' *Journal of Abnormal Child Psychology 34*, 1, 87–102. https://doi.org/10.1007/s10802-005-9003-x

Dillard, R. and Beaujolais, B. (2019) 'Trauma and adolescents who engage in sexually abusive behavior: A review of the literature.' *Journal of Child Sexual Abuse 28*, 6, 629–648. https://doi.org/10.1080/10538712.2019.1598528

Dozier, C.L., Iwata, B.A. and Worsdell, A.S. (2011) 'Assessment and treatment of foot-shoe fetish displayed by a man with autism.' *Journal of Applied Behavior Analysis 44*, 1, 133–137. https://doi.org/10.1901/jaba.2011.44-133

Duane, Y. and Morrison, T. (2004) 'Families of Young People Who Sexually Abuse.' In G. O'Reilly, W.L. Marshall, A. Carr and R.C. Beckett (eds) *The Handbook of Clinical Intervention with Young People Who Sexually Abuse* (Chapter 4). London: Psychology Press.

Dubin, N. (2017) 'An Autistic Universe: The Perspectives of an Autistic Registrant.' In L.A. Dubin and E. Horowitz (eds) *Caught in the Web of the Criminal Justice System: Autism, Developmental Disabilities and Sex Offences* (pp.248–274). London: Jessica Kingsley Publishers.

Dubin, L.A. and Horowitz, E. (2017) *Caught in the Web of the Criminal Justice System: Autism, Developmental Disabilities, and Sex Offenses*. London and Philadelphia, PA: Jessica Kingsley Publishers.

Dudley, C. and Herbert, E.J.C. (2014) *The Value of Caregiver Time: Costs of Support and Care for Individuals Living with Autism Spectrum Disorder*. 15 January. SPP Research Paper No. 7-1. https://papers.ssrn.com/sol3/papers.cfm?abstract_id=2379633

Dziobek, I., Rogers, K., Fleck, S., Bahnemann, M., *et al.* (2008) 'Dissociation of cognitive and emotional empathy in adults with Asperger syndrome using the Multifaceted Empathy Test (MET).' *Journal of Autism and Developmental Disorders 38*, 3, 464–473. https://doi.org/10.1007/s10803-007-0486-x

Embrace Autism (2018) 'Meltdowns & shutdowns.' https://embrace-autism.com/melt-downs-and-shutdowns

Everall, I.P. and Lecouteur, A. (1990) 'Firesetting in an adolescent boy with Asperger's syndrome.' *The British Journal of Psychiatry 157*, 2, 284–287. https://doi.org/10.1192/bjp.157.2.284

Fanniff, A.M., Schubert, C.A., Mulvey, E.P., Iselin, A.-M.R. and Piquero, A.R. (2017) 'Risk and outcomes: Are adolescents charged with sex offenses different from other adolescent offenders?' *Journal of Youth and Adolescence 46*, 7, 1394–1423. https://doi.org/10.1007/s10964-016-0536-9

Fenigstein, A. and Vanable, P.A. (1992) 'Paranoia and self-consciousness.' *Journal of Personality and Social Psychology 62*, 1, 129–138. https://doi.org/10.1037//0022-3514.62.1.129

Fernandes, L.C., Gillberg, C.I., Cederlund, M., Hagberg, B., Gillberg, C. and Billstedt, E. (2016) 'Aspects of sexuality in adolescents and adults diagnosed with autism spectrum disorders in childhood.' *Journal of Autism and Developmental Disorders 46*, 9, 3155–3165. https://doi.org/10.1007/s10803-016-2855-9

Finkelhor, D., Turner, H. and Colburn, D. (2022) 'Prevalence of online sexual offenses against children in the US.' *JAMA Network Open 5*, 10, e2234471. https://doi.org/10.1001/jamanetworkopen.2022.34471

Firmin, C. (2020) 'School rules of (sexual) engagement: Government, staff and student contributions to the norms of peer sexual-abuse in seven UK schools.' *Journal of Sexual Aggression 26*, 3, 289–301. https://doi.org/10.1080/13552600.2019.1618934

Firmin, C., Lloyd, J. and Walker, J. (2019) 'Beyond referrals: Levers for addressing harmful sexual behaviours between students at school in England.' *International Journal of Qualitative Studies in Education 32*, 10, 1229–1249. https://doi.org/10.1080/09518398.2019.1659442

Fisher, M.H., Moskowitz, A.L. and Hodapp, R.M. (2013) 'Differences in social vulnerability among individuals with autism spectrum disorder, Williams syndrome, and Down syndrome.' *Research in Autism Spectrum Disorders 7*, 8, 931–937. https://doi.org/10.1016/j.rasd.2013.04.009

Fitzgerald, M. and Bellgrove, M.A. (2006) 'The overlap between alexithymia and Asperger's syndrome.' *Journal of Autism and Developmental Disorders 36*, 4, 573–576. https://doi.org/10.1007/s10803-006-0096-z

Fletcher-Watson, S. and Happé, F. (2019) *Autism: A New Introduction to Psychological Theory and Current Debate*. London: Routledge.

Foster, S. (2015) 'Autism is not a tragedy...ignorance is: Suppressing evidence of Asperger's Syndrome and High-Functioning Autism in capital trials prejudices defendants for a death sentence.' *Lincoln Memorial University Law Review 2*, 9. https://digital-commons.lmunet.edu/lmulrev/vol2/iss1/4

Foucault, M. (1990) *The History of Sexuality, Volume 1*. New York: Vintage Books.

Foucault, M. (1992a) *The History of Sexuality Vol. 1: The Will to Knowledge.* London: Penguin.

Foucault, M. (1992b) *The History of Sexuality Vol. 2: The Use of Pleasure.* London: Penguin.

Foy, W., Furrow, J. and McManus, S. (2011) 'Exposure to Violence, Post-Traumatic Symptomatology and Criminal Behaviours.' In V. Ardino (ed.) *Post-Traumatic Syndromes in Children and Adolescents* (pp.199–210). Chichester: Wiley/Blackwell Publishers.

Franklin, A., Raws, P. and Smeaton, E. (2015) *Unprotected, Overprotected: Meeting the Needs of Young People with Learning Disabilities Who Experience, or Are at Risk of, Sexual Exploitation.* September, Northern Ireland Briefing: Mary Anne Webb. Ilford: Barnardo's. www.barnardos.org.uk

Freckelton, I. (2011a) 'Asperger's disorder and the criminal law.' *Journal of Law and Medicine 18*, 4, 677–694.

Freckelton, I. (2011b) 'Autism Spectrum Disorders and the Criminal Law.' In M.R. Mohammadi (ed.) *A Comprehensive Book on Autism Spectrum Disorders* (pp.249–272). Zagreb: Intech Press.

Freckelton, I. (2013) 'Forensic Issues in Autism Spectrum Disorder: Learning from Court Decisions.' In M. Fitzgerald (ed.) *Recent Advances in Autism Spectrum Disorders – Volume II* (Chapter 8). IntechOpen.

Freckelton, I. (2021) 'Expert Evidence about Autism Spectrum Disorder.' In F.R. Volkmar, R. Loftin, A. Westphal and M. Woodbury-Smith (eds) *Handbook of Autism Spectrum Disorder and the Law* (pp.39–69). Cham, Switzerland: Springer.

Freckelton, I. and List, D. (2009) 'Asperger's disorder, criminal responsibility and criminal culpability.' *Psychiatry, Psychology and Law 16*, 1, 16–40. https://doi.org/10.1080/13218710902887483

Freckelton, I. and Selby, H. (2009) *Expert Evidence: Law, Practice, Procedure and Advocacy.* Sydney: Lawbook Company.

Friedrich, W.N. (2007) *Children with Sexual Behavior Problems: Family-Based Attachment-Focused Therapy.* New York and London: W.W. Norton & Co.

Gallagher, H.L. and Frith, C.D. (2003) 'Functional imaging of "theory of mind".' *Trends in Cognitive Sciences 7*, 2, 77–83. https://doi.org/10.1016/s1364-6613(02)00025-6

Galvin, C., Taylor, M., Milburn, P., Kearney, R., Crawford, E. and Kennedy, P.J. (2024) 'A descriptive evaluation of children presenting with Technology Assisted-Harmful Sexual Behaviour (TA-HSB) within a regional Forensic Child and Adolescent Mental Health Service (FCAMHS).' *Journal of Sexual Aggression*, 1–13. https://doi.org/10.1080/13552600.2024.2378020

Gardner, L., Campbell, J.M. and Westdal, J. (2019) 'Brief report: Descriptive analysis of law enforcement officers' experiences with and knowledge of autism.' *Journal of Autism and Developmental Disorders 49*, 3, 1278–1283. https://doi.org/10.1007/s10803-018-3794-4

Gardner, L., Cederberg, C., Hangauer, J. and Campbell, J.M. (2022) 'Law enforcement officers' interactions with autistic individuals: Commonly reported incidents and use of force.' *Research in Developmental Disabilities 131*, 104371. https://doi.org/10.1016/j.ridd.2022.104371

George, R. and Stokes, M.A. (2016) '"Gender Is Not on My Agenda!" Gender Dysphoria and Autism Spectrum Disorder.' In L. Mazzone and B. Vitiello (eds) *Psychiatric Symptoms and Comorbidities in Autism Spectrum Disorder* (pp.139–150). Cham, Switzerland: Springer.

Gibbs, V. and Haas, K. (2020) 'Interactions between the police and the autistic community in Australia: Experiences and perspectives of autistic adults and parents/

carers.' *Journal of Autism and Developmental Disorders 50*, 12, 4513–4526. https://doi.org/10.1007/s10803-020-04510-7

Gilmore, D., Radford, D., Haas, M.K., Shields, M., Bishop, L. and Hand, B. (2024) 'Building community and identity online: A content analysis of highly viewed #autism TikTok videos.' *Autism in Adulthood 6*, 1, 95–105. https://doi.org/10.1089/aut.2023.0019

Glidden, D., Bouman, W.P., Jones, B.A. and Arcelus, J. (2016) 'Gender dysphoria and autism spectrum disorder: A systematic review of the literature.' *Sexual Medicine Reviews 4*, 1, 3–14. https://doi.org/10.1016/j.sxmr.2015.10.003

Goddard, L., Howlin, P., Dritschel, B. and Patel, T. (2007) 'Autobiographical memory and social problem solving in Asperger's syndrome.' *Journal of Autism and Developmental Disorders 37*, 2, 291–300. https://doi.org/10.1007/s10803-006-0168-0

Gougeon, N.A. (2010) 'Sexuality and autism: A critical review of selected literature using a social-relational model of disability.' *American Journal of Sexuality Education 5*, 4, 328–361. https://doi.org/10.1080/15546128.2010.527237

Gould, J. and Smith, A. (2011) 'Missed diagnosis or misdiagnosis? Girls and women on the autism spectrum.' *Good Autism Practice (GAP) 12*, 1, 34–41.

Gralton, E. (2013) 'Inpatient assessment of young people with developmental disabilities who offend.' *Advances in Mental Health and Intellectual Disabilities 7*, 2, 108–116. https://doi.org/10.1108/20441281311310207

Green, J., Gilchrist, A., Burton, D. and Cox, A. (2000) 'Social and psychiatric functioning in adolescents with Asperger syndrome compared with conduct disorder.' *Journal of Autism and Developmental Disorders 30*, 4, 279–293. https://doi.org/10.1023/a:1005523232106

Griffiths, D., Hingsburger, D., Hoath, J. and Ioannou, S. (2013) '"Counterfeit deviance" revisited.' *Journal of Applied Research in Intellectual Disabilities 26*, 5, 471–480. https://doi.org/10.1111/jar.12034

Grossman, H. (2021) 'An introduction to CBT for people with an autism spectrum disorder.' Beck Institute, Cognitive Behaviour Therapy, 8 June. https://beckinstitute.org/blog/an-introduction-to-cbt-for-people-with-an-autism-spectrum-disorder

Grotevant, H.D. and Cooper, C.R. (1985) 'Patterns of interaction in family relationships and the development of identity exploration in adolescence.' *Child Development 56*, 2, 415–428. https://doi.org/10.2307/1129730

Gruber, J. (ed.) (2001) *Risky Behavior Among Youths: An Economic Analysis.* London: The University of Chicago Press.

Gudjonsson, G.H. (2003) *The Psychology of Interrogations and Confessions: A Handbook.* New York: John Wiley & Sons.

Gudorf, C.E. (1994) *Body, Sex, and Pleasure: Reconstructing Christian Sexual Ethics.* Cleveland, OH: The Pilgrim Press.

Haas, K. and Gibbs, V. (2021) 'Does a person's autism play a role in their interactions with police: The perceptions of autistic adults and parent/carers.' *Journal of Autism and Developmental Disorders 51*, 5, 1628–1640. https://doi.org/10.1007/s10803-020-04663-5

Hackett, S. (2014) *Children and Young People with Harmful Sexual Behaviours.* Totnes: Dartington, Research in Practice. https://tce.researchinpractice.org.uk/wp-content/uploads/2020/05/children_and_young_people_with_harmful_sexual_behaviours_research_review_2014.pdf

Hackett, S., Branigan, P. and Holmes, D. (2019) *Operational Framework for Children and Young People Displaying Harmful Sexual Behaviours*, 2nd edn. London: NSPCC.

Hackett, S., Holmes, D. and Branigan, P. (2019) *Harmful Sexual Behaviour Framework: An Evidence-Informed Operational Framework for Children and Young People Displaying Harmful Sexual Behaviours*, 2nd edn. London: NSPCC.

Hackett, S., Phillips, J., Masson, H. and Balfe, M. (2013) 'Individual, family and abuse characteristics of 700 British child and adolescent sexual abusers.' *Child Abuse Review 22*, 4, 232–245. https://doi.org/10.1002/car.2246

Hackett, S., Darling, A.J., Balfe, M., Masson, H. and Phillips, J. (2024) 'Life course outcomes and developmental pathways for children and young people with harmful sexual behaviour.' *Journal of Sexual Aggression 30*, 2, 145–165. https://doi.org/10.10 80/13552600.2022.2124323

Haidt, J. (2024) *The Anxious Generation: How the Great Rewiring of Childhood Is Causing an Epidemic of Mental Illness.* New York: Penguin Press.

Hamilton-Giachritsis, C., Hanson, E., Whittle, H., Alves-Costa, F. and Beech, A. (2020) 'Technology assisted child sexual abuse in the UK: Young people's views on the impact of online sexual abuse.' *Children and Youth Services Review 119*, 105451. https://doi.org/10.1016/j.childyouth.2020.105451

Hancock, G.I.P., Stokes, M.A. and Mesibov, G.B. (2017) 'Socio-sexual functioning in autism spectrum disorder: A systematic review and meta-analyses of existing literature.' *Autism Research 10*, 11, 1823–1833. https://doi.org/10.1002/aur.1831

Happé, F. and Frith, U. (2006) 'The weak coherence account: Detail-focused cognitive style in autism spectrum disorders.' *Journal of Autism and Developmental Disorders 36*, 1, 5–25. https://doi.org/10.1007/s10803-005-0039-0

Harkins, L., Beech, A.R. and Goodwill, A.M. (2010) 'Examining the influence of denial, motivation and risk on sexual recidivism.' *Sexual Abuse 22*, 1, 78–94. https://doi.org/10.1177/1079063209358106

Hartwig, M. and Bond Jr, C.F. (2011) 'Why do lie-catchers fail? A lens model meta-analysis of human lie judgments.' *Psychological Bulletin 137*, 4, 643–659. https://doi.org/10.1037/a0023589

Haskins, B.G. and Silva, J.A. (2006) 'Asperger's disorder and criminal behavior: Forensic-psychiatric considerations.' *Journal of the American Academy of Psychiatry and the Law 34*, 3, 374–384.

Hellemans, H., Colson, K., Verbraeken, C., Vermeiren, R. and Deboutte, D. (2007) 'Sexual behavior in high-functioning male adolescents and young adults with autism spectrum disorder.' *Journal of Autism and Developmental Disorders 37*, 260–269. https://doi.org/10.1007/s10803-006-0159-1

Hellemans, H., Roeyers, H., Leplae, W., Dewaele, T. and Deboutte, D. (2010) 'Sexual behavior in male adolescents and young adults with autism spectrum disorder and borderline/mild mental retardation.' *Sexuality and Disability 28*, 2, 93–104. http://hdl.handle.net/1854/LU-1092003

Heller, S., Larrieu, J.A., D'Imperio, R. and Boris, N.W. (1999) 'Research on resilience to child maltreatment: Empirical considerations.' *Child Abuse and Neglect 23*, 4, 321–338. https://doi.org/10.1016/s0145-2134(99)00007-1

Helton, J.J., Gochez-Kerr, T. and Gruber, E. (2018) 'Sexual abuse of children with learning disabilities.' *Child Maltreatment 23*, 2, 157–165. https://doi.org/10.1177/1077559517733814

Henshaw, M., Ogloff, J.R. and Clough, J.A. (2015) 'Looking beyond the screen: A critical review of the literature on the online child pornography offender.' *Sexual Abuse: A Journal of Research and Treatment 29*, 5, 416–445. https://doi.org/10.1177/1079063215603690

Hickman & Rose (2023) 'Everyone's Invited: What has been the sexual abuse website's impact on the criminal law?' 30 June. www.hickmanandrose.co.uk/everyones-invited-what-has-been-the-sexual-abuse-websites-impact-on-the-criminal-law

Hill, E., Berthoz, S. and Frith, U. (2004) 'Brief report: Cognitive processing of own emotions in individuals with autistic spectrum disorder and in their relatives.' *Journal of Autism and Developmental Disorders 34*, 2, 229–235. https://doi.org/10.1023/b:jadd.0000022613.41399.14

Hingsburger, D., Griffiths, D. and Quinsey, V. (1991) 'Detecting counterfeit deviance: Differentiating sexual deviance from sexual inappropriateness.' *Habilitation Mental Health Care Newsletter 10*, 9, 51–54.

Hinnebusch, A.J., Miller, L.E. and Fein, D.A. (2017) 'Autism spectrum disorders and low mental age: Diagnostic stability and developmental outcomes in early childhood.' *Journal of Autism and Developmental Disorders 47*, 12, 3967–3982. https://doi.org/10.1007/s10803-017-3278-y

Hlavatá, P., Kašpárek, T., Linhartová, P., Ošlejšková, H. and Bareš, M. (2018) 'Autism, impulsivity and inhibition: A review of the literature.' *Basal Ganglia 14*, 44–53. https://doi.org/10.1016/j.baga.2018.10.002

HM Inspectorate of Probation (2023) 'Socio-ecological framework.' https://hmiprobation.justiceinspectorates.gov.uk/our-research/evidence-base-youth-justice/general-models-and-principles/social-ecological-framework

Hodgins, S., Cree, A., Alderton, J. and Mak, T. (2008) 'From conduct disorder to severe mental illness: Associations with aggressive behaviour, crime and victimization.' *Psychological Medicine 38*, 7, 975–987. https://doi.org/10.1017/S0033291707002164

Hollis, V., Belton, E. and Team, N.E. (2017) *Children and Young People Who Engage in Technology Assisted Harmful Sexual Behaviour.* London: NSPCC (National Society for the Prevention of Cruelty to Children). https://learning.nspcc.org.uk/research-resources/2017/children-young-people-technology-assisted-harmful-sexual-behaviour

Holloway, C.A., Munro, N., Jackson, J., Phillips, S. and Ropar, D. (2020) 'Exploring the autistic and police perspectives of the custody process through a participative walkthrough.' *Research in Developmental Disabilities 97*, 103545. https://doi.org/10.1016/j.ridd.2019.103545

Holmes, L.G. and Himle, M.B. (2014) 'Brief report: Parent–child sexuality communication and autism spectrum disorders.' *Journal of Autism and Developmental Disorders 44*, 11, 2964–2970. https://doi.org/10.1007/s10803-014-2146-2

Hopkins, P.E. (2006) 'Youthful Muslim masculinities: Gender and generational relations.' *Transactions of the Institute of British Geographers 31*, 3, 337–352. https://doi.org/10.1111/j.1475-5661.2006.00206.x

Hughes, D. (2004) 'An attachment-based treatment of maltreated children and young people.' *Attachment & Human Development 6*, 3, 263–278. https://doi.org/10.1080/14616730412331281539

Iglesias, O.B., Gómez Sánchez, L.E. and Alcedo Rodríguez, M.Á. (2019) 'Do young people with Asperger syndrome or intellectual disability use social media and are they cyberbullied or cyberbullies in the same way as their peers?' *Psicothema 31*, 1, 30–37. https://doi.org/10.7334/psicothema2018.243

Im, D.S. (2016a) 'Template to perpetrate: An update on violence in autism spectrum disorder.' *Harvard Review of Psychiatry 24*, 1, 14–35. https://doi.org/10.1097/HRP.0000000000000087

Im, D.S. (2016b) 'Trauma as a contributor to violence in autism spectrum disorder.' *The Journal of the American Academy of Psychiatry and the Law 44*, 2, 184–192.

Jack, J. (2012) 'Gender copia: Feminist rhetorical perspectives on an autistic concept of sex/gender.' *Women's Studies in Communication 35*, 1, 1–17. https://doi.org/10.10 80/07491409.2012.667519

Jackson, J., Rhodes, C. and Kotera, Y. (2022) 'Parents' attitudes towards conversations with their young children about sex: A cross-sectional study.' *British Journal of Child Health 3*, 4. https://doi.org/10.12968/chhe.2022.3.4.183

Jackson-Perry, D. (2020) 'The autistic art of failure? Unknowing imperfect systems of sexuality and gender.' *Scandinavian Journal of Disability Research 22*, 1, 221–229. https://doi.org/10.16993/sjdr.634

Jacobsen, P. (2003) *Asperger Syndrome and Psychotherapy*. London: Jessica Kingsley Publishers.

Jawaid, A., Riby, D.M., Owens, J., White, S.W., Tarar, T. and Schulz, P.E. (2012) '"Too withdrawn" or "too friendly": Considering social vulnerability in two neuro-developmental disorders.' *Journal of Intellectual Disability Research 56*, 4, 335–350. https://doi.org/10.1111/j.1365-2788.2011.01452.x

Jay, A., Evans, M., Frank, I. and Sharpling, D. (2018) *Full Interim Report of the Independent Inquiry into Child Sexual Abuse*. April, HC 954-1. A report of the Inquiry Panel. IICSA (Independent Inquiry into Child Sexual Abuse). London: The Stationery Office. www.iicsa.org.uk/document/full-interim-report-independent-inquiry-child-sexual-abuse.html

Johnson, J.L., Goodman, G.S. and Mundy, P.C. (2018) *The Wiley Handbook of Memory, Autism Spectrum Disorder, and the Law*. Hoboken, NJ: John Wiley & Sons, Ltd.

Judicial College (2021) *Equal Treatment Bench Book*. February. Valuation Tribunal. https://valuationtribunal.gov.uk/app/uploads/2021/11/Equal-Treatment-Bench-Book-February-2021-1.pdf

Jurek, L., Longuet, Y., Baltazar, M., Amestoy, A., *et al.* (2019) 'How did I get so late so soon? A review of time processing and management in autism.' *Behavioural Brain Research 374*, 112121. https://doi.org/10.1016/j.bbr.2019.112121

Kana, R.K., Maximo, J.O., Williams, D.L., Keller, T.A., *et al.* (2015) 'Aberrant functioning of the theory-of-mind network in children and adolescents with autism.' *Molecular Autism 6*, 59. https://doi.org/10.1186/s13229-015-0052-x

Kellaher, D.C. (2015) 'Sexual behavior and autism spectrum disorders: An update and discussion.' *Current Psychiatry Reports 17*, 4, 562. https://doi.org/10.1007/s11920-015-0562-4

King-Hill, S. (2013) 'Teenage mothers' experiences of the transition to parenthood in relation to education: An interpretative phenomenological analysis.' *MIDIRS Midwifery Digest 23*, 4, 426.

King-Hill, S. (2021) 'Assessing sexual behaviours in children and young people: A realistic evaluation of the Brook Traffic Light tool.' *Child Abuse Review 30*, 1, 16–31. https://doi.org/10.1002/car.2664

King-Hill, S. (2022) 'Knowledge translation and evidence-informed policy challenges: The implementation of the Brook Traffic Light Tool in Cornwall.' *Journal of Sexual Aggression 29*, 2, 208–225. https://doi.org/10.1080/13552600.2022.2052770

King-Hill, S. (2023) 'Changing the age of consent is not the solution to protecting young people from unhealthy relationships with adults.' *The Conversation*, 23 September. https://theconversation.com/changing-the-age-of-consent-is-not-the-solution-to-protecting-young-people-from-unhealthy-relationships-with-adults-214099

King-Hill, S. (2024a) *Young People's Voices: Relationships, Health and Sex Education*. University of Birmingham. https://pure-oai.bham.ac.uk/ws/portalfiles/portal/223027932/Young_Peoples_Voices_RSHE_Report_Dr_Sophie_King-Hill_2024.pdf

King-Hill, S. (2024b) 'Proposed sex education guidance in England goes against evidence and may well lead to harm.' *The Conversation*, 16 May. https://theconversation.com/proposed-sex-education-guidance-in-england-goes-against-evidence-and-may-well-lead-to-harm-207248

King-Hill, S. and Gilsenan, A. (2023) *Sibling Sexual Behaviour: Practitioner Mapping Tool*. University of Birmingham. www.birmingham.ac.uk/documents/college-social-sciences/social-policy/hsmc/sibling-sexual-behaviour.pdf

King-Hill, S. and McCartan, K. (2024a) 'Tackling and preventing inter-partner abuse in young people through evidence based relationships and sex education.' ATSA Blog, 19 December. https://blog.atsa.com/2024/12/tackling-and-preventing-inter-partner.html

King-Hill, S. and McCartan, K. (2024b) 'Education and understanding is vital when tackling rising reports of harmful sexual behaviour by children.' The Conversation, 17 January. https://theconversation.com/education-and-understanding-is-vital-when-tackling-rising-reports-of-harmful-sexual-behaviour-by-children-220922

King-Hill, S., Gilsenan, A. and McCartan, K. (2023a) 'Professional responses to sibling sexual abuse.' *Journal of Sexual Aggression 29*, 3, 359–373. https://doi.org/10.1080/13552600.2023.2241482

King-Hill, S., McCartan, K., Gilsenan, A., Beavis, J. and Adams, A. (2023b) *Understanding and Responding to Sibling Sexual Abuse*. London: Palgrave Macmillan. https://doi.org/10.1007/978-3-031-34010-9

Kinnaird, E., Stewart, C. and Tchanturia, K. (2019) 'Investigating alexithymia in autism: A systematic review and meta-analysis.' *European Psychiatry 55*, 80–89. https://doi.org/10.1016/j.eurpsy.2018.09.004

Kirby, D. (2007) 'Abstinence, sex, and STD/HIV education programs for teens: Their impact on sexual behavior, pregnancy, and sexually transmitted disease.' *Annual Review of Sex Research 18*, 1, 143–177. https://doi.org/10.1080/10532528.2007.10559850

Kobayashi, R. (1991) 'Psychosexual development of autistic children in adolescence.' *Japanese Journal of Child and Adolescent Psychiatry 32*, 3, 1–14.

Kolta, B. and Rossi, G. (2018) 'Paraphilic disorder in a male patient with autism spectrum disorder: Incidence or coincidence.' *Cureus 10*, 5, e2639. https://doi.org/10.7759/cureus.2639

Kroncke, A.P., Willard, M. and Huckabee, H. (2016) 'Forensic Assessment for Autism Spectrum Disorder.' In A.P. Kroncke, M. Willard and H. Huckabee (eds) *Assessment of Autism Spectrum Disorder: Critical Issues in Clinical, Forensic and School Settings* (pp.345–373). Cham, Switzerland: Springer.

Kumar, S., Devendran, Y., Radhakrishna, A., Karanth, V. and Hongally, C. (2017) 'A case series of five individuals with Asperger syndrome and sexual criminality.' *Journal of Mental Health and Behaviour 22*, 1, 63. https://doi.org/10.4103/0971-8990.210703

Kuusikko, S., Pollock-Wurman, R., Jussila, K., Carter, A.S., *et al.* (2008) 'Social anxiety in high-functioning children and adolescents with autism and Asperger syndrome.' *Journal of Autism and Developmental Disorders 38*, 9, 1697–1709. https://doi.org/10.1007/s10803-008-0555-9

Lazaratou, H., Giannopoulou, I., Anomitri, C. and Douzenis, A. (2016) 'Case report: Matricide by a 17-year-old boy with Asperger's syndrome.' *Aggression and Violent Behavior 31*, 61–65. https://doi.org/10.1016/j.avb.2016.07.007

Ledingham, R. and Mills, R. (2015) 'A preliminary study of autism and cybercrime in the context of international law enforcement.' *Advances in Autism 1*, 1, 2–11. https://doi.org/10.1108/AIA-05-2015-0003

Leonard, M. and Donathy, M.L. (2017) 'Understanding Normal Sexual Functioning to Assess Sexual Deviancy.' In D. Wilcox, M. Donathy, R. Gray and C. Baim (eds) *Working with Sex Offenders: A Guide for Practitioners* (Chapter 5). London: Routledge.

Letourneau, E.J., Henggeler, S.W., Borduin, C.M., Schewe, P.A., *et al.* (2009) 'Multisystemic therapy for juvenile sexual offenders: 1-year results from a randomized effectiveness trial.' *Journal of Family Psychology 23*, 1, 89. https://doi.org/10.1037/a0014352

Letourneau, E.J. and Shields, R.T. (2017) 'Ending child sexual abuse: A look at prevention efforts in the United States.' In M. Israelashvili and J.L. Romano (eds) *The Cambridge Handbook of International Prevention Science* (pp. 728–752). Cambridge University Press. https://doi.org/10.1017/9781316104453.032

Lévi-Strauss, C. (1966) *The Savage Mind (Nature of Human Society)*. New York: Oxford University Press.

Lewis, J. (1992) 'Gender and the development of welfare regimes.' *Journal of European Social Policy 2*, 3, 159–173. https://doi.org/10.1177/095892879200200301

Lewis, R. (2018) 'Literature review on children and young people demonstrating technology-assisted harmful sexual behavior.' *Aggression and Violent Behavior 40*, 1–11. https://doi.org/10.1016/j.avb.2018.02.011

Lewis, R., Tanton, C., Mercer, C.H., Mitchell, K.R., *et al.* (2017) 'Heterosexual practices among young people in Britain: Evidence from three national surveys of sexual attitudes and lifestyles.' *Journal of Adolescent Health 61*, 694e702.

Li, B., Blijd-Hoogewys, E., Stockmann, L., Vergari, I. and Rieffe, C. (2023) 'Toward feeling, understanding, and caring: The development of empathy in young autistic children.' *Autism 27*, 5, 1204–1218. https://doi.org/10.1177/13623613221117955

Lindsey, L.L. (2008) *Gender: Sociological Perspectives*. New York: Routledge.

Lloyd, J. (2019) 'Response and interventions into harmful sexual behaviour in schools.' *Child Abuse & Neglect 94*, 104037. https://doi.org/10.1016/j.chiabu.2019.104037

Lordan, R., Storni, C. and De Benedictis, C.A. (2021) 'Autism Spectrum Disorders: Diagnosis and Treatment.' In A.M. Grabrucker (ed.) *Autism Spectrum Disorders* (Chapter 2). Brisbane: Exon Publications. www.ncbi.nlm.nih.gov/books/NBK573609

Loveland, K.A., McEvoy, R.E., Tunali, B. and Kelley, M.L. (1990) 'Narrative story telling in autism and Down's syndrome.' *British Journal of Developmental Psychology 8*, 1, 9–23. https://doi.org/10.1111/j.2044-835X.1990.tb00818.x

Maggio, M.G., Calatozzo, P., Cerasa, A., Pioggia, G., Quartarone, A. and Calabrò, R.S. (2022) 'Sex and sexuality in autism spectrum disorders: A scoping review on a neglected but fundamental issue.' *Brain Sciences 12*, 11, 1427. https://doi.org/10.3390/brainsci12111427

Mahoney, M.J. (2009) *Asperger's Syndrome and the Criminal Law: The Special Case of Child Pornography*. www.harringtonmahoney.com/content/Publications/AspergersSyndromeandtheCriminalLawv26.pdf

Mahoney, M.J. (2017) 'Introduction.' In A. Lawrence, J.D. Dubin and E. Horowitz (eds) *Caught in the Web of the Criminal Justice System: Autism, Developmental Disabilities, and Sex Offenses* (pp.11–20). London: Jessica Kingsley Publishers.

Mahoney, M.J. (2021) 'Defending Men with Autism Accused of Online Sexual Offenses.' In F.R. Volkmar, R. Loftin, A. Westphal and M. Woodbury-Smith (eds) *Handbook of Autism Spectrum Disorder and the Law* (pp.269–306). Cham, Switzerland: Springer.

Maister, L., Simons, J.S. and Plaisted-Grant, K. (2013) 'Executive functions are employed to process episodic and relational memories in children with autism spectrum disorders.' *Neuropsychology 27*, 6, 615–627. https://doi.org/10.1037/a0034492

Malloy, L.C., Mugno, A.P. and Arndorfer, A. (2018) 'Interviewing Children with Autistic Spectrum Disorder: The NICHD Protocol and Ten-Step Investigative Interview.'

In J.L. Johnson, G.S. Goodman and P.C. Mundy (eds) *The Wiley Handbook of Memory, Autism Spectrum Disorder, and the Law* (pp.292–310). Oxford: Wiley Blackwell.

Manocha, K. and Mezey, G. (1998) 'British adolescents who sexually abuse: A descriptive study.' *Journal of Forensic Psychiatry 9*, 3, 488–508. https://doi.org/10.1080/09585189808405375

Maras, K.L. and Bowler, D.M. (2012) 'Brief report: Suggestibility, compliance and psychological traits in high-functioning adults with autism spectrum disorder.' *Research in Autism Spectrum Disorders 6*, 3, 1168–1175. https://doi.org/10.1016/j.rasd.2012.03.013

Maras, K.L., Memon, A., Lambrechts, A. and Bowler, D.M. (2013) 'Recall of a live and personally experienced eyewitness event by adults with autism spectrum disorder.' *Journal of Autism and Developmental Disorders 43*, 8, 1798–1810. https://doi.org/10.1007/s10803-012-1729-z

Marco, E.J., Hinkley, L.B.N., Hill, S.S. and Nagarajan, S.S. (2011) 'Sensory processing in autism: A review of neurophysiologic findings.' *Pediatric Research 69*, 5 Pt 2, 48R–54R. https://doi.org/10.1203/PDR.0b013e3182130c54

Mattison, M. and Allely, C. (2022) 'Questioning Autistic People: Police and Courts.' In N. Tyler and A. Sheeran (eds) *Working with Autistic People in the Criminal Justice and Forensic Mental Health Systems: A Handbook for Practitioners* (pp.55–66). London: Routledge.

Mattison, M.L.A., Dando, C.J. and Ormerod, T.C. (2015) 'Sketching to remember: Episodic free recall task support for child witnesses and victims with autism spectrum disorder.' *Journal of Autism and Developmental Disorders 45*, 6, 1751–1765. https://doi.org/10.1007/s10803-014-2335-z

McAuliffe, T., Vaz, S., Falkmer, T. and Cordier, R. (2017) 'A comparison of families of children with autism spectrum disorders in family daily routines, service usage, and stress levels by regionality.' *Developmental Neurorehabilitation 20*, 8, 483–490. https://doi.org/10.1080/17518423.2016.1236844

McCann, J. and Peppé, S. (2003) 'Prosody in autism spectrum disorders: A critical review.' *International Journal of Language & Communication Disorders 38*, 4, 325–350. https://doi.org/10.1080/1368282031000154204

McCartan, K., Eason, A., Senker, S., Addis, N. and Porter, C. (2025) *Developing and Implementing a Public Health and Criminological Approach to Tackling Sexual Abuse: Prevention, Treatment and Integration.* Palgrave Studies in Risk, Crime and Society. London: Palgrave Macmillan.

McCrory, E., Henry, L.A. and Happé, F. (2007) 'Eye-witness memory and suggestibility in children with Asperger syndrome.' *Journal of Child Psychology and Psychiatry 48*, 5, 482–489. https://doi.org/10.1111/j.1469-7610.2006.01715.x

McGeeney, E. and Kehily, M.J. (2016) 'Young people and sexual pleasure – where are we now?' *Sex Education 16*, 3, 235–239. https://doi.org/10.1080/14681811.2016.1147149

McGhee Hassrick, E., Holmes, L.G., Sosnowy, C., Walton, J. and Carley, K. (2021) 'Benefits and risks: A systematic review of information and communication technology use by autistic people.' *Autism in Adulthood 3*, 1, 72–84. https://doi.org/10.1089/aut.2020.0048

McGrath, R.J., Cumming, G.F., Burchard, B.L., Zeoli, S. and Ellerby, L. (2010) *Current Practices and Emerging Trends in Sexual Abuser Management.* Brandon, VT: Safer Society Press.

McInnes, E. and Ey, L.-A. (2020) 'Responding to problematic sexual behaviours of primary school children: Supporting care and education staff.' *Sex Education 20*, 1, 75–89. https://doi.org/10.1080/14681811.2019.1621827

McKibbin, G., Humphreys, C. and Hamilton, B. (2017) '"Talking about child sexual abuse would have helped me": Young people who sexually abused reflect on preventing harmful sexual behavior.' *Child Abuse & Neglect 70*, 210–221. https://doi.org/10.1016/j.chiabu.2017.06.017

McNay, L. (1992) *Foucault and Feminism: Power, Gender, and the Self.* Cambridge: Polity Press.

McNeil, B., Reeder, N. and Rich, J. (2012) *A Framework of Outcomes for Young People.* July. London: The Young Foundation. www.youngfoundation.org/wp-content/uploads/2012/10/Framework-of-outcomes-for-young-people-July-2012.pdf

Mehzabin, P. and Stokes, M.A. (2011) 'Self-assessed sexuality in young adults with High-Functioning Autism.' *Research in Autism Spectrum Disorders 5*, 1, 614–621. https://doi.org/10.1016/j.rasd.2010.07.006

Meigham, R. and Harber, C. (2007) *A Sociology of Educating*, 5th edn. London: Continuum International Publishing Group

Mercer, C.H., Tanton, C., Prah, P., Erens, B., *et al.* (2013) 'Changes in sexual attitudes and lifestyles in Britain through the life course and over time: Findings from the National Surveys of Sexual Attitudes and Lifestyles (Natsal).' *Lancet (London, England) 382*, 9907, 1782–1794. doi: 10.1016/S0140-6736(13)62035-8.

Mesibov, G. and Sreckovic, M. (2017) 'Child and Juvenile Pornography and Autism Spectrum Disorder.' In L.A. Dubin and E. Horowitz (eds) *Caught in the Web of the Criminal Justice System: Autism, Developmental Disabilities, and Sex Offenses* (Chapter 2). London: Jessica Kingsley Publishers.

Miller, D. (1990) *Market State and Community: Theoretical Foundations of Market Socialism.* Oxford: Oxford University Press.

Milton, J., Duggan, C., Latham, A., Egan, V. and Tantam, D. (2002) 'Case history of co-morbid Asperger's syndrome and paraphilic behaviour.' *Medicine, Science and the Law 42*, 3, 237–244. https://doi.org/10.1177/002580240204200308

Ministry of Justice (2011) *Achieving Best Evidence in Criminal Proceedings. Guidance on Interviewing Victims and Witnesses, and Guidance on Using Special Measures.* March. www.cps.gov.uk/sites/default/files/documents/legal_guidance/Achieving%2520Best%2520Evidence%2520in%2520Criminal%2520Proceedings.pdf

Mogavero, M.C. (2016) 'Autism, sexual offending, and the criminal justice system.' *Journal of Intellectual Disabilities and Offending Behaviour 7*, 3, 116–126. https://doi.org/10.1108/JIDOB-02-2016-0004

Morgan, L.W., McClendon, L.S., McCarty, J. and Zinck, K. (2016) 'Supporting every child: School counselors' perceptions of juvenile sex offenders in schools.' *Journal of School Counseling 14*, 1, n1. https://files.eric.ed.gov/fulltext/EJ1089428.pdf

Moultrie, D. (2006) 'Adolescents convicted of possession of abuse images of children: A new type of adolescent sex offender?' *Journal of Sexual Aggression 12*, 2, 165–174. https://doi.org/10.1080/13552600600823670

Mouridsen, S.E., Rich, B., Isager, T. and Nedergaard, N.J. (2008) 'Pervasive developmental disorders and criminal behaviour: A case control study.' *International Journal of Offender Therapy and Comparative Criminology 52*, 2, 196–205. https://doi.org/10.1177/0306624X07302056

Murphy, D. (2018) 'Interviewing individuals with an autism spectrum disorder in forensic settings.' *International Journal of Forensic Mental Health 17*, 4, 310–320. https://doi.org/10.1080/14999013.2018.1518939

Murrie, D.C., Warren, J.I., Kristiansson, M. and Dietz, P.E. (2002) 'Asperger's syndrome in forensic settings.' *International Journal of Forensic Mental Health 1*, 1, 59–70. https://doi.org/10.1080/14999013.2002.10471161

Myers, S. (2007) '(De)constructing the risk categories in the AIM assessment model for children with sexually harmful behaviour.' *Children & Society 21*, 5, 365–377. https://doi.org/10.1111/j.1099-0860.2006.00053.x

Myles, B.S. and Simpson, R.L. (2002) 'Asperger syndrome: An overview of characteristics.' *Focus on Autism and Other Developmental Disabilities 17*, 3, 132–137. https://doi.org/10.1177/10883576020170030201

Myles, B.S., Adreon, D., Hagen, K., Hoverstott, J., Hubbard, A. and Smith, S. (2005) *Life Journey through Autism: An Educator's Guide to Asperger's Syndrome*. Arlington, VA: Organization for Autism Research.

Nathanson, D.L. (1992) *Shame and Pride*. New York: Norton.

National Autistic Society (2020a) 'Meltdowns.' Advice and Guidance. www.autism.org.uk/advice-and-guidance/topics/behaviour/meltdowns

National Autistic Society (2020b) 'Obsessions and repetitive behaviour.' Advice and Guidance. www.autism.org.uk/advice-and-guidance/topics/behaviour/obsessions

National Autistic Society (2023) 'What is autism?' www.autism.org.uk/advice-and-guidance/what-is-autism

NeuroLaunch (2024) 'Autism and consent: Navigating relationships and boundaries.' 11 August. https://neurolaunch.com/autism-and-consent

Newman, S.S. and Ghaziuddin, M. (2008) 'Violent crime in Asperger syndrome: The role of psychiatric comorbidity.' *Journal of Autism and Developmental Disorders 38*, 10, 1848–1852. https://doi.org/10.1007/s10803-008-0580-8

NHS Lothian (2006) *The Big Question: Assessing Sexual Knowledge: An Assessment for People with Learning Disabilities*.

NICE (National Institute for Health and Care Excellence) (2019) *Learning Disability: Behaviour that Challenges*. www.nice.org.uk

North, A.S., Russell, A.J. and Gudjonsson, G.H. (2008) 'High functioning autism spectrum disorders: An investigation of psychological vulnerabilities during interrogative interview.' *The Journal of Forensic Psychiatry and Psychology 19*, 3, 323–334. https://doi.org/10.1080/14789940701871621

NPCC (National Police Chiefs Council) (2024) *National Analysis of Police-Recorded Child Sexual Abuse & Exploitation (CSAE) Crimes Report, January 2022 to December 2022*. www.vkpp.org.uk/assets/Files/Publications/National-Analysis-of-police-recorded-CSAE-Crimes-Report-2022-external.pdf

NSPCC (2021) *Harmful Sexual Behaviour: Learning from Case Reviews*. December. https://learning.nspcc.org.uk/research-resources/learning-from-case-reviews/harmful-sexual-behaviour

NSPCC (2024) 'Why language matters: Why we should avoid the term "victim" when talking about children who have experienced abuse.' Blog, 26 January. https://learning.nspcc.org.uk/news/why-language-matters/avoid-victim-talking-about-children-experienced-abuse

O'Nions, E., Petersen, I., Buckman, J.E.J., Charlton, R., *et al.* (2023) 'Autism in England: Assessing underdiagnosis in a population-based cohort study of prospectively collected primary care data.' *The Lancet Regional Health. Europe 29*, 100626. https://doi.org/10.1016/j.lanepe.2023.100626

O'Rourke, S., Whalley, H., Janes, S., MacSweeney, N., *et al.* (2020) *The Development of Cognitive Emotional Maturity in Adolescents and Its Relevance in Judicial Contexts: Literature Review*. Edinburgh: University of Edinburgh. www.scottishsentencing-council.org.uk/media/2044/20200219-ssc-cognitive-maturity-literature-review.pdf

O'Sullivan, O.P. (2018) 'Autism spectrum disorder and criminal responsibility: Historical perspectives, clinical challenges and broader considerations within the criminal justice system.' *Irish Journal of Psychological Medicine 35*, 4, 1–7. https://doi.org/10.1017/ipm.2017.13

Ofcom (2024) *Children and Parents: Media Use and Attitudes Report 2024*. www.ofcom.org.uk/media-use-and-attitudes/media-habits-children/children-and-parents-media-use-and-attitudes-report-2024-interactive-data

Ofsted (2021) *Review of Sexual Abuse in Schools and Colleges*. June. www.gov.uk/government/publications/review-of-sexual-abuse-in-schools-and-colleges

Ogloff, J.R., Cutajar, M.C., Mann, E.C. and Mullen, P.E. (2012) 'Child sexual abuse and subsequent offending and victimisation: A 45 year follow-up study.' *Trends & Issues in Crime and Criminal Justice 2012*, 440, 1–6.

Orsmond, G.I., Shattuck, P.T., Cooper, B.P., Sterzing, P.R. and Anderson, K.A. (2013) 'Social participation among young adults with an autism spectrum disorder.' *Journal of Autism and Developmental Disorders 43*, 11, 2710–2719. https://doi.org/10.1007/s10803-013-1833-8

Ousley, O.Y. and Mesibov, G.B. (1991) 'Sexual attitudes and knowledge of high-functioning adolescents and adults with autism.' *Journal of Autism and Developmental Disorders 21*, 4, 471–481. https://doi.org/10.1007/BF02206871

Palmer, M., Clarke, L., Ploubidis, G., Mercer, C., *et al.* (2016) 'Is "sexual competence" at first heterosexual intercourse associated with subsequent sexual health status?' *Journal of Sexual Research 54*, 1, 91–104. https://doi.org/10.1080/00224499.2015.1134424

Pecora, L., Mesibov, G. and Stokes, M.A. (2016) 'Sexuality in high-functioning autism: A systematic review and meta-analysis.' *Journal of Autism and Developmental Disorders 46*, 11, 3519–3556. https://doi.org/10.1007/s10803-016-2892-4

Peterson, C.C., Slaughter, V.P. and Paynter, J. (2007) 'Social maturity and theory of mind in typically developing children and those on the autism spectrum.' *Journal of Child Psychology and Psychiatry 48*, 12, 1243–1250. https://doi.org/10.1111/j.1469-7610.2007.01810.x

Philander, R. (2018) 'Management of Children with Sexual Behaviour Problems, between the Ages of Five to Nine Years Old, by Educators and Social Workers.' Thesis, Department of Social Work, Faculty of Community and Health Sciences, University of the Western Cape. https://uwcscholar.uwc.ac.za:8443/server/api/core/bitstreams/3e12f6d8-ef6d-4f0d-b112-5fde93c9705b/content

Philaretou, A.G. and Allen, K.R. (2001) 'Reconstructing masculinity and sexuality.' *The Journal of Men's Studies 9*, 3, 301–321. https://doi.org/10.3149/jms.0903.301

Phoenix, A. (1991) *Young Mothers?* Cambridge, MA: Polity Press.

Polusny, M.A. and Follette, V.M. (1995) 'Long-term correlates of child sexual abuse: Theory and review of the empirical evidence.' *Applied and Preventive Psychology 4*, 3, 143–166. https://doi.org/10.1016/S0962-1849(05)80055-1

Postman, N. (1994) *The Disappearance of Childhood*. New York: Vintage Books.

Preece, D., Becerra, R., Allan, A., Robinson, K. and Dandy, J. (2017) 'Establishing the theoretical components of alexithymia via factor analysis: Introduction and validation of the attention-appraisal model of alexithymia.' *Personality and Individual Differences 119*, 341–352. https://doi.org/10.1016/j.paid.2017.08.003

Prentky, R. and Righthand, S. (2003) *Juvenile Sex Offender Assessment, Protocol-II (J-SOAP-II), Manual*. Office of Juvenile Justice and Delinquency Prevention's Juvenile Justice Clearinghouse. www.ojp.gov/pdffiles1/ojjdp/202316.pdf

Pressman, S.D., Matthews, K.A., Cohen, S., Martire, L.M., *et al.* (2009) 'Association of enjoyable leisure activities with psychological and physical well-being.' *Psychosomatic Medicine 71*, 7, 725–732. https://doi.org/10.1097/PSY.0b013e3181ad7978

Pritchard, D., Graham, N., Penney, H., Owen, G., Peters, S. and Mace, F.C. (2016) 'Multicomponent behavioural intervention reduces harmful sexual behaviour in a 17-year-old male with autism spectrum disorder: A case study.' *Journal of Sexual Aggression 22*, 33, 368–378. https://doi.org/10.1080/13552600.2015.1130269

Print, B. (2013) *The Good Lives Model for Adolescents Who Sexually Harm*. Brandon, VT: Safer Society Foundation.

Pugh, V.-M. and King-Hill, S. (2024) 'Teaching Relationships and Sex Education.' In S.-L. McPhee and V.-M. Pugh (Eds) *Developing Quality PHSE in Secondary Schools and Colleges*. London: Bloomsbury. www.bloomsbury.com/uk/developing-quality-pshe-in-secondary-schools-and-colleges-9781350336957

Quadara, A., O'Brien, W., Ball, O., Douglas, W. and Vu, L. (2020) *Good Practice in Delivering and Evaluating Interventions for Young People with Harmful Sexual Behaviours*. Research Report. ANROWS. www.anrows.org.au/publication/good-practice-in-delivering-and-evaluating-interventions-for-young-people-with-harmful-sexual-behaviours

Radford, L., Allnock, D. and Hynes, P. (2015) *Preventing and Responding to Child Sexual Abuse and Exploitation: Evidence Review*. www.unicef.org/media/84081/file/Preventing-Responding-to-Child-Sexual-Abuse-Exploitation-Evidence-Review.pdf

Radford, L., Allnock, D., Hynes, P. and Kelly, L. (2020) *Sexual Violence and Abuse: A Global Evidence Review*. London: University of Bedfordshire and University of London.

Ragaglia, B., Caputi, M. and Bulgarelli, D. (2023) 'Psychosexual education interventions for autistic youth and adults – A systematic review.' *Education Sciences 13*, 3, 224. https://doi.org/10.3390/educsci13030224

Rava, J., Shattuck, P., Rast, J. and Roux, A. (2017) 'The prevalence and correlates of involvement in the criminal justice system among youth on the autism spectrum.' *Journal of Autism and Developmental Disorders 47*, 2, 340–346. https://doi.org/10.1007/s10803-016-2958-3

Reed, L.A., Lawler, S.M., Cosgrove, J.M., Tolman, R.M. and Ward, L.M. (2021) '"It was a joke:" Patterns in girls' and boys' self-reported motivations for digital dating abuse behaviors.' *Children and Youth Services Review 122*, 105883.

Rees, C. (2007) 'Childhood attachment.' *The British Journal of General Practice 57*, 544, 920–922. https://doi.org/10.3399/096016407782317955

Reitzel, L.R. and Carbonell, J.L. (2006) 'The effectiveness of sexual offender treatment for juveniles as measured by recidivism: A meta-analysis.' *Sexual Abuse 18*, 4, 401–421. https://doi.org/10.1177/107906320601800407

Ringrose, J., Regehr, K. and Milne, B. (2021) *Understanding and Combatting Youth Experiences of Image-Based Sexual Harassment and Abuse*. School of Sexuality Education & Association of School and College Leaders.

RJC (Restorative Justice Council) (2016) *RJC Practitioners Handbook*. Norwich: RJC. https://restorativejustice.org.uk/sites/default/files/resources/files/Practitioners%20Handbook_0.pdf

Rodger, S. and Umaibalan, V. (2011) 'The routines and rituals of families of typically developing children compared with families of children with autism spectrum disorder: An exploratory study.' *British Journal of Occupational Therapy 74*, 1. https://doi.org/10.4276/030802211X12947686093567

Ross, E. and Rapp, R. (1981) 'Sex and society: A research note from social history and anthropology.' *Comparative Studies in Society and History 23*, 1, 51–72. https://doi.org/10.1017/S0010417500009683

Russell, D., McCartan, K. and King-Hill, S. (2025) 'Multi-systemic responses and understanding to the prevention and intervention of harmful sexual behaviour in autistic children and young people.' ATSA Blog, 5 March. https://blog.atsa.com/2025/03/multi-systemic-responses-and.html

Salerno, A.C. and Schuller, R.A. (2019) 'A mixed-methods study of police experiences of adults with autism spectrum disorder in Canada.' *International Journal of Law and Psychiatry 64*, 18–25. https://doi.org/10.1016/j.ijlp.2019.01.002

Sandvik, M., Nesset, M.B., Berg, A. and Søndenaa, E. (2017) 'The voices of young sexual offenders in Norway: A qualitative study.' *Open Journal of Social Sciences 5*, 82–95. https://doi.org/10.4236/jss.2017.52009

Schloredt, K.A. and Heiman, J.R. (2003) 'Perceptions of sexuality as related to sexual functioning and sexual risk in women with different types of childhood abuse histories.' *Journal of Traumatic Stress 16*, 3, 275–284. https://doi.org/10.1023/A:1023752225535

Schnitzer, G., Terry, R. and Joscelyne, T. (2020) 'Adolescent sex offenders with autism spectrum conditions: Currently used treatment approaches and their impact.' *The Journal of Forensic Psychiatry & Psychology 31*, 1, 17–40.

Schoeneberg, C., Underwood, L., Newmeyer, M. and Gomez, M. (2020) 'Protective factors and sub-groups of sexually offending adolescents: Implications for conceptualization and practice.' *Journal of Child and Adolescent Counseling 6*, 3, 149–165. https://doi.org/10.1080/23727810.2020.1835416

Schöttle, D., Briken, P., Tüscher, O. and Turner, D. (2017) 'Sexuality in autism: Hypersexual and paraphilic behavior in women and men with high-functioning autism spectrum disorder.' *Dialogues in Clinical Neuroscience 19*, 4, 381–393. https://doi.org/10.31887/DCNS.2017.19.4/dschoettle

Schwartz-Watts, D.M. (2005) 'Asperger's disorder and murder.' *The Journal of the American Academy of Psychiatry and the Law 33*, 3, 390–393. PMID: 16186206.

Scottish Government, The (2011) *Diversion from Prosecution Toolkit: Diverting Young People from Prosecution.* Young People Who Offend (Managing High Risk and Transitions). June. Edinburgh: The Scottish Government. www.gov.scot/binaries/content/documents/govscot/publications/advice-and-guidance/2011/06/diversion-prosecution-toolkit-diverting-young-people-prosecution/documents/0118158-pdf/0118158-pdf/govscot%3Adocument/0118158.pdf

Scottish Government, The (2014) *Framework for Risk Assessment Management and Evaluation (FRAME) for Local Authorities and Partners: For Children and Young People under 18.* November. Edinburgh: The Scottish Government. www.gov.scot/binaries/content/documents/govscot/publications/advice-and-guidance/2014/12/framework-risk-assessment-management-evaluation-frame-local-authorities-partners-incorporating/documents/00466882-pdf/00466882-pdf/govscot%3Adocument/00466882.pdf

Scottish Government, The (2020) *The Expert Group on Preventing Sexual Offending Involving Children and Young People: Prevention of and Responses to Harmful Sexual Behaviour by Children and Young People.* Edinburgh: The Scottish Government, January. https://dera.ioe.ac.uk/id/eprint/34909

Scottish Government, The (2021) *Trauma Informed Practice: A Toolkit for Scotland.* Edinburgh: The Scottish Government, January. www.gov.scot/publications/trauma-informed-practice-toolkit-scotland

Seto, M.C. and Lalumière, M.L. (2010) 'What is so special about male adolescent sexual offending? A review and test of explanations through meta-analysis.' *Psychological Bulletin 136*, 4, 526–575. https://doi.org/10.1037/a0019700

Setty, E. (2022) 'Pornography as a cultural resource for constructing and expressing gendered sexual subjectivities among students in a co-educational boarding school.' *Porn Studies 9*, 2, 159–175. https://doi.org/10.1080/23268743.2021.1875028

Setty, E. (2023) 'Young people and sexual consent: Contextualising "miscommunica-tion" amid "grey areas" of ambiguity and ambivalence.' *Sex Education 25*, 1, 140–155. https://doi.org/10.1080/14681811.2023.2259321

Setty, E., Ringrose, J. and Hunt, J. (2024) 'From "harmful sexual behaviour" to "harmful sexual culture": Addressing school-related sexual and gender-based violence among young people in England through "post-digital sexual citizenship".' *Gender and Education 36*, 5, 434–452. https://doi.org/10.1080/09540253.2024.2348534

Sevin, J.A., Rieske, R.D. and Matson, J.L. (2015) 'A review of behavioral strategies and support considerations for assisting persons with difficulties transitioning from activity to activity.' *Review Journal of Autism and Developmental Disorders 2*, 329–342. https://doi.org/10.1007/s40489-015-0056-7

Sevlever, M., Roth, M.E. and Gillis, J.M. (2013) 'Sexual abuse and offending in autism spectrum disorders.' *Sexuality and Disability 31*, 189–200. https://doi.org/10.1007/s11195-013-9286-8

Sex Education Forum (2017) *Relationships and Sex Education: Contributing to the Safe-guarding, Sexual & Reproductive Health and Wellbeing of Children and Young People.* https://rsehub.org.uk/media/1252/rse_hub-briefing-document_final.pdf

Sex Education Forum (2022) 'Young People's RSE Poll 2021.' 22 January. www.sexedu-cationforum.org.uk/resources/evidence/young-peoples-rse-poll-2021

Silva, J.A., Leong, G.B. and Ferrari, M.M. (2003) 'Paraphilic psychopathology in a case of autism spectrum disorder.' *American Journal of Forensic Psychiatry 24*, 3, 5–20.

Sinclair, J. (1992) 'Don't mourn for us.' *Autonomy, the Critical Journal of Interdisciplinary Autism Studies 1*, 1. https://philosophy.ucsc.edu/SinclairDontMournForUs.pdf

Siponmaa, L., Kristiansson, M., Jonson, C., Nydén, A. and Gillberg, C. (2001) 'Juvenile and young adult mentally disordered offenders: The role of child neuropsychiat-ric disorders.' *The Journal of the American Academy of Psychiatry and the Law 29*, 420–426. https://jaapl.org/content/jaapl/29/4/420.full.pdf

Smahel, D., Machackova, H., Mascheroni, G., Dedkova, L., *et al.* (2020) *EU Kids Online 2020: Survey Results from 19 Countries.* London: London School of Economics and Political Science. www.lse.ac.uk/media-and-communications/research/research-projects/eu-kids-online

Smallbone, S., Marshall, W.L. and Wortley, R. (2008) *Preventing Child Sexual Abuse: Evidence, Policy and Practice.* London: Willan.

Smallbone, S., Rayment-McHugh, S.N. and Smith, D. (2013) 'Youth sexual offending: Context, good-enough lives, and engaging with a wider prevention agenda.' *Interna-tional Journal of Behavioral Consultation and Therapy 8*, 3–4, 49–54. https://psycnet.apa.org/fulltext/2014-12592-010.pdf

Soble, A. (1998) *The Philosophy of Sex and Love: An Introduction.* St Paul, MN: Paragon House.

Sperry, L., Hughes, C. and Forsee, M.J. (2020) 'Vulnerabilities of Defendants with ASD and Strategies for Improving Outcomes.' In E. Kelley (ed.) *Representing People with Autism Spectrum Disorders: A Practical Guide for Criminal Defense Lawyers* (Chapter 14). Chicago, IL: American Bar Association.

Stabenow, T. (2011) 'A method for careful study: A proposal for reforming the child pornography guidelines.' *Federal Sentencing Reporter 24*, 2, 108–136. www.jstor.org/stable/10.1525/fsr.2011.24.2.108

Stagg, S., Tan, L.-H. and Kodakkadan, F. (2022) 'Emotion recognition and context in adolescents with autism spectrum disorder.' *Journal of Autism and Developmental Disorders 52*, 9, 4129–4137. https://doi.org/10.1007/s10803-021-05292-2

Stewart, R. (1995) *Philosophical Perspectives on Sex and Love.* New York: Oxford University Press.

Stokes, M.A. and Attwood, T. (2020) 'Testing.' In E. Kelley (ed.) *Representing People with Autism Spectrum Disorders: A Practical Guide for Criminal Defense Lawyers* (Chapter 9). Chicago, IL: American Bar Association.

Stokes, M.A. and Newton, N. (2004) 'Autistic spectrum disorders and stalking.' *Autism 8*, 337–338.

Stokes, M., Newton, N. and Kaur, A. (2007) 'Stalking, and social and romantic functioning among adolescents and adults with autism spectrum disorder.' *Journal of Autism and Developmental Disorders 37*, 10, 1969–1986. https://doi.org/10.1007/s10803-006-0344-2

Stonard, K.E. (2018) 'The prevalence and overlap of technology-assisted and offline adolescent dating violence.' *Current Psychology 40*, 1056–1070. https://doi.org/10.1007/s12144-018-0023-4

Stonard, K.E. (2020) '"Technology was designed for this": Adolescents' perceptions of the role and impact of the use of technology in cyber dating violence.' *Computers in Human Behavior 105*, 106211. https://doi.org/10.1016/j.chb.2019.106211

Sugrue, D.P. (2017) 'Forensic Assessment of Individuals with Autism Spectrum Charged with Child Pornography Violations.' In L.A. Dubin and E. Horowitz (eds) *Caught in the Web of the Criminal Justice System: Autism, Developmental Disabilities, and Sex Offenses* (Chapter 4). London: Jessica Kingsley Publishers.

Tantam, D. (2000) 'Psychological disorder in adolescents and adults with Asperger syndrome.' *Autism 4*, 1, 47–62. https://doi.org/10.1177/1362361300004001004

Tanton, C., Jones, K.G., Macdowell, W., Clifton, S., *et al.* (2015) 'Patterns and trends in sources of information about sex among young people in Britain: Evidence from three National Surveys of Sexual Attitudes and Lifestyles.' *BMJ Open 5*, e007834. http://bmjopen.bmj.com/content/5/3/e007834.full

Taylor, K., Mesibov, G. and Debbaudt, D. (2009) 'Autism in the criminal justice system.' *North Carolina Bar Journal 14*, 4, 32–36. https://autismriskmanagement.com/wp-content/uploads/2016/07/Autism_Criminal_Justice.pdf

Taylor, S.E. and Armor, D.A. (1996) 'Positive illusions and coping with adversity.' *Journal of Personality 64*, 4, 873–898. https://doi.org/10.1111/j.1467-6494.1996.tb00947.x

Ten Hoopen, L.W., de Nijs, P.F.A., Duvekot, J., Greaves-Lord, K., *et al.* (2020) 'Children with an autism spectrum disorder and their caregivers: Capturing health-related and care-related quality of life.' *Journal of Autism and Developmental Disorders 50*, 1, 263–277. https://doi.org/10.1007/s10803-019-04249-w

Thorn (2023) *Youth Perspectives on Online Safety, 2022: An Annual Report of Youth Attitudes and Experiences.* www.thorn.org/research/library/youth-perspectives-on-online-safety-2022-an-annual-report-of-youth-attitudes-and-experiences

Tint, A., Palucka, A.M., Bradley, E., Weiss, J.A. and Lunsky, Y. (2017) 'Correlates of police involvement among adolescents and adults with autism spectrum disorder.' *Journal of Autism and Developmental Disorders 47*, 9, 2639–2647. https://doi.org/10.1007/s10803-017-3182-5

Torralbas-Ortega, J,. Valls-Ibáñez, V,. Roca, J,. Sastre-Rus, M,. *et al.* (2023) 'Affectivity and sexuality in adolescents with autism spectrum disorder from the perspective of education and healthcare professionals: A qualitative study.' *International Journal of Environmental Research & Public Health 20*, 3, 2497. https://doi.org/10.3390/ijerph20032497

Tracy, J.L., Shaver, P.R., Albino, A.W. and Copper, M.L. (2003) 'Attachment Styles and Adolescent Sexuality.' In P. Florsheim (ed.) Adolescent Romantic Relations and

Sexual Behaviour: Theory, Research and Practical Implications (pp.137–159). Mahwah, NJ: Lawrence Erlbaum Associates Publishers.

Uljarevic, M. and Hamilton, A. (2013) 'Recognition of emotions in autism: A formal meta-analysis.' *Journal of Autism and Developmental Disorders 43*, 7, 1517–1526. https://doi.org/10.1007/s10803-012-1695-5

UN (United Nations) (1989) *United Nations Convention on the Rights of the Child*. www.ohchr.org/en/instruments-mechanisms/instruments/convention-rights-child

UNESCO (United Nations Educational, Scientific and Cultural Organization) (2009) *International Technical Guidance on Sexuality Education: An Evidence-Informed Approach*. Paris, Geneva, New York: UNESCO, UNAIDS Secretariat, United Nations Population Fund (UNPFA), United Nations Children's Fund (UNICEF) and UN Women. https://unesdoc.unesco.org/ark:/48223/pf0000260770

van der Put, C.E. and Asscher, J.J. (2015) 'Protective factors in male adolescents with a history of sexual and/or violent offending: A comparison between three subgroups.' *Sexual Abuse 27*, 1, 109–126. https://doi.org/10.1177/1079063214549259

Vaswani, N., Mullen, L., Efthymiadou, E. and Allardyce, S. (2022) *The Risk of Online Sexual Abuse (ROSA) Project*. The Faithfull Papers. Glasgow: The Lucy Faithfull Foundation. https://pure.strath.ac.uk/ws/portalfiles/portal/138597671/Vaswani_etal_CYPCJ_2022_The_Risk_of_Online_Sexual_Abuse.pdf

Vizard, E., Hickey, N., French, L. and McCrory, E. (2007) 'Children and adolescents who present with sexually abusive behaviour: A UK descriptive study.' *The Journal of Forensic Psychiatry & Psychology 18*, 1, 59–73. https://doi.org/10.1080/14789940601056745

Vosmer, S., Hackett, S. and Callanan, M. (2009) 'Normal and "inappropriate" childhood sexual behaviours: from a Delphi study of professionals in the United Kingdom.' *Journal of Sexual Aggression 15*, 3, 275–288. https://doi.org/10.1080/13552600902915984

Wachtel, L.E. and Shorter, E. (2013) 'Self-injurious behaviour in children: A treatable catatonic syndrome.' *Australian & New Zealand Journal of Psychiatry 47*, 12. https://doi.org/10.1177/0004867413506500

Walsh, D., Brooks, G., Naka, M., Oxburgh, G. and Kyo, A. (2023) 'Forensic interviews conducted with autistic adults in Japan: A review of the literature and directions for future research.' *Psychiatry, Psychology and Law 31*, 2, 216–234. https://doi.org/10.1080/13218719.2023.2192255

Waters, J. (2019) 'Turning a Blind Eye? Teachers' Lived Experiences of Child-on-Child Harmful Sexual Behaviour at Three Schools in the UK. An Interpretative Phenomenological Analysis.' Thesis, Cardiff University. https://orca.cardiff.ac.uk/id/eprint/127462/1/J.pdf

Weir, E., Allison, C. and Baron-Cohen, S. (2021) 'Understanding the substance use of autistic adolescents and adults: A mixed-methods approach.' *The Lancet Psychiatry 8*, 8, 673–685. https://doi.org/10.1016/S2215-0366(21)00160-7

Weiss, J.A. and Fardella, M.A. (2018) 'Victimization and perpetration experiences of adults with autism.' *Frontiers in Psychiatry 9*, 203. https://doi.org/10.3389/fpsyt.2018.00203

Wellings, K., Nanchahal, K., Macdowall, W., McManus, S., *et al.* (2001) 'Sexual behaviour in Britain: Early heterosexual experience.' *Lancet (London, England) 358*, 9296, 1843–1850. https://doi.org/10.1016/S0140-6736(01)06885-4

Williams, F. (1989) *Social Policy: A Critical Introduction*. London: Polity Press.

Williams, G.L. (2023) 'Autistic people experience loneliness far more acutely than neurotypical people – new research.' The Conversation. https://theconversation.com/autistic-people-experience-loneliness-far-more-acutely-than-neurotypical-people-new-research-216471

Wing, L. (1997) 'Asperger's syndrome: Management requires diagnosis.' *Journal of Forensic Psychiatry 8*, 2, 253–257. https://doi.org/10.1080/09585189708412008

Wood, R., Hirst, J., Wilson, L. and Burns-O'Connell, G. (2019) 'The pleasure imperative? Reflecting on sexual pleasure's inclusion in sex education and sexual health.' *Sex Education 19*, 1, 1–14. www.tandfonline.com/doi/full/10.1080/14681811.20118. 1468318

Woodbury-Smith, M.R., Robinson, J., Wheelwright, S. and Baron-Cohen, S. (2005) 'Screening adults for Asperger syndrome using the AQ: A preliminary study of its diagnostic validity in clinical practice.' *Journal of Autism and Developmental Disorders 35*, 3, 331–335. https://doi.org/10.1007/s10803-005-3300-7

Worling, J.R. and Curwen, T. (2001) 'The "ERASOR": Estimate of Risk of Adolescent Sexual Offense Recidivism.' Version 2.0. https://safersociety.org/wp-content/uploads/2023/06/Worling-Curwen_2001_The-ERASOR-2.0.pdf

Yates, P. and Allardyce, S. (2021) *Sibling Sexual Abuse: A Knowledge and Practice Overview.* January. Ilford: Centre of Expertise on Child Sexual Abuse. www.csacentre.org.uk/app/uploads/2023/09/Sibling-sexual-abuse-report.pdf

Yoder, J.R., Hansen, J., Ruch, D. and Hodge, A. (2016) 'Effects of school-based risk and protective factors on treatment success among youth adjudicated of a sexual crime.' *Journal of Child Sexual Abuse 25*, 3, 310–325. https://doi.org/10.1080/10538 712.2016.1137668

Young, E. (2019) 'For people with alexithymia, emotions are a mystery.' The Transmitter, Spectrum, News, 22 February. www.thetransmitter.org/spectrum/people-alexithymia-emotions-mystery

Young, R.L. and Brewer, N. (2020) 'Brief report: Perspective taking deficits, autism spectrum disorder, and allaying police officers' suspicions about criminal involvement.' *Journal of Autism and Developmental Disorders 50*, 2234–2239. https://doi.org/10.1007/s10803-019-03968-4

Youth Justice Board (2023) 'Youth Justice Statistics: 2021 to 2022 | Things you need to know.' www.gov.uk/government/statistics/youth-justice-statistics-2021-to-2022/youth-justice-statistics-2021-to-2022-accessible-version#things-you-need-to-know

Zolyomi, A., Begel, A., Waldern, J.F., Tang, J., *et al.* (2019) 'Managing stress: The needs of autistic adults in video calling.' *Proceedings of the ACM on Human-Computer Interaction 3*, CSCW, 134, 1–29. https://doi.org/10.1145/3359236

Index

16th century 27–8
17th century 30
19th century 30

abuse 24
accessories to crimes 154
ACEs 82, 97–8
'acting' 166
ADHD 16, 152, 170
adolescent dating violence 154
adult supervision 121
adverse childhood
    experiences see ACEs
adverse experiences 82
adversity 81, 83–4, 107, 116, 118
aggression 129, 151
AIDS crisis 35
alexithymia 49, 104–5
anime 108, 148
anxiety 23, 50, 60, 89, 101,
    103, 118, 127, 171
arrest 155
articulated sketching 160
ASEM 23, 66–8, 93–5, 112–13,
    131, 133–4, 143, 177
asexuality 20
'Asperger time' 128
attachment styles 113
attention deficit hyperactivity
    disorder see ADHD

autism socio-ecological
    model see ASEM
autistic subculture and advocacy 16
autobiographical memory 168

BDSM 73
befriend and mate crimes 154
bestiality 111
beyond Referrals 138
black-and-white thinking 135
'blank slates' 30
bondage, discipline, sadism and
    masochism see BDSM
brain maturation 97
British National Survey of Sexual
    Attitudes and Lifestyles see Natsal
Brook Traffic Light Tool 67–8
bullying 82, 100, 151, 154, 180

cartoons 108
CBT 78, 81
child development 96
child maltreatment 154
child protection 24, 79, 83, 144, 146–7
child sexual abuse 106, 119
child sexual abuse reports 70
child's experience of developmental
    adversity 95
child-centred and holistic approach 47
child-centred approach 80, 122, 134

child-centred interventions 146
child-focused 15
childhood adversity *see* ACEs
Children's Commissioner's Office 61
Christian church 28
Christian religion 28
CJS 99, 126, 149–50, 155–6
coercion 58, 60
coercive interviewing techniques 160
cognitive rigidity 135, 157
cognitive style 167
cognitive-behavioural therapy *see*
    CBT
community rejection 141
'compass of shame' 103
compliance 158, 163
compulsivity 43, 69
concepts of privacy 58
conduct disorder 153
confidentiality 144
consensual relationship 88
consent 20, 58, 62, 91, 95, 120, 145
Conservative coalition 32, 35
Conservative governments 32, 36
Conservative MP Miriam Cates 35
contact abuse 85
contact sexual abuse 60
context reinstatement 161
contextual safeguarding 138
contraception 32
counterfeit deviance 26, 149
Courting Behaviour Scale 125
courtroom 171
courtroom proceedings 24, 157
COVID-19 35, 50, 174
Criminal Justice System *see* CJS
criminal responsibility 44
critical risk indicator 46
'cry for help' 152
CSAM 44, 51, 55, 58, 60, 89, 91, 107–9,
    123–4, 134–5, 139, 141, 148–9, 174
curiosity 140
cyberbullying 60
cybercrimes 51

dating behaviour 56
defendant 150, 157
deficit model 17
denial 23, 102–3, 115
depression 153
depressive mood 131, 140
developmentally orientated 77
deviance 61, 102
deviant sexuality 149
diaper fetishism 73
digital communication 50
digital direct aggression 52
digital monitoring and control 52
digital sexual abuse 52
digital technologies 49
disinhibited online behaviour 26
disordered in timing 162
distress 60
diversion 173–4
Diversion from Prosecution Toolkit
    173
diversity 77
DSM-5 (*The Diagnostic and Statistical
    Manual of Mental Disorders,
    Fifth Edition*) 16, 109, 111

early socialisation 141
echolalia 84, 158
Elementary Education Act 30
emerging sexuality 31
emotional awareness 104
emotional expressions 163
emotional intonation 163
emotional recognition 26
emotional regulation 26, 96
'emotions thermometer' 172
empathy 48–9, 59, 81, 97, 127, 157
EpiCrim (Epidemiological
    Criminology) 67
episodic memory 158
Equal Treatment Bench Book 167–8
equality 120
Everyone's Invited [website] 70
exploitation 98, 100, 154, 184

exploitation online 60
extra-familial harm 138
extreme pornography 54
eye contact 157, 167

facial expression 123–4, 149
family dynamics 113
family ecosystems 113
family engagement 134
family environment 117–19
family trauma 96
fathers 119–20
FBA 129
fetish-based interests 110
fetishist preoccupations 73
fidget spinners 101
Fisher Education Act 30
flirting 56–7
foster carers 116
free-recall narratives 159
free-recall performance 160
functional behavioural
    assessment see FBA

gender dysphoria 21
gender expectations 120
gender identity 21
gender inequality 103
gender socialisation 119
GIRFEC (getting it right
    for every child) 144
Glasgow 54
GLM (Good Lives Model) 75
grooming 54
group work 78–9
guilt 53
gullibility 151

Hackett Continuum 40, 44, 68, 94
heterogenous 16, 106
holistic 77
hope 102
hopelessness 102

hyper- or hyposensitive sensory
    response 43, 100, 110, 165
hypersexuality 110

I/PSB 40–2, 67, 69–71
ICD-11 (International Classification
    of Diseases, 11th revision) 16
imagination 59
imitation 58
inappropriate affect or
    expressions 140, 157
inappropriate and problematic
    sexual behaviours see I/PSB
incarceration 151, 157
indecent images of children 24, 53
Industrial Revolution 28
inflexibility of thought 135, 158
Inform Young People's programme 90
intergenerational experiences 119
internet 20, 49, 90, 123, 140
internet use 50
internet-based sexual
    communication 91
interpersonal violence victimisation
    153
interpersonally isolated 127
intimacy 62, 96
intimate partner violence 89, 154
intrafamilial or sibling sexual abuse 80
IQ 130
isolation 86

juror 150

kissing 56

labelling 15, 94, 147
law enforcement officers see LEOs
learning disabilities 16, 45,
    54, 98, 107, 129, 144
learning style see learning type
learning type 85, 100
LEOs 156

literal thinking or cognitive
    style 149, 157
longitudinal studies 64
low-level problematic sexual
    behaviour 185
low-level sexual concerns 184
Lucy Faithfull Foundation Parents
    Protect Tool (PP) 67

major depressive disorder 140
major psychiatric disorders 152
male role modelling 120
masculine fluidity 120
masculinity 120
masturbation 43, 56, 62, 85, 87, 112, 140
media 50, 124
medical model 16
'meltdowns' 96
memory 158–9
mental health 43
mental health disorders
    24, 54, 99, 152–3
mental illness 50
mental processing speed weakness 128
mind blindness 16
minimisation 102, 114–15
'mimicking' 166
misleading questions 160
mistrust 127–8, 158
mobile phone 49
modelling see imitation
monotonous voice 163
moral repair 24
multi-agency approach 77, 139, 147
multidimensional assessment 91
multilevel approach 48
multimodal 77
multisystemic 66

National Analysis of Police-Recorded
    Child Sexual Abuse and Exploitation
    Crimes Report 2022 53
National Society for the Prevention
    of Cruelty to Children see NSPCC

Natsal 39
NeuroLaunch (2024) website 95
neurodevelopmental
    disorders 16, 152, 170
neurodivergence 55
neurodiverse 46
neurodiversity 24, 48
'neurotypical' 48
NGO 52
NHS Lothian assessment tool
    'The Big Question' (2006) 87
non-government organisation see
    NGO
normative sexual behaviours 145
NSPCC 67, 69, 71

obsessional interests 26
Obsessive-compulsive
    disorder see OCD
OCD 139
OCSA 51, 53
Ofcom 50
offending behaviour 24, 150–2
Ofsted report 70
olfactophilia 109
one-to-one support 78
online and technology
    obsessional behaviour 88
online child sexual abuse see OCSA
online dating 52
online harassment behaviours 89
online media 50
online sexual harmful behaviour 51
online sexual offending 55
online technologies 49
open-ended questions 169
open-ended recall 160

paedophiliac 141
paranoia 127, 158
Paranoia Scale 127
paraphilias 44, 109, 111
paraphilic fantasies or behaviours 110
parental gender role modelling 119

PECS 87, 130
peer isolation 121
peer pressure 32
peer-on-peer sexual abuse 136, 138
penetrative abuse 83
perception of time 162
perpetrator 15, 90, 154, 179
personal computers 51
personal safety 164
personal, social, health and
   economic education *see* PSHE
personality disorder 170
person-first 17
physical arousal responses *see*
   physical sexual arousal
physical health 62
physical sexual arousal 56, 96
Picture Exchange Communication
   System *see* PECS
place-based situational prevention
   139
podophilia 109
police custody 172
police interactions 24, 155
police investigative interviews 24
police involvement 155
police officers 156
pornography 20, 38, 43, 53, 58, 60-3,
   105, 121, 123, 141, 145, 174
positive attachment 96
positive role models 183
post-traumatic stress 82
predisposing factors 141
pre-pubescent children 45
prevention 131, 177-9, 182-4, 187
pro offending behaviour 180
probative value 150
problematic sexual development 43
procedural court adaptations 150, 171
proportionate 77
prosocial 133
prosody 163
protective factors 136, 181
PSHE 35

psychiatric co-morbidity 164, 170
psychoeducation 77
psychological risk 136
psychopathy 170
psychosexual 101
psychosexual development 45, 99
psychosexuality 103, 119
psychosis 99, 170
psychosocial development 21
public health models 178
punitive measures 48, 147

rape 60
Rape Crisis England &
   Wales website 94
rejection 86
relationships and sex
   education *see* RSE
relationships, sex, health and
   education *see* RSHE
religious beliefs 134
remorse 97, 157
residential living environments
   116-17
resilience 79, 84, 97
responsibility 97
restorative approaches 78, 80
restorative justice 45, 80-1
Restorative Justice Council 80
restricted and repetitive patterns
   of behaviours, activities
   or interests *see* RRBIs
rights-respecting approach 187
rigidity in interests 58
risk 46, 65, 72, 137, 147, 178-9, 181-2
risk assessment 89-90, 164
risk factors *see* Risk
risk management 24, 74, 147
RJ *see* restorative justice
role-playing exercises 90
romantic functioning 126-7
RRBIs 16, 58, 61, 111, 158
RSE 32, 35, 62-3, 87, 120
RSHE 34-8, 40, 70

safeguarding 24, 146
safety plan 86, 147–8
schizoaffective disorder 153
schizophrenia 99
school environment 135–6
school-based protective factors 139
secure care 116
secure children's home 129
self-blame 53
self-efficacy 84
self-esteem 84
self-harm 131
self-regulation 97, 110
semantic memory 158
SEND 36
sensory art techniques 101
sensory processing difficulties 58
sensory profile checklist 165
sensory sensitivity 26, 151, 172, 184
sensory techniques 100
serious offence 157
sexual abuse 17, 71, 98
sexual abuse and neglect 82
sexual abuse images of
    children see CSAM
sexual arousal 85
sexual crime 19, 177–8
sexual curiosity 121
sexual development 20–1,
    24, 30, 43, 57, 96, 180
sexual diversity 35
sexual dysfunction 85
sexual education 122
sexual exploitation and
    abuse online 52, 59
sexual exploration and
    experimentation 19
sexual fantasies 111
'sexual fetishism' 44
sexual harassment behaviours 70
sexual harassment online 54
sexual harassment see sexual
    harassment behaviours
sexual harm 52

sexual identity 19, 180
sexual intercourse 56
sexual intimacy 56
sexual knowledge 57
sexual offending 21, 51, 53, 128, 181
sexual physical development 140
sexual sadism 44
sexual violence 44
sexually abused see sexual offending
sexually abusive behaviour 15
sexually assaulted 60
sexually explicit material 20
sexually naïve 134
sexually transmitted infections see STIs
sexual-related fixated interests 58
shame 103
shame 23, 28, 36–7, 53
Shore resource (UK, Lucy Faithfull
    Foundation, 2023) 91
'shutdowns' 96–7
sibling or intrafamilial sexual abuse
    45
sibling sexual behaviour
    and abuse see SSB/A
sibling Sexual Behaviour
    Mapping Tool see SSBMT
sibling sexual behaviours 45
sleep deprivation 62
'small adults' 29
smartphones 50–1
social and peer isolation
    see social isolation
social competence 126
social ecological approach 45
social ecological framework 66
social ecological model 17, 67,
    69, 71–2, 74, 79–80, 92
social exclusion 98
social functioning 127
social isolation 43, 50, 57,
    61, 75, 85, 134, 180
social maturity 57, 122–3, 149
social media 49, 139, 148
social model 16

social naivety 149, 151
social skills 95
social stories 184
social understanding or
    misunderstanding 62, 150
social-ecological interpersonal
    domain 115
social-emotional immaturity 151
societal expectations 19
societal norms 64
socio-ecological model 22–3, 46–7,
    65–6, 68–9, 75, 79, 84, 90
soliciting 54
special educational needs and
    disabilities see SEND
spiky profile 123
SSB/A 96
SSBMT 46–7
stalking 124
Star Wars 62
stigma 36, 84, 94, 103, 149, 178
STIs 34–5, 39
strengths-based approach 15, 77, 92, 133
stress 51, 89, 101, 133, 171
stress-adaptive behaviours 103
suggestible 160, 167
suggestive interviewing techniques
    160
survivor 17
suspiciousness 127
sympathy 49
systemic approaches 135

TA-HSB 49, 54–6, 59
'tabula rasa' 30
TAS-20 104–5
Taylor's 'continuum of denial' 102
technological-assisted harmful
    sexual behaviour see TA-HSB 49
technological-assisted sexual
    behaviours 25–6
technology-assisted abuse 85
technology-assisted harm 38
teenage pregnancy 35

The Diagnostic and Statistical
    Manual of Mental Disorders,
    Fifth Edition see DSM-5
theory of mind see ToM
time perception 162
time to respond 158
ToM 16, 42, 58, 135, 149
Toolkit 14: Using Communication Aids
    in the Criminal Justice System (The
    Advocate's Gateway) 162, 171–2
Toronto Alexithymia Scale see TAS-20
transitory period 31
transvestism 73
trauma 54, 74, 81–2, 95, 98, 107, 130,
    133
trauma-informed practice
    or approach 81, 101
trichotillomania 131

United Nations Convention on the
    Rights of the Child see UNCRC
'unformed adults' 29
UNCRC 17, 26, 29, 31, 33, 35

VAWC 70
verbal communication 101
victim 17, 46, 80, 83, 90, 115, 156, 179
victim-blaming narratives 103
victim-centred approach 146
victimisation 24, 54, 60, 151, 153–4, 184
video calling 51
violence 153–4
violence against women and
    children see VAWC
violent behaviours 99
violent pornography 61
visual aids 100, 184
visual communication guides 100
visual techniques 100
visual timetables 171–2
vulnerability 23–4, 42, 45, 50, 53,
    55, 57–60, 98, 100, 152–4
vulnerability assessment 98

Wechsler Intelligence Scale
    for Children, Fourth
    Edition *see* WISC-IV
Western culture 31–2
What's OK resource (US) 91
WHO 31
whole-child approach 144
whole-family engagement 131
whole-family support approach 119

whole-school perspective 139
whole-systems approach 150
WISC-IV 128
World Health Organization *see* WHO

youth-produced sexual images 89

zoophilia 109, 111